A Western Horseman Book

THE HANK WIESCAMP STORY

The Authorized Biography of the Legendary Colorado Horseman

By Frank Holmes

THE HANK WIESCAMP STORY

Published by
Western Horseman Inc.
3850 North Nevada Ave.
Box 7980
Colorado Springs, CO 80933-7980

Design, Typography, and Production
Western Horseman
Colorado Springs, Colorado

Cover painting of Hank Wiescamp with Skip Napoleon
Dwayne Brech

Printing
Publisher's Press
Salt Lake City, Utah

Third Printing: December 1998

ISBN 0-911647-38-4

Dedication

This book is dedicated to
my late wife, Freda, and to our children.

Special Recognition

I would like to also pay special recognition to the CS Ranch of Cimarron, New Mexico. The daughters of Plaudit whom I got from the Philmont Ranch were all out of CS-bred mares. The blood of those CS mares was instrumental in the establishment of my early horse breeding program.

Hank Wiescamp

HANK WIESCAMP

INTRODUCTION

THE CHANCE to write the authorized biography of Hank Wiescamp was a once-in-a-lifetime opportunity for me. At the same time, it was a project that I approached with a certain amount of apprehension.

It wasn't that I felt unfamiliar with Hank's personal history or the history of his horses. I made my first trip to Alamosa as a teenager in the late 1960s. As I would confess to Hank years later, it was a trip that changed the way I viewed horses.

Up to that point, I had never seen large groups of horses—breeding stallions, broodmares, and young stock—that were stamped in the consistent, definitive way that the Wiescamp horses were.

Hank had rows of stallion pens, pastures full of broodmares, and corrals full of yearling and 2-year-old replacement fillies. They all looked as if someone had taken a cookie cutter and stamped them out, adding a little different color and chrome to each for the sake of variety.

Each one of those stallions, mares, and fillies was of the same general height and weight. They had the same type of head, ear, throatlatch, and neck. Their necks tied into their shoulders the same way, their hips were the same length and angle, and their muscling was almost identical.

Skips Magistrate, a 1975 stallion by Skip Cadet and out of Skip Whiskers by Skipper's King, exhibits the hallmark characteristics of a Wiescamp-bred Quarter Horse stallion. His fox ears, wide-set eyes, and prominent jaws mark him as "one of Hank's," as surely as the Quarter Circle I brand on his left jaw.

For the first time in my life, I realized that I was viewing a *family* of horses—bred to be consistent in type and temperament. I marveled at those Wiescamp horses of the 1960s, and they became the barometer by which I measured every other horse breeding program that I studied from then on.

Long after that first visit to Hank's, I remained a student of his horses and their accomplishments. I read and saved every article written about them; I traveled around the country, visiting with people who had them; I collected photographs and pedigrees, and pored over them, trying to find the elusive key that would enable me to see exactly how Hank Wiescamp could consistently breed the kind of horses that he did.

So, it wasn't unfamiliarity with the subject that gave me pause as I sank my teeth into this project. It was the complexity of the man himself.

Hank Wiescamp is one of those larger-than-life men you often read about, but seldom encounter firsthand. One of the greatest testimonials to his stature, in my opinion, is the fact that over the past 30 years I've discussed him with hundreds of people who have had passionate feelings about that him, pro and con, and yet have never met him personally. He is that kind of man.

Hank is a study in contrasts. He is at home as the focal point of a group of people, and yet he is a loner by nature. He can be charming, intimidating, warm, and distant, all within the same moment. He can be talkative one instant, and taciturn the next. He has only an eighth-grade formal education, and yet he is one of the most literate and well-read men I've ever met.

Hank Wiescamp raised himself out of

poverty and built a multimillion-dollar land and livestock empire in the San Luis Valley of southern Colorado on the strength of his vision and energy.

In the process, he outsmarted, outdealt, and outhustled a legion of his contemporaries. As would be expected, he accumulated his share of both supporters and detractors. This is not unique. For almost every extremely successful, self-made man or woman, the situation is the same.

Hank has also been involved in his share of controversy over the years. He has often been at odds with registries over their rules, particularly those that deal with excess white in Quarter Horses and solid color in Appaloosas and Paints.

Whether Hank's stance on these subjects was the popular one at the time has never made any difference to him. That's just the way he is.

There is also an air of mystery that surrounds both the man and his horses. Hank, to this day, shares the intricacies of his personal life and his horse breeding program with very few outsiders. Why should he? Part of the Wiescamp mystique lies in the veil of secrecy that surrounds him, both as an individual and as a horse breeder.

The bottom line to all of this is that he has bred, and still is, breeding and raising some of the best Quarter Horses in the world. And that's why so many people have made the journey to southern Colorado over the years to meet him and to try to buy his best horses.

As for myself, I have chosen to place the emphasis of this book where I firmly feel it belongs.

This is the story of a man who single-handedly created one of the most easily recognizable and enduring *families* of horses in the history of modern horse breeding.

And this is also the story of that family of horses: where they came from, how they evolved, what accomplishments they made, and how they have influenced the Quarter Horse, Palomino, Appaloosa, and Paint Horse registries.

The Hank Wiescamp Story is one whose telling is long overdue. I hope you enjoy it.

—Frank Holmes

I've never seen a photograph that captures the consistency of type of the Wiescamp horses any better than this one that was taken by Darrell Dodds in the early 1990s. There are four mares in this photo (although only three can be readily seen): two palominos, a sorrel, and a buckskin directly behind the sorrel. They are as alike as four peas in a pod.

The Man . . .

"One man can make a fortune selling shoes on a street corner, and another can go broke selling the same shoes on the corner across the street. It's not the shoes or the corner that are responsible for either result. It's the man who's doing the selling."

—*Hank Wiescamp*

Henry J. "Hank" Wiescamp.

. . . AND HIS BRAND

"I bought the Quarter Circle I brand in the 1930s from Roy Boyd of Denver, Colorado. I gave $100 for it when you could buy almost any brand for $10. I liked this brand because it is neat and will never blotch on the jaw."

—***Hank Wiescamp***

ACKNOWLEDGEMENTS

The writing of *The Hank Wiescamp Story* took the better part of a year. Along the way, I was fortunate enough to receive the help of numerous people, and I would like to take this opportunity to thank them for their assistance.

Staff members in the records research departments of the American Quarter Horse Association, the Appaloosa Horse Club, and the American Paint Horse Association provided me with the show and production records that I needed to document the achievements of the Wiescamp horses.

Carolyn Bignall of Topeka, Kan., a Wiescamp pedigree researcher *par excellence,* furnished me with detailed pedigrees and production information on virtually every one of the early Wiescamp horses.

Staff members of *The Quarter Horse Journal, The Appaloosa Journal, The Paint Horse Journal,* and *Palomino Horses* very graciously researched their photo files to provide me with a significant portion of the photographs that appear in the book. So did Darol Dickinson of Ellicott, Colorado.

The folks at the American Quarter Horse Heritage Center & Museum, Amarillo, Tex., also helped me secure some of the priceless photographs of the Philmont and Ghost Ranch mares that are included in the book.

Steve Zimmer, curator of the Philmont Museum, Cimarron, N.M., furnished photos of such horses as Plaudit and Lani Chief, and staff members of the Nebraska State Historical Society supplied the photos of Maple Prince (TB) and Chimney Sweep (TB).

The entire Wiescamp clan tolerated my repeated rifling through their family albums in search of "just one more photograph" to be included in the book. While I'm on the subject of photographs, you will notice that some of the most noted horse photographers of all time are credited with many of the fine photographs. Without their efforts, much of the visual record of western horse history would have been lost.

I am also indebted to the many owners of past and present Wiescamp-bred horses from throughout the country who graciously loaned photographs to me for inclusion in the book. I have given credit to them for the photographs used.

There is little doubt about how important good photographs are to books of historical content. I hope you will agree with me that the photographs that appear in *The Hank Wiescamp Story* are one of the best sets ever assembled to pay homage to a single family of horses.

Frank Holmes

FRANK HOLMES

CONTENTS

1 THE CHILDHOOD

Early on, Hank showed a tendency for goal-setting and hard work that would characterize his entire life.

HENRY J. "HANK" Wiescamp (pronounced Wheeze-camp) was born on May 21, 1906, near Holland, Neb., a small farming community located south of Lincoln.

His paternal grandparents, Gerrit and Janna Wiescamp, had immigrated to that area from Winterswijk, Holland, with their six children in 1888. This was shortly after their home in Holland had burned to the ground.

"My dad, Christiaan, and his family came to this country when he was 12 years old," relates Hank Wiescamp. "They crossed over on a freight boat because they couldn't afford tickets on a regular passenger liner."

The Wiescamps settled on a tract of prairie between the small southeastern Nebraska communities of Holland and Panama. With a team of oxen and an 8-inch sod plow, they first carved the virgin Nebraska soil into bricks that went into the construction of a home and a barn. Later on, a hand-dug well was added, and the first fields were prepared for planting. Christiaan Wiescamp was one of the two oldest boys in the family and, because of this, was not allowed to attend school, but was kept at home to help run the farm. Deprived of a formal education, Christiaan continued to ply the only trade that he had ever learned, farming, once he reached maturity.

In 1898 he married the former Catherine

Hank Wiescamp is shown here as a boy in a family portrait taken on the Wiescamp farm in southeastern Nebraska. Hank is the youngster to the far left in the back row. His father and mother are in the center of the middle row.

Schneider and, from this union, 14 children were born. Twelve of the fourteen lived to reach maturity. Twin girls, born prematurely, died shortly after birth.

Henry J., Christiaan and Catherine Wiescamp's fifth child and third son, was born on the original Wiescamp homestead.

Later on, the family moved to a 200-acre farm between Holland and Hickman.

"We raised mostly corn and wheat and did all the work with horse-drawn machinery," remembers Hank. "And I'm here to tell you that in July and August, when it got to up to 110 degrees in the shade, cultivating corn behind a team of horses or mules was work."

Early on, Hank showed a tendency for goal-setting and hard work that would characterize his entire life. "When I was about 9 years old," he relates, "I wanted a bicycle. I finally twisted around and got a dollar put together and bought one from a neighbor boy. The only reason I could buy it so cheap was because it had about a third of the spokes broke out of the wheels.

"Then I saw an ad in the *Farm Journal* about winning a Shetland pony by selling Cloverine™ salve. I wanted a pony of some kind so I ordered the salve. I think they sent me ten little tins of it to sell at 25 cents each.

"So, every night after school, I'd get on that old bicycle and I'd pedal to all the neighbors and sell salve. Before long, everybody in that whole community had Cloverine salve because I never left anybody's place until I had sold them some. But I never did sell enough to win a Shetland pony."

Undeterred by this setback, Hank looked for other means of making the money he needed to buy a pony.

"I attended a country school in District 142 that was about a mile from home. I got along pretty good there. As I got older, I did the janitor work for the school. And I ran a trap line. I'd trap muskrats, rabbits, and skunks—any pelts I could sell for any money at all.

"During the winter, I'd get up at 4 o'clock every morning and run my trap line. Then I'd milk the cows and get the wood in at home. Then I'd go to school and fire up the coal furnace. After school, I'd sweep the floors—they paid me $2 a week.

The one-room schoolhouse where Hank received his formal education. This photo was taken in the 1950s, hence the electric power lines. There was no electricity in the building when Hank attended classes there.

"After school, I'd run my trap line again and then do my evening chores. After supper, I was ready to go to bed. And I didn't need a sleeping pill to go to sleep either.

"By the time I turned 10, I had enough saved to buy a Shetland pony and I guess he was the first horse I ever had."

Even at that early age, Hank showed a marked interest in an area that would one day become the source of his livelihood—auctioneering.

"There were 12 of us kids in the family, including 9 boys," he recollects, "and there wasn't a one of us boys who was

Hank Wiescamp at the time of his graduation from Reppart's Auctioneer School in 1926.

"I've always been drawn to horses. That's the way it is. I never could change it; I never did want to."

what you would've called puny. In fact, when we got older, we used to call ourselves the '1-ton litter,' because together we weighed over a ton.

"Anyway, we had a big old table, and when those food bowls got passed around, you better make sure you got all you needed the first time, because when they came around again, there wouldn't be much left in 'em.

"Now, even as a kid, I was fascinated by auctioneering. So, about the time we'd all get settled around the table, I'd start auctioning off the knives, the forks, and the dishes—anything that was on the table that I could get to selling.

"Dad would be gettin' ready to ask the blessing, and they just couldn't get me to shut up. So my mother would pick me up and lock me in the broom closet, and she'd keep me there until everyone else was practically done eating—that was my punishment.

"But she never did get me cured. She didn't know it then, but I was just practicing for what would be my career someday."

At the same early age, Wiescamp also showed a definite interest in horses. "I don't know where it came from; I don't know when it came; it's just always been there, as far back as I can remember.

"Back in Nebraska, when supper was over and the chores were all done, I'd spend most of my time before bed out in the barn, with the horses.

"We had our work horses and we also had three buggy horses; we had one team we drove on the buggy and one single horse we drove on the carriage. I'd spend most of my time after supper currying those work horses and buggy horses. I'd brush out their manes and tails, rub all the sweat marks off of 'em, and trim their hoofs.

"I don't know why I did it; I just did. And I was out there most of the time by myself. I've always been drawn to horses. That's just the way it is. I never could change it; I never did want to.

"I suppose I could look back at my childhood and complain about this thing or that thing," Wiescamp continues. "It's true that I came from a pretty big family, and it's true that I might not have had as much as some others did; I sure enough got my formal education cut short.

"But, I'm not complaining about when I was raised, or where I was raised, or how I was raised. I came from good, hard-working Dutch stock, and that has stood me in good stead over the years."

As time went on, the Wiescamp family began to feel the crunch of too little land and too many sons who were nearing the age at which they would want to strike out on their own.

"We had 200 acres of land in Nebraska," recalls Hank. "But there were five older boys wantin' something to do. Land was hard to come by back there. We just couldn't seem to find any more to buy or rent.

"So in 1922, when I was 16, we moved here—to the San Luis Valley (in south-central Colorado). My mother's family already lived here, and I suppose that was why we wound up looking for land in this part of the country. We were able to find a 320-acre farm that gave us a little more room to grow, so we just moved out here—lock, stock, and barrel.

"We shipped our milk cows, our work horses, our household goods, and some of our machinery to Colorado by boxcar—immigrant cars as they used to call them. It took 4 or 5 days to make the trip, and my brother John had to ride in the boxcar with the stock, to feed and water them.

"When we got to Alamosa and got unloaded, I hopped up on our saddle horse, bareback, and drove the work horses and milk cows out to the new place. It was in the Bowen (school) district, 14 miles west of town. And it was a long, slow ride 'cause those milk cows just didn't travel too fast. And I didn't really know where I was going, but I found my way and I finally made it.

"I had just graduated from the eighth grade when we moved. We wound up living 12 miles from the nearest high school, so my formal schooling ended right there and then.

"Of course, we didn't know anything about valley farming, how and when to irrigate, and so on; but we still raised a pretty good crop of potatoes that first year. But I remember we didn't get much for 'em; potatoes were only worth 35 cents a hundredweight then. Barley was only worth 25 cents a hundred. You just couldn't get anything for anything in those days.

"Well, we couldn't make the payments on the Bowen place. So we lost it and moved over to the Waverly district, south of town, and rented a place there. And all of us kids who were old enough went to work to help the family survive.

"My older brother got a job in a garage for $1.50 a day. My sisters hired out on farms and ranches, doing housework for 50 cents a day. I went to work for Clyde Helms, who lived in the Carmel district, for a dollar a day. During the winter, I worked for the Denver & Rio Grande Railroad, building boxcars in their Alamosa yard for 32 cents an hour. In the spring, I'd go back to work for Clyde at the farm.

"That's how we made enough money to eat and buy clothes. In those days there wasn't any charity; there wasn't any food stamps; there wasn't any give-away programs. You did the best you could with what you had.

"By this time, my dad was getting up in years, and we never did buy another place. Eventually all of us boys branched

In 1926, Hank decided it was time for him to choose a permanent career. He was torn between two choices—the ministry and auctioneering.

Fred Reppart (right), owner and instructor of Reppart's Auctioneer School, in a photo taken in 1942 with Freddie Chandler, a top student. Reppart had playfully messed up Chandler's hat and wanted the photo taken that way.

out, and my sisters got married, and we all finally got places of our own."

Hank continued to work for Clyde Helms for almost 4 years, from early spring to late fall. At one point, he was encouraged to quit Helms and go to work for the railroad company on a year-round basis.

"About the second winter that I worked for the railroad," he recalls, "Ol' Swede Lingerholm, the big boss, came to me and said, 'Hank, I don't understand you. You're making 32 cents an hour here, and you can put together boxcars about as fast as anybody here. You make it through the coldest part of the year, and don't ever miss a day. Then, when spring hits, and the weather gets nice, you quit and go to work for a farmer, for a dollar a day. I don't understand it.'

"'Well,' I said, 'I don't mind working here, but it's not the same as working out on the farm. Out there, I'm doing what I really enjoy, and I'm gettin' room and board on top of the wages. What's more, I'm workin' for one of the best farmers in the valley, and I'm learnin' a lot from him.

"'And I need to learn it all because one of these days, when I'm financially able, I'm going to own me a ranch or two. And no matter how much I make, or how much I learn about puttin' boxcars together, I have no intentions of ever owning a railroad.'"

In 1926, Hank decided that it was time for him to choose a permanent career.

He was torn between two choices—the ministry and auctioneering. Although at first glance the two would seem to have absolutely nothing in common, upon closer examination it becomes easier to understand how a young man with Hank Wiescamp's personality could be drawn to both.

Hank was then, as he is now, people-oriented. He was at ease among people, whether it was a one-on-one encounter, or in the middle of a crowd. And, from an early age on, Hank has been a master of assessing personalities and reading the moods of a single individual as well as crowds. Finally, he was then, as he is now, a gifted storyteller, able to almost mesmerize people by virtue of the energy he puts into whatever tale he is spinning.

Certainly, these qualities are essential to both the successful preacher and the successful auctioneer.

In the end, Hank's love of the ranching lifestyle, coupled with his love of horses, led to his decision to go to auctioneer's school.

"In the spring of 1926, after saving for several years to get the $500 tuition, I decided to attend Reppart's Auction School, in Decatur, Ind.," he recalls. "Fred Reppart, who ran the school, was one of the best-known auctioneers in America. He was the dean of the Hereford cattle auctioneers back when Herefords ruled the world. Anyway, I traveled back there in a used Model T Ford that I had bought for $200. The route I took was what they used to call the Pikes Peak Ocean to Ocean Highway. It's U.S. Highway 24 today.

"In 1926 it was mostly gravel, and traveling it was something of an adventure for a 20-year-old who had never been away from home. I didn't have any money to stay in motels, but I had a tent that fit onto the side of the Model T. I took my frying pan along and my eating utensils, and I just sort of roughed it.

"I attended a summer session of the school so I could camp out while I was back there, too, and saved money that way. I stayed at the fairgrounds and lived on Post Toasties™, sardines, pork & beans, ginger snaps, and Carnation™ milk.

"Every night, after supper, all us students would have to go back into Decatur from the fairgrounds—it was about a mile—to a sale that was held on the courthouse square. Mr. Reppart would buy up everything from brooms to pots and pans, so we could get some practice in selling.

"Those sales would last until about 11 o'clock at night, and then we'd have to get up at the crack of dawn to go to class. This was our schedule from Monday through Saturday. On Sundays, we had to attend church; Mr. Reppart was a stickler about that.

"He was a hard ol' row, and he worked us some pretty long hours. When it was all said and done though, I made the grade, graduated, and came on back home with the skills I needed to make a better living.

"And I took to heart what Clyde Helms used to always tell me: 'You need to figure out where you're goin' in life. If you don't know where you're going, how are you going to know when you get there?'

"And he also used to tell me, 'Once you've got a destination in mind, set yourself a stake way out there and then, just aim for that stake and work straight toward it. Don't veer off to the left or the right.'

"I set my stake, in life and in horses, a long time ago, and I've been headed toward it ever since."

2 Career and Family

"When I got back home, I still had to prove to people that I could do a good job handling their sales."

SUCCESS AS an auctioneer did not come overnight for young Hank Wiescamp. As is usually the case when a new business is born, building up clientele was a slow but steady process.

"When I got back home," notes Hank, "I still had to prove to people that I could do a good job handling their sales. In the meantime I had to make a living, so I sold Maytag washing machines for a while.

"I took the trunk lid off my Model T and built a platform on the back of it—sort of made me a pickup truck. In those days we didn't have electricity out in the country, so those washing machines had gas motors. I'd travel around the country, putting on demonstrations and selling gasoline-driven Maytag washing machines. This way I was in contact with all the farmers.

"In October of 1926 I got my first sale. It was for two bachelors who lived out northeast of town. I heard they were going to have a sale, so I went out there and told them that I thought I could sell it. I convinced them and got the sale and did a pretty good job for them. From then on, it just sort of took off and kept on gettin' a little better."

For the next several years, Hank was

Hank Wiescamp's Alamosa Sale Barn saw a lot of action during its heyday, as this photo taken in the early 1960s shows. That's Hank on the right in the auctioneer's box.

continually on the move, crisscrossing the San Luis Valley in search of auction sales to manage and cry. As the country's economy began to falter and then fail, and the Great Depression took hold, the young auctioneer's calendar began to fill.

"Those were tough times here in the valley," recalls Hank. "It wasn't that people weren't working just as hard as they ever had. But when the banks failed, and those people lost their life savings overnight, there wasn't anything for them to do but sell their farms and equipment, fold their tents, and move on.

"Handling those folks' dispersal sales was not the easiest way to make a living. But it was a job that had to be done, and it was a job that I was trained for and good at, so I just did the best I could."

It was at this same time, as he was struggling to establish and build his career as an auctioneer, that Hank made a contact of a slightly different nature.

"Shortly after I got back from auctioneer's school," he reminisces, "I went to a school program one evening out in the Waverly district. I noticed a girl sitting over by a window in a red coat with a fur collar.

"She was sitting there with some people I knew so, after the program was over, I ducked around to the front door. When they came out, I introduced myself, and talked with 'em for a while. I found out that the girl's name was Freda Flint. She had moved to the valley from Okeene, Okla., to live with her cousins, and find work.

"I finally said to Freda, 'I don't want you to think I'm forward, but you seem to be a stranger in this country. I haven't seen you before. How about going to church with me Sunday night?"

She said that she would.

"We had a church here called Seven Gables Church, with a cowboy preacher. Gil Traveler was his name and he was a pretty good cowboy. He could ride a bronc, he could rope a calf, and he was a pretty good horsetrader. But he was a good preacher too. Every Sunday night, he'd fill that church. He almost broke all the theatres in Alamosa because he was such a good entertainer.

"My brother had a Star coupe, so I borrowed it and Freda and I went to that church. After church was over, we went and had a couple of 5-cent soda pops. We were gettin' along pretty

Hank met his bride-to-be, Freda Flint, at a social gathering in 1926, in this schoolhouse south of Alamosa.

Freda Flint Wiescamp, as she looked shortly after she and Hank were married.

On their first date, Hank took Freda to church to hear the cowboy preacher, Gil Traveler, deliver a sermon. In addition to being a man of the cloth, Traveler was also quite a horseman and, in fact, sold Hank his first good mare in 1926. In this photo taken in 1924, Traveler works with three of his trick horses.

"I had never had anything to do with a sale barn before, but I had the nerve to try."

good, so I asked her, 'If you're not doing anything next Sunday, how about if I come and pick you up and we go to church again?' She said okay, and 2 years later I married her."

After Hank and Freda were wed, they moved to a place in the country, south of Alamosa.

"The place had a log house on it, and a log barn," recalls Hank. "It was nice-looking from the outside, but it wasn't insulated and it was a cold son-of-a-gun in the winter.

"In those days, we didn't have electricity out in the country. We didn't have any oil-burning stoves. We just had to burn wood. That first winter it seemed like it was 35 and 40 below zero every morning.

"Freda was working in town at the confectionery store. She was gettin' $6 a week for working 6 days. Later on, she got a better job working for the Singer Sewing Machine people. They paid her $1.50 a day. Anyway, I'd have to take her to work every morning, but sometimes I couldn't get our old Model T started when the weather got bitterly cold.

"I had an old mare who would pull, but wouldn't run off, so I'd hook her to that car every morning out on the highway where the road was bare (of snow). I'd get the car started and turn that ol' mare loose. She'd bee-line it back to the barn and I'd take Freda to work.

"Then I'd go out for the rest of the day and try to make a living. I'd work sales, trade horses and cows, just do whatever I had to do to make a dollar.

"Freda and I made a pact when we first got married. We agreed that, no matter how tough it got, we would never charge any groceries. And we never did. But I'll tell you one thing: We ate a lot of rabbits and potatoes. In fact, I ate so many rabbits that first winter that I started to think like one. Every time the dog would bark, I had to fight to keep from running under the bed," Hank laughed.

"But we made it. That was before there were food stamps, or charity, or anything. You either made it or you didn't. It was as simple as that."

The Sale Barn

Several years later, an opportunity to expand and solidify his efforts in the auction business presented itself to Wiescamp,

Billy Carson, son of the mountain man and explorer Kit Carson, worked for Hank for over 30 years. Carson and this pair of buckskin draft mares were a familiar sight around the Alamosa area in the 1940s as they hauled loose hay from the countryside into town to feed the Wiescamp livestock. Hank, Loretta, and Ron Wiescamp are barely visible in front of their sale barn home in this photo.

and he was quick to recognize its potential and act on it.

"About 1932," he remembers, "some folks from Kansas named McKinley and Eally built a sale barn out here. They ran it about 4 months and couldn't make it work. So I went to 'em and said, 'You know, if you'd consider leasing this thing, I might be interested.' They jumped at the chance to get shed of the place and made me a good deal.

"I had never had anything to do with a sale barn before, but I had the nerve to try. I talked my next-door neighbor and friend, Frank Burns, into coming in with me and we leased the place for 6 months.

"When the lease came due, I asked Frank if he wanted to go again, and he replied, 'No! It's too much hard work! I'm just going to go with my running horses.'

"'Well,' I replied, 'I'm not only going to go again, I'm going to buy the thing.'

"Frank gave me a kind of funny look and snorted, 'What's the matter with you? Did you fall out of bed and land on your head?'

"'No, I didn't,' I shot back. 'I think I can make it work.' So I bought it for $3,500. I gave 'em $250 down and my payment was $100 a month.

"At that time, the sale barn was clear out in the country.

"There wasn't a house this side of the railroad tracks. There wasn't any electricity out here. There was no telephone. There was no water. So I put in my own power plant and drilled a well.

"The whole area was really just a mess

Here's a rare photo of Hank on a horse. He's riding Holy Smoke, one of his first registered Quarter Horse stallions. This shot was taken behind the sale barn in the late 1940s.

when I took it over. It was a dump grounds. But I hired a fella with a 'dozer and he flattened it all out and buried all the tin cans.

"When I first bought it, it was a city block. It was in the country, but it had been platted with the idea that it would some day be subdivided and annexed into the city.

"I added on to it during the late 1930s by buying some adjoining land from the county. There hadn't been any taxes paid on it for 36 years so I bought it, went through court, and quieted the title. It had also been platted for streets and lots, but I

Here is one of the few photos ever taken of Skipper W under saddle. George Mueller is up on the 2-year-old chestnut colt, to the right, in this shot taken in 1947. Next to George and Skipper W are Clyde Swift and Show Boat, and next to them are Charlotte Wiescamp and Teddy.

Photo Courtesy of Clyde Swift

put it all back into acreage. I dug five more wells and put in my own sewer system that I hooked on to the city's.

"I fenced it all and started building corrals. And it was just like a tree; it just kept a-growin' from then on."

When young Hank Wiescamp started his sale barn business, the San Luis Valley farm economy was a lot more diverse than it is today.

"I started out having my sales on Saturday," he recalls, "and then it got so big that I had sales 2 days a week. I'd sell cattle on Friday and hogs and sheep on Saturday.

"That was when they had a lot of hogs and sheep in this country. Many's the day that we'd sell hogs for 4 hours. And I'd sell it all by myself. I never had any other auctioneers to help me. Then the irrigation pivots came along, and the fences came down and people quit raising hogs. Pretty soon we were just selling cattle and sheep.

"We sold a lot of work horses when farmers changed over to tractors. Once in a while, we'd have a special horse sale, but I had to quit those because the horse traders would bring those horses in from everywhere and they'd have shipping fever and distemper and everything else and, the first thing you'd know, my yards were infected and my horses would get it, so I had to quit that."

From the day it began, until the day it ended, the Wiescamp Sale Barn was a family affair.

"When I bought the sale barn," says Hank, "it had a restaurant between the office and the ring. We didn't want to run a restaurant, so we made living quarters out of it. We built some rooms upstairs. After our kids were born, we just added some more rooms. We lived there for 16 years.

"When I bought the sale barn, it had a restaurant between the office and the ring. We didn't want to run a restaurant, so we made living quarters out of it. We built some rooms upstairs. After our kids were born, we just added some more rooms. We lived there for 16 years."

"Freda clerked the sales for 48 years," states Hank. "She did all the book work. She took care of everything until her health failed, and then Charlotte took over. Ron started selling calves when he was 9 years old. By the time he was 15, he was selling most of it.

"We ran that sale barn for 58 years," continues Hank. "We ran it as a family. Even after Freda passed away, we kept after it. Finally, in 1990, I woke up one sale-day morning and decided I'd had enough. After the sale was over that evening, I got on the microphone and said, 'Well folks, this was the last one. This is the end of it.'

"I didn't know I was going to do it until that morning. The people couldn't believe it. They tried to lease it. They tried to buy it. But I said, 'Nope, It's all over with. When I'm through, I'm through.' I enjoyed the sale barn business, and I made a little money at it. But I also knew when it was time to quit it, and I did."

To promote the sale barn during its infancy, Hank had a replica of it built on a flatbed trailer. Inside the replica he placed a Shetland pony, calf, lamb, and piglet. He then mounted his family and sale barn help on typey riding horses and participated in parades in Alamosa and the surrounding communities. This shot of the group, in the early 1950s, was taken at the Monte Vista Stampede. Freda Wiescamp is mounted on the far left, and is next to Hank's brother, Lawrence "Shorty" Wiescamp. Perry McDonald is at the lines of the buckskin team, and Loretta, Ron, and Hank are to the right.

The Children

Hank and Freda Wiescamp had five children. Loretta, the oldest, was born in 1933, followed by Ron in 1937, Charlotte in 1943, Larry in 1950, and Grant in 1957. From the onset, the Wiescamp children were involved with the horses.

"All the kids were good hands," states Hank. "They could all handle horses and ride, and they all showed horses for me at one time or another.

"Loretta and Larry showed the most. Loretta was a natural on a horse. She could show one at halter and then come back and ride him in the cutting. And Larry was one of the toughs when it came to calf roping. He was the AQHA honor roll youth at that 2 years runnin'.

"When things were runnin' hot and heavy around here with the show horses, it was a family affair, that's for sure."

Throughout the 1950s and 1960s, Hank Wiescamp, his family, and his horse program prospered. The Alamosa sale barn became the best known and most successful in the valley. As will be chronicled in the following chapter, Hank also built a highly successful secondary career crying registered Quarter Horse sales throughout the West. And the fame of the Wiescamp Quarter Horses continued to mushroom.

As the material successes added up,

Even as youngsters, the Wiescamp children had access to some better-than-average riding horses. Here is Ron Wiescamp at around the age of 3 with Sam, a gelding of Lani Chief (TB) breeding. Sam was Hank's personal riding horse for a number of years before being sold to Wiley Post as a hunter-jumper prospect. Post was Will Rogers' friend and pilot.

Charlotte Wiescamp attended Colorado State University where she was a member of the CSU rodeo team. She's shown here in May 1962, running barrels on Skip Kid.

Larry Wiescamp was a top youth competitor and won the AQHA Honor Roll title in calf roping in 1967 and 1968. Here he is mounted on Skipette, the Skipper W daughter who carried him to his wins.

Photo by Conde

Ron Wiescamp also showed horses for his father. Here he is in 1958 with Skipper's King, receiving the grand champion stallion trophy at the Denver National Western Stock Show from an unidentified woman. The man on the right is J.L. "Dusty" Rhoades, who was a well-known Colorado horseman and judge.

Photo by Ralph Morgan, Courtesy of Morgan Gerard Studio

however, so did the personal tragedies.

In 1965 Ron, then only 28 years old, was killed when a generator that he was using to weld with exploded. His death was a blow that affected Hank deeply.

"Ronnie was my right-hand man," he reflects. "He had all the makings of a top cow- and horseman, and he was following in my footsteps as an auctioneer. I always used to tell him that I paved the way for him; I smoothed out as many of the rough spots as I could.

"But he would have made it even without my help. He was a good auctioneer, he knew livestock, he was smooth, and he was better with people than I was. His death was a bitter pill for Freda and me to swallow."

Three years later, Charlotte contracted Hodgkin's disease, or lymphatic cancer. After intensive treatment, over a period of 5 years, she recovered. In 1969, Loretta suffered a massive stroke. Although she survived, it left her permanently disabled.

Then, in 1982, Freda passed away after a lengthy battle against breast cancer. She and Hank had recently celebrated their 55th wedding anniversary. Finally, in 1991, at the age of 41, Larry Wiescamp passed away.

In reflecting on his family and the misfortunes that have beset it over the years, Hank remains philosophical.

"Life on this earth is a temporary thing," he notes. "You never know how long you're here for. You just have to make the best of it as it comes.

"I sit back and think a lot of those days when we were puttin' it all together," he continues. "I was too dumb to realize it then, but those were the happiest days of my life. I had my health, I had my family, and I was puttin' something together that I believed in and was excited about. Maybe I should have slowed down some back then and enjoyed it all a little more.

"Freda was a good wife and mother. My kids had talent.

"Maybe I should have spent more time with them.

"At the time, all I could think about was building up that business, building up the horses. My eye was on that stake that I'd set way out there. I didn't know how to be any different.

"Looking back, there's times I wish I had."

Young Grant Wiescamp often accompanied Hank to the various Quarter Horse sales that he cried. Here, Grant takes to the mike to thank the folks for attending an Oklahoma sale in the early 1960s. **Photo by Wayne Hunt**

Loretta Wiescamp often showed Hank's horses during the late 1940s and early 1950s. Here she is with Joker W, a halter, racing, and cutting champion who was one of her regular mounts during that time period.

3 Buckin' Broncs and Quarter Sales

"The bucking string was never a big money-maker for us. It was more or less our entertainment."

THROUGHOUT HIS life, Hank Wiescamp showed that he was willing to tackle any kind of business endeavor that would help him achieve his financial goals. One of the more interesting ventures he was involved with was a string of bucking horses that he owned and managed in partnership with Frank Burns.

Burns was one of the great horsemen to come out of southern Colorado. He was the same age as Hank, having been born in 1906 in Missouri. As a teenager, he rode his

Throughout the 1940s, '50s, and '60s, Hank Wiescamp was one of the most sought-after Quarter Horse auctioneers in the country. Here he is at work at an Oklahoma sale in the early 1960s.

During his selling career, Hank auctioned off some of the Quarter Horse breed's most famous horses. At the R.L. Underwood dispersal sale in 1956, he sold the renowned palomino cutting horse Cutter Bill as a yearling. Western Horseman *field representative Ray Davis was at that sale and took this random shot of some of the sale horses. Cutter Bill is the third colt from the left.*

***Western Horseman* Photo**

father's race horses at bush tracks and county fairs. Throughout the 1920s and early 1930s, he worked as a cowboy and jockey for the legendary Colonel C.B. Irwin of the Irwin Brothers Wild West Show.

While with Irwin, Burns developed into one of the greatest relay race riders of his day. He won the relay race at the 1933 World's Fair Rodeo in Chicago and also won that event 5 years in succession, 1935-39, at the Cheyenne Frontier Days.

Burns also followed the rodeo circuit for over 40 years, roping and riding rough-stock. He won his last saddle in a calf roping competition at the Monte Vista (Colo.) Mile-High Stampede in 1963, when he was 57 years old. And, from the days of his youth, he always maintained some involvement in horse racing, fielding both his own string, and training for such established racing stables as the CS Ranch of Cimarron, New Mexico.

Beginning in the late 1920s, Hank Wiescamp and Frank Burns formed a sort of loose partnership to pool their talents in horse trading. They traveled around southern Colorado and northern New Mexico, buying up horses and mules. The best of the horses would be marketed by the pair as cavalry, carriage-trade, and polo prospects. The mules would go to the southern cotton fields.

In the process of buying and selling high-quality animals, Wiescamp and Burns also began to accumulate a string of salty bucking horses. At first, they leased their rough-stock to rodeo stock contractors. Eventually though, they began contracting rodeos themselves.

"The bucking string was never a big money-maker for us," notes Hank. "It was more or less our entertainment. If we took the string to a rodeo at Cimarron or Monte

Hank was the auctioneer for the Rocky Mountain Quarter Horse Association's sale from 1947 to 1965. This sale was held every January in conjunction with the Denver National Western Stock Show. As this photo of horses being sifted for the 1955 sale shows, the Colorado weather did not always cooperate with the venture. **Photo by William Mueller**

Vista, and came home $200 or $300 to the good, we thought we'd stabbed a fat hog.

"But we had fun! We only gave $40 or $50 apiece for those horses. Most of 'em were half-Thoroughbreds. You take a horse that's about half-Thoroughbred, who's been ridden 3 or 4 years and then messed up, he'll stay a bucking horse for a long time.

"A young, unbroke horse won't last long. Two or three outs, and they're broke to ride. They start running off with you. I always liked those ol' horses with saddle marks on 'em who'd turned buckin' horse. They would stay with you a long time.

"We had one little horse named Tom Thumb. He wouldn't weigh 900 pounds, but he could sure buck 'em off. We had another horse—a gray named Little Boy Blue—that was pure poison.

"One time, at Monte Vista, Earl Thode drew Little Boy Blue. Now Earl was one of the good saddle bronc riders. He was the world's champ in '29 and '31. Anyway, Earl spoke with a Scandinavian brogue and, after he'd drawn Little Boy Blue, he looked at me and said, 'Vell, a man come all the vay up here, pay a $50 entry fee, and draw a Shetland pony!'

"Now you could put your saddle on Little Boy Blue and ride him all day, corral the cattle, do whatever you wanted to do. But when you put a flank strap on him, it took a bronc rider to stay on him.

"So, Earl got up on Little Boy Blue. We opened the chute and, boom! He lost his right stirrup. Then he lost his left stirrup. Then he grabbed the saddle horn. And then he bucked off! He couldn't even ride that Shetland pony pullin' leather!

"I had a lot of fun with those buckin' horses. There wasn't very much sale barn business in the summer, so they were my summer entertainment.

"Finally, when I started working a lot of registered Quarter Horse sales and bull sales, and Frank got more involved with his running horses, there was no time left

In order to evaluate the horses at the early RMQHA sales, you had to be able to look through some winter hair. Here is Sky Raider, one of the sale-toppers from the 1955 sale. The 1953 stallion, by Star Duster and out of Mary K by Ding Bob, was consigned by Quentin Semotan of Steamboat Springs, Colorado. He sold for $2,675 to Don Wilson of the Flying W Ranch in Colorado Springs, who is at his halter.

Photo by Clarence Coil/Stewart's Photographers

to be rodeo stock contractors. So we sold the whole string to McCarty and Elliott and that was the end of it."

Eddie McCarty, of Chugwater, Wyo., and Verne Elliott, of Platteville, Colo., were partners in the stock contracting business from 1920 to 1940. They furnished the rough stock for rodeos held in Madison Square Garden and Yankee Stadium in New York and Soldier's Field in Chicago, and at Cheyenne Frontier Days, Pendleton Round-Up, Fort Worth, Denver, and Omaha. Two of their better-known bucking horses were Midnight and Five Minutes to Midnight.

The Sales

By the late 1950s and early 1960s, Wiescamp was in great demand as a Quarter Horse auctioneer. It might have seemed to some people that he simply arrived on the scene at that time and was an overnight success. This was not true.

Like every other venture that he tackled in his life, Hank had spent a long time preparing for his career as a "pedigreed livestock" auctioneer.

"I didn't even start out in the auctioning business selling livestock," he comments. "I had to work up to that. I started out selling box lunches at social events. Then I worked my way up to furniture consignment sales. And then I got into farm sales. Finally I started selling some livestock.

"In the early 1930s, Frank Burns and I were buying and selling horses and mules," he says, "and we would take some of the better ones up to Denver to sell at the Colorado Horse and Mule Company sale.

"The Colorado Horse and Mule Company was owned by Charley Powell and Ray Hays. They held their sales every 2 weeks, on a Monday. Buyers would come in by train from all over the country. And I'm here to tell you that they were sharp—especially those mule buyers. They could tell you within $2 what every mule in the sale was worth.

"Anyway, we took some horses and mules up there one Monday, and when one of 'em came into the ring to be sold, Frank started kidding Charley Powell a little.

"'My partner's a pretty good auctioneer himself,' he said, 'Why don't you just let

"Working the Quarter Horse sales was never a chore to me. I liked getting out and meeting the people. And I really appreciated the opportunity to evaluate horses and breeding programs throughout the West."

Hank cried the record-setting R.S. Bar Ranch sale, Overland Park, Kan., in May 1957. The sale grossed $149,625 on 44 head—the first time any Quarter Horse auction had topped the $100,000 mark. The Paul A. daughter Paulyana also set a mare record when she sold for $10,400. Here is Hank, R.S. Bar owner R.Q. Sutherland, Paulyana, and her new owner, J.P. Davidson of Albuquerque.

Photo Courtesy of *The Quarter Horse Journal*

him give you a hand selling our stock?' After listening to Frank for a while, Charley told me to get on up in the auctioneer's box and have a go at it. So I did.

"I got along pretty good selling a few of our horses and mules. After they passed through, I went to get down from the box. Charley just motioned for me to stay up there, so I did. After the sale, he asked me if I'd go to work for him. It looked like a great opportunity to me, so I said I would.

"I sold the Denver Horse and Mule Company sales for 4 or 5 years. Charley Powell sort of took me under his wing and taught me a lot about the auction business.

"He taught me things that you can't learn in school, like how to read a person's body language from across a crowded room, how to know when to push and when to back off, and how to put the kind of energy and enthusiasm into crying a sale that would help it be a success.

"Charley's also the man who taught me that color sells horses. 'I've never left tire marks on the highway backing up to look at a solid brown horse,' he'd say, 'but I've left my share of rubber on the road backing up to look at a sorrel with a lot of white on his face and his legs.'"

In the late 1940s, Hank's growing reputation as a livestock auctioneer led to another long-standing assignment.

"The Rocky Mountain Quarter Horse Association had started having an auction during the Denver Stock Show in 1945," he says. "They were having a little trouble getting it off the ground. As I recall, their first sale only averaged $375 or so.

"They hired me to cry the 1947 sale. This was my first registered Quarter Horse sale, and I sure wanted it to be a success.

"I can remember crawling into the auctioneer's box as if it were just yesterday. There, down on the front row sat Fred Reppart. About two seats down from him was Charley Powell. And they were both grinning up at me. There I was, their student, and I was sitting in the same chair that they had both occupied for years, working sales.

"The first horse to go through the sale, a daughter of Leo, came into the ring and I started her off. One of the ringmen started pulling in bids left and right. I thought to myself, 'Man, where'd that hot-fire little son-of-a-buck come from. He's a good 'un.'

"I got up there to around $1,000 and said to him, 'That's you.' 'Oh no,' he hollered, 'I haven't got a live bid!'

"So there I sat—at my first Denver sale—standing at $1,000 on the first horse in the auction, and nobody home!

"Freda was there with me and later on she said, 'My gosh, Hank, you looked like a rainbow sittin' up there. First you were white, then you were red, then you were blue, and then you were yellow.'

"There was nothing left for me to do but start over. I stuttered and stammered; I preached and pleaded; I told stories. Finally I got back to the $1,000 I thought

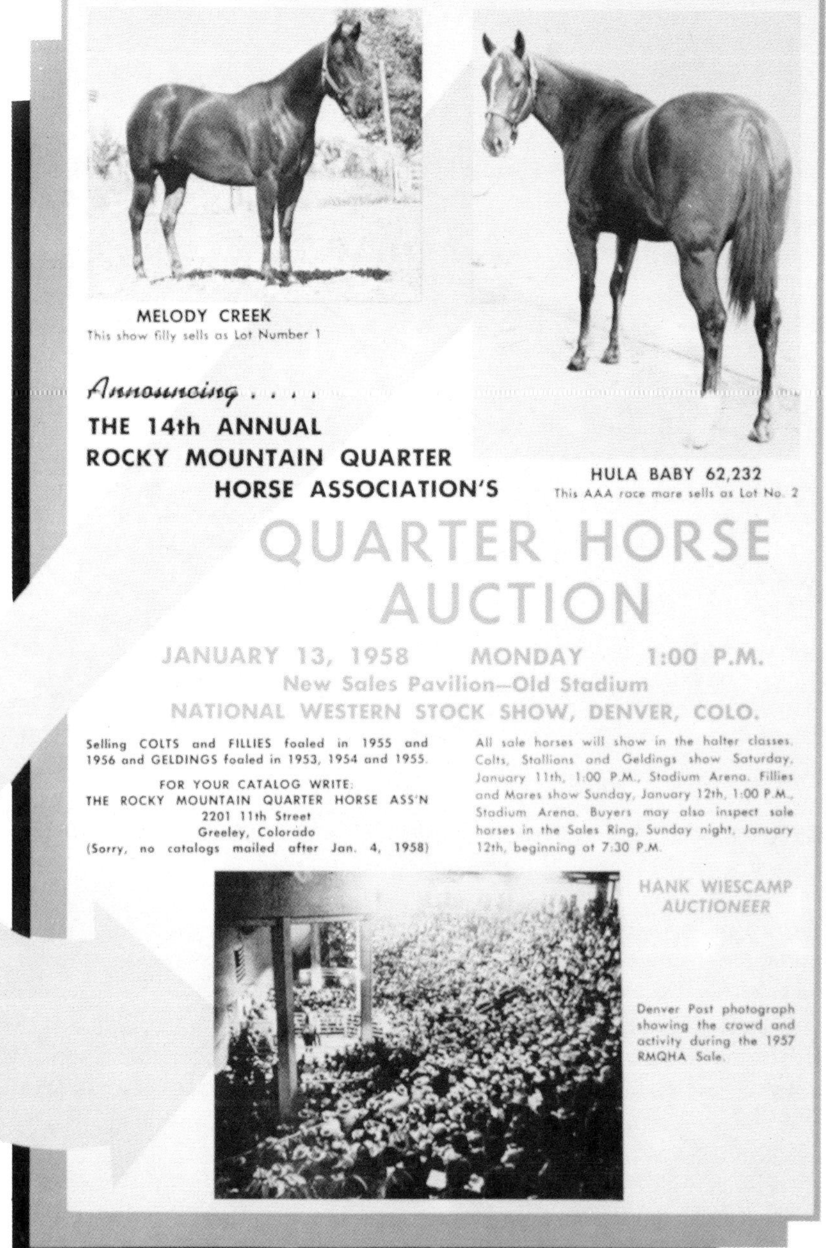

Here is a copy of the RMQHA sale's full-page ad that appeared on the inside back cover of the January 1958 Western Horseman *The sale was a record-setter in terms of numbers, total sales, and average price. One hundred eleven head sold for $139,420, or an average of $1,256.*

Photo by James Cathey

Hank cried the Denver Quarter Horse Sale for the next 19 years. As his reputation began to spread, leading breeders from throughout the West sought him out to help market their horses.

Hoss Inman, Lamar, Colo., consigned the two top-selling horses at the 1958 RMQHA sale, and G.B. Howell, Dallas, Tex., purchased them. Hula Baby, by Lightning Bar and out of Hula Girl, topped the sale at $5,400. Melody Creek, by Beaver Creek and out of Lynn Blackburn, was the second-high seller at $4,000. Here is a good shot of the record-setting quartet, with Howell (left) at the halter of Melody Creek, and Inman holding Hula Baby.

I'd had earlier, and I said to myself, 'Now what do I do?'

"Francis Dressor, who used to work for *Western Farm Life,* was another one of the ringmen. He was workin' on a fella from Billings, Mont., and I picked up on it and started workin' on that guy too. I started givin' him all the arguments.

"I talked and pleaded with that ol' boy, and I could see he was inhaling it all. Finally, Francis looked up at me and said, 'Hank, I have n-e-e-e-e-ws for you!'

"We were playin' to the crowd by this time. 'Is it good news,' I asked?

"'$1,100,' he crowed!

"'You sound just like a voice from heaven,' I laughed.

"By now, the crowd was really gettin' into the spirit of things. They were hootin' and hollerin' and, from that point on, it just took off.

"The mare wound up bringing around $1,125."

Hank cried the Denver Quarter Horse Sale for the next 19 years. As his reputation began to spread, leading breeders from throughout the West sought him out to help market their horses. The King Ranch, E. Paul Waggoner, Ed Honnen, B.F. Phillips, Walter Merrick, Hoss Inman, Frank Vessels, and Robert Sutherland were just a few of the top breeders who hired Hank to auction their sales.

"The King Ranch and Waggoner Ranch horses always seemed very similar to me," notes Hank. "They were good horses for that time and that country, but they weren't my kind of horse. They were 'bulldogs.'

"But the Walter Merrick, B.F. Phillips, and Hoss Inman horses were my type. They had that half-Thoroughbred look that I liked. In fact, although I made it a personal practice to not try to buy horses at the sales that I cried, I did make exceptions to that rule on a couple of occasions.

"In the early 1960s, I was searching the country over for good sons and daughters of Three Bars (TB). I wound up buying two of his daughters, Twin Bar (TB) and Anna Bar, at sales that I cried. They both did a good job for me in the broodmare band."

Over the years, Hank sold some of the greatest Quarter Horses of all time. Among his many memories of the horses and people that he crossed paths with through the sales that he cried is the one involving Cutter Bill and Rex Cauble.

"I was crying R.L. Underwood's dispersal sale in the spring of 1956," he states. "Cutter Bill was a yearling at the time and he was a nice-looking colt. I was having a little trouble getting what I thought he was worth. I spotted Rex Cauble standing with a group of guys near the back of the tent.

"I knew Rex well enough to know that, at that time, he could've bought and sold me a hundred times. But I singled him out anyway and hollered, 'Rex, you're not paying attention. This is a good colt. You need this colt. He'll make you money.'

"I had his attention, so I laid it on him. 'I'm so sure that this is the colt you need, that I'll tell you what I'm gonna' do.

"'You bid on this colt and, if you get him, I'll loan you the money right here and now to pay for him. You can just take him home and pay me back whenever you can.'

"Man, that did it! Ol' Rex's hand started flyin' up and he bought Cutter Bill for $1,500, which was a big price for a yearling stallion at that time. And he never borrowed the money from me to pay for him either."

Cutter Bill went on to become the 1962 National Cutting Horse Association's World Champion Cutting Horse and a leading sire.

For all practical purposes, Hank's career as a Quarter Horse auctioneer ended in the mid-1960s.

"I did work a few select Quarter Horse sales after 1965," he says, "but that was the summer that Ron died. He had been handling a lot of the responsibilities around the ranch and the sale barn. That had freed me up to book sales. With him gone, I just had to cut a lot of the traveling out.

"Working the Quarter Horse sales was never a chore to me. I liked getting out and meeting the people. And I really appreciated the opportunity to evaluate horses and breeding programs throughout the West.

"When I had a big sale to work, like E. Paul Waggoner's or B.F. Phillips', I'd arrive a day early just to study the horses. I'd try to pick out the best ones—the ones I thought would top the sale. But I'd make mental notes on all the horses. It just helped me sell 'em.

"As my sale barn business at home grew, and my own horse breeding program expanded, it got harder and harder for me to get away. So I finally had to put an end to the outside sales.

"If I was a good auctioneer—and I think I was—it was because I enjoyed it, and I took the time to study it and learn it right. Auctioneering was always a love of mine. I only quit it for the one thing that I loved more, and that was the horses."

4 Early Horse Influences

"The U.S. Army was without a doubt the biggest single buyer of good young horses at the time I got into the horse trading business."

TO BETTER understand the origins of the Wiescamp horse breeding program, we must take into consideration both the time and climate in which it was formed.

Hank Wiescamp returned to Alamosa from auctioneer's school in the fall of 1926. At this time, the horse was still very much a part of the country's urban, rural, and military cultures. Although it loomed on the horizon, the Age of Mechanization had not yet completely displaced the horse on the nation's city streets, in farm fields, and on cavalry posts.

As a result, a broad-based horse market still existed. Demand was high for quality prospects for use as buggy and carriage horses, cavalry mounts, polo ponies, and hunter/jumpers.

And young Hank Wiescamp, all of 20 years old at the time, was quick to capitalize on the situation.

"The U.S. Army was without a doubt the biggest single buyer of good young horses at the time I got into the horse

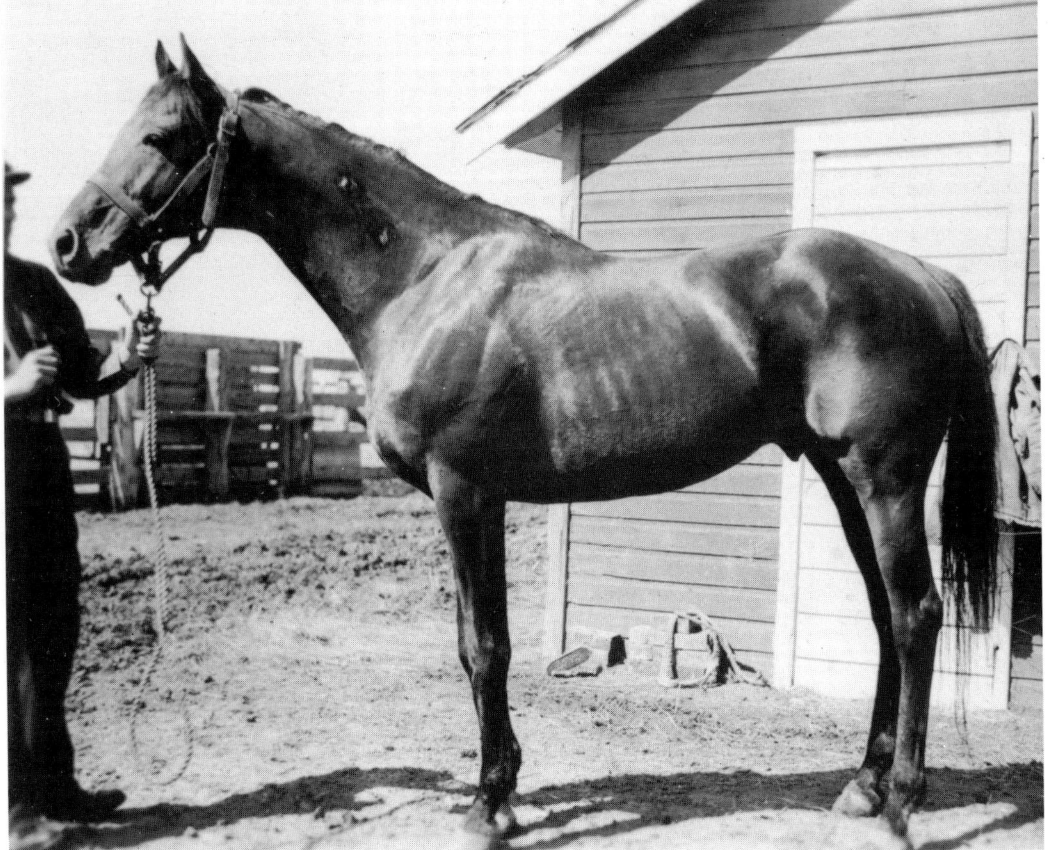

Maple Prince, the Thoroughbred stallion Hank Wiescamp utilized prior to the advent of his Quarter Horse breeding program.

Photo Courtesy of the Nebraska State Historical Society

Flamette, the first horse Wiescamp registered with the American Quarter Horse Association. On the left, she stands in front of the sale barn that the Wiescamp family called both business and home for many years. Below, she is in front of a hay wagon with a pretty fancy towing vehicle hooked to it.

Photos Courtesy of the American Quarter Horse Museum & Heritage Center, Amarillo, Texas

trading business," he recalls. "I began dealing in cavalry horses almost immediately after returning to Alamosa from auctioneer's school.

"There was also quite a market back east for polo prospects and fancy buggy and carriage horses and, as far as I could see, there just wasn't a lot of difference in the type of horse that would satisfy the needs in all three of those areas."

That type, according to Wiescamp, was a middle-of-the road horse—15 to 15.1 hands and 1,000 to 1,250 pounds in weight—built on a heavily muscled Thoroughbred frame.

The U.S. Cavalry Remount program was in full swing during the mid-1920s. This program, which was administered by the U.S. government, allotted registered Thoroughbred stallions, at no cost, to horsemen throughout the country to be crossed on native mares. The program's goal was the production of a pool of horses of consistent

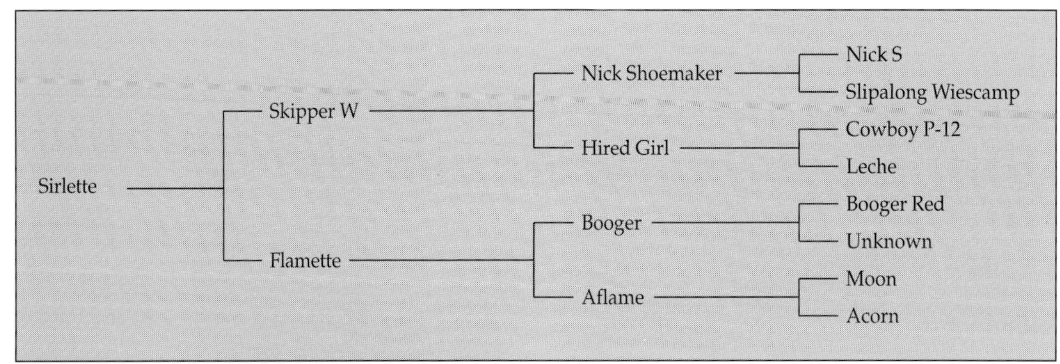

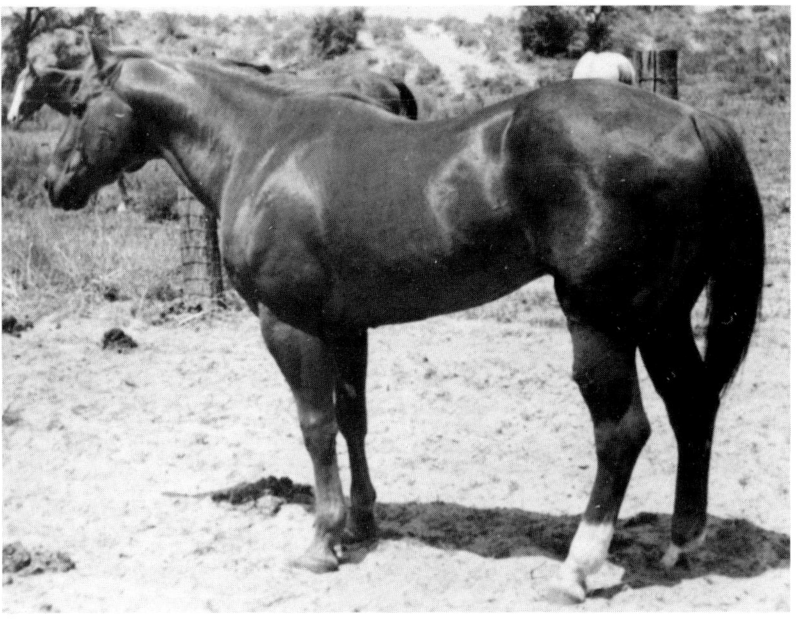

Sirlette, by Skipper W and out of Flamette, was foaled in 1952. He sired a number of excellent show horses over the years, but his greatest claim to fame was as a broodmare sire. He is shown here in 1971 at Leroy Webb's ranch near Monte Vista, Colorado.
Photo Courtesy of Sharlis Irwin

type and known breeding that could be bought by the Army in a very short time should the need arise.

Although all of the foals who resulted from this program were the property of the mare owners to do with as they saw fit, a high percentage of them were eventually sold to the government. Hank capitalized on the Remount program in two ways—by putting together a small broodmare band and breeding them to local Remount stallions, and, eventually, by acquiring a top-notch Remount stallion himself.

Wiescamp's first broodmares were acquired as a result of his constant travels throughout southern Colorado and northern New Mexico during the middle 1920s to late 1930s.

As Hank traveled through the San Luis Valley, first building up his farm sale business, and later his sale barn business, he was constantly on the lookout for top cavalry and "eastern-trade" prospects, and also good young mares for his own use. He established a pattern of buying, selling, and trading mares during this time period that would remain constant for the next 15 years.

"This country was full of horses when I got into the business," recalls Wiescamp. "Every farmer had at least a pair of work horses and maybe a buggy or saddle horse. And if he were so inclined, he might have a broodmare or two.

"As the '30s rolled around, and the Great Depression took hold, people started going broke and selling out. I was handling a lot of their farm sales—sometimes two a day—so I got a firsthand look at a lot of the horses who were in this country. Every once in a while, a good mare would come to my attention and I'd deal for her. Then, when I got into the sale barn business, I was on the road even more. I was traveling all over the valley, visiting with farmers and ranchers, buying a few cattle, sheep, and hogs outright, but mostly just trying to encourage folks to give me and my sale barn a try.

"Here again, I'd run across a pretty good type of mare every once in a while, and I'd deal for her. Most of the mares I bought during this time were of Thoroughbred breeding. They showed Remount breeding in their frames and bone structure. They weren't the best mares in the world, but they weren't the worst either.

"My mare band wasn't too big during those days, and I was always working to improve it. If I'd run across a mare somewhere who was better than any of my mares, I'd pick her up and deal off one of my lesser mares. Even back then, I was trying to put together a like set of mares, a set of mares who could produce cavalry mounts, or polo ponies, or fancy buggy horses, and I made a little progress."

Although these first mares set the stage for the great broodmares who were yet to come, few of them had any lasting effect on the Wiescamp program. Two notable exceptions would be the mares Aflame and Busy Bee, both acquired by Hank in the mid-1930s.

At around this same time, Hank had acquired the first of the stallions who would have any impact on his breeding program. This was Booger, a young, crippled stallion sired by Booger Red, by Rancocas (TB), and bred by the Trinchera Ranch of Fort Garland, Colorado.

In 1935 Hank bred Aflame, who was sired by Moon, by Concho Colonel, to Booger and she produced Flamette, the first horse Wiescamp registered with the American Quarter Horse Association. Flamette went on to be the grand champion mare at the first Quarter Horse show ever held at the Denver National Western Livestock Show, in 1944, and she also

Sir Leyban, by Sirlette and out of Leyba Fe Ana, was one of the top show horses in the Rocky Mountain region in the mid-1960s. An AQHA Champion, he earned a Superior in halter, and stood grand champion in Palomino competition at the Denver National Western and the New Mexico State Fair.

Photo by Darol Dickinson, Courtesy of *The Quarter Horse Journal*

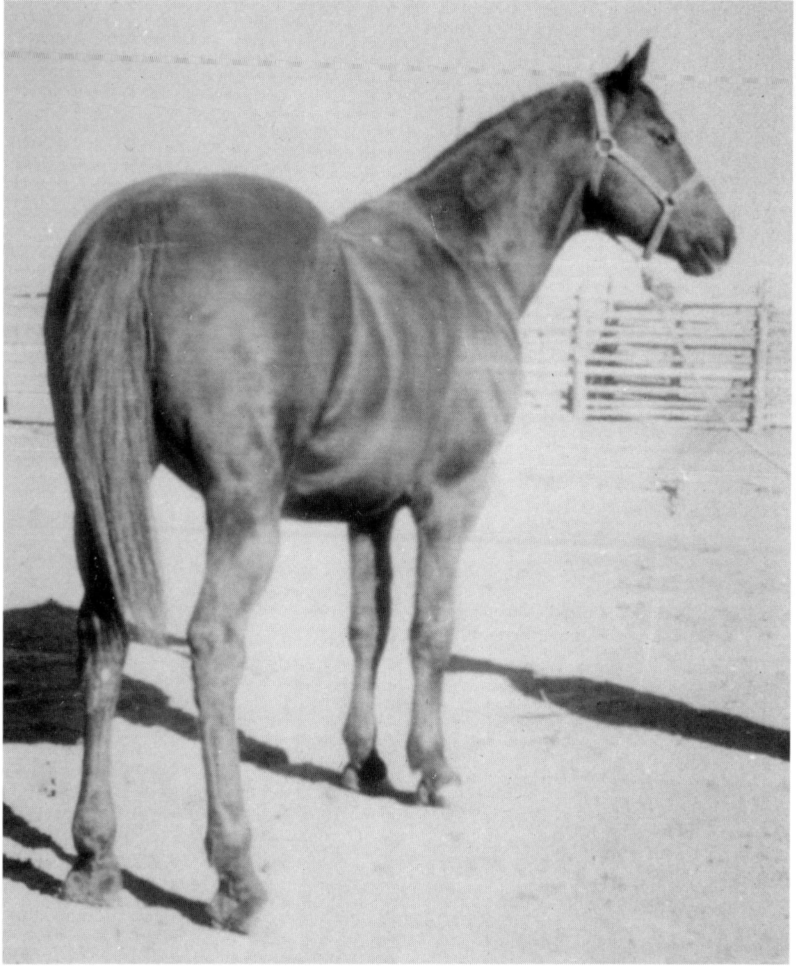

Barney Owens was the first of a long line of Quarter Horse stallions utilized by Hank. The stallion's most lasting contribution to the Wiescamp program was through a number of top-producing daughters.

Photo Courtesy of the American Quarter Horse Museum & Heritage Center, Amarillo, Texas

became one of the cornerstones of the early Wiescamp breeding program.

Among the good horses that Flamette produced for Hank were H.J. Sir Nick, by Nick W., a halter and performance point-earner; Sirlette, by Skipper W, a top sire; Sis Nick, by Nick W, an AQHA Champion producer; and Spotette, by Spot Cash, also an AQHA Champion producer.

Busy Bee was a CS Ranch-bred mare, sired by Little Joe, by Harmon Baker, by Peter McCue. When taken by Hank to the court of the Remount Thoroughbred named Galus, Busy Bee produced the good show mare and producer Night Nurse, who also figured prominently in the early Wiescamp breeding program.

Night Nurse was the dam of the good breeding stallions Super Cash, by Spot Cash, and Skip Comet, by Skipper's King. She was also the dam of several top-producing mares such as Skip Nurse and Skip's Aid, by Skipper W, and Skip A Nurse and Skip's Art, by Skipper's King.

In addition to breeding mares to Galus, Hank utilized several other area Remount stallions in his early breeding program. The services of Coventry (winner of the 1925 Preakness), Captain Alcock, Advantage, Light Carbine, and Reighlock were all used by the young Colorado horse breeder at one time or another.

Again, only a few of the horses resulting from these early breedings found their way into Hank's permanent breeding band. One mare who did was Hollyhock W., a brown mare foaled in 1938, sired by Reighlock (TB) and out of Miss Hall, by Light Carbine (TB).

Hollyhock W. lived out her entire life at Wiescamp's and proved to be a stellar producer for him. Among her produce were Joker W., by Nick Shoemaker, a 1944 dun stallion who was a halter, racing, and cutting champion; H.J. Scootalong, by Scooter W., a 1950 sorrel mare who, like her dam, was a solid producer; and Speedster, by Nick W, a 1952 dun gelding who placed in the NCHA top 10 in 1962 and who earned 250 AQHA cutting points.

In later years the influence of a Remount stallion by the name of Chimney Sweep (TB), who had been allotted to the CS Ranch, would also have a significant effect on the Wiescamp program, primarily through his palomino son, Brushmount.

All during the years that he was breeding mares to local Remount stallions, however, Hank kept his eye peeled for just the right type of Thoroughbred stallion to bring back to Alamosa to use on his mares on an extensive basis. He

Nye's Barney Google, an AQHA Champion by Barney Owens, out of Southern Queen.

found him in 1938 at the Fort Robinson, Neb., Remount depot.

"It was in the spring of the year when I went to Fort Robinson," recalls Hank. "They still had most of their studs right there at the station. I must have looked at 125 stallions and, when I was through, Major Adamson, who was in charge of the breeding end of the operation, asked me how many of the studs I liked.

"'Two,' I told him. He got a little offended over that answer—he kind of jumped up and down a little—but he finally asked me, 'Which two?'

"'Above Par and Maple Prince,' I said. Above Par was a big chestnut horse. I liked him a lot. He was a heavier-made horse than Maple Prince. He had more muscle. But he was a little sickle-hocked, and I didn't care for that. And he had already been assigned to Doc Hilton at Cheyenne anyway, so that left only Maple Prince.

"Maple Prince was a son of Sweep, by Ben Brush. I never made the connection then—in fact, I never made it until years later—but the best, most consistent results I ever got from my Thoroughbred outcrosses came when I went to Ben Brush horses. It just always seemed to work out that way.

"Anyway, Maple Prince was a Ben Brush horse—and a good one. He stood a little over 15 hands. He had a beautiful head and neck, and he had a lot of rear end and hind leg muscle. I liked him and I was

"The best, most consistent results I ever got from my Thoroughbred outcrosses came when I went to Ben Brush horses."

No Butt, the 1962 World Champion Quarter Running Horse, was out of Red Bottom, a Wiescamp-bred daughter of Barney Owens.

Photo Courtesy of *The Quarter Horse Journal*

"After Mr. Baca passed away, his family wanted to get rid of the horses. I got wind of it and went down there and bought 'em all—92 head."

ready to bring him back home with me."

As it turned out, however, Maple Prince was not assigned to the southern Colorado area, and Hank was forced to return to Alamosa without him.

"It didn't look like I was going to ever get Maple Prince," Hank continued, "so I sort of forgot about him for awhile.

"Then, one day, I got a telegram. We had just bought the sale barn. We didn't have a telephone in it yet. A boy on a bicycle came by with a telegram from Major Adamson, and it read, 'Do you like Maple Prince as well as you did?' I just turned it over and wrote on the back, 'The U.S. Remount Service has one stallion—Maple Prince, signed, Hank Wiescamp.' I sent it back with the boy and didn't pay any more attention to it.

"About 2 weeks later, I came home one evening and Freda told me that the Army had been by and dropped off a beautiful bay stud. I went into the sale barn, and there was Maple Prince, standing in the ring.

"I finally had him and I kept him until he died. I was the only one to use him. I had enough of my own mares that the Army didn't make me stand him to outside mares. He was a good horse. His colts could run, they could perform, they could do about anything that you wanted them to."

During the years that Hank used Maple Prince, most of the good young horses sired by him went either to the Army, for use as cavalry mounts, or back east, to be turned into polo ponies or fancy carriage horses.

Hank made a present of Cherioca (TB), one of the daughters of Maple Prince, to Kenneth Gann, who was working for him at the time. Gann bred Cherioca to Joe Mac R, a grandson of Jack McCue, and got Cheri Mac, a Register of Merit race mare and one of the first AQHA Champions ever named.

Later, when Gann fell terminally ill, Hank bought back Cherioca and several of her daughters and granddaughters, including Cheri Mac.

Cheri Mac, when bred to Skipper W, produced Skipador, a grand champion halter horse and multiple AQHA Champion sire. She also produced a trio of mares for Wiescamp who went on to become solid performers: Spanish Cheri, by Spanish Nick, and Skip Irish and Skip's Rose, by Skipper's King.

Cheri Barta, by Bart B.S., a AAA-rated racing daughter of Cheri Mac who was raised and raced by Gann, was bred to Skipper's King after she was acquired by Wiescamp. From this mating she produced the AQHA champion show horse and sire Skip Barta.

Like the early Wiescamp Quarter-type sire Booger, Maple Prince does not at first appear to have had any broad-based, lasting effect on the modern Wiescamp breeding program.

Both stallions, however, are responsible for at least one of the foundation mare lines that Wiescamp has become so renowned for. More importantly, they each helped put food on the table and keep a roof over the head of the young Colorado horseman and his family as they struggled to make ends meet during the hard times of the Great Depression.

In 1941, Hank made the first of several large mare purchases that, more than anything else he did at the start of his horse-breeding endeavors, marked him as a man who dared to tackle any horse-related venture that he believed could work.

"N.T. Baca and his family were still running cattle and horses on the Baca Grant in northeastern New Mexico," recalls Hank "They had leased a lot of that country between Gallegos and Mos-

Toppereno descended from Barney Owens through his sire, Shorty Bill. This smutty-colored palomino gelding dominated the western riding event in AQHA competition during the mid-1960s, and was Honor Roll champion in the event in 1963, 1964, 1965, and 1967.

Cheri Mac was bred by long-time Wiescamp employee Kenneth Gann. When purchased from Gann by Wiescamp, she became one of his foundation mares. Cheri Mac was both a champion race horse and an early AQHA Champion. Gann is holding her after one of her halter wins. **Photo by James Cathey**

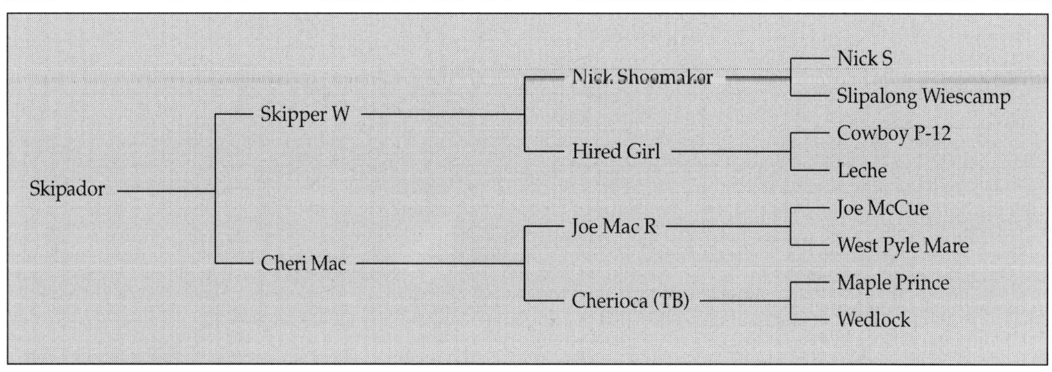

Skipador, by Skipper W and out of Cheri Mac, was an early Wiescamp show champion who went on to be a top sire.

quero. After Mr. Baca passed away, his family wanted to get rid of the horses. I got wind of it and went down there and bought 'em all—92 head.

"I'm here to tell you that they were just a little wild, too. The Baca hands ran 'em in off the range and we loaded 'em into boxcars—28 to a car 'cause that's all a car was supposed to hold. When the train engineer got ready to go, he took a big pull on the whistle and those horses all ran to one end of the cars. I wound up with just a half a carload in each car. That's how wild they were," grinned Hank. "I could have put another 28 horses in each one.

"I gave $35 apiece for 'em. There were some mules in the bunch, too. I sold them to the Army. I think I got about $250 apiece for 'em. There were also seven or eight geldings and I sold all those to the Army. I made a pretty good chunk of money on that deal."

The bulk of the Baca horses were brood-

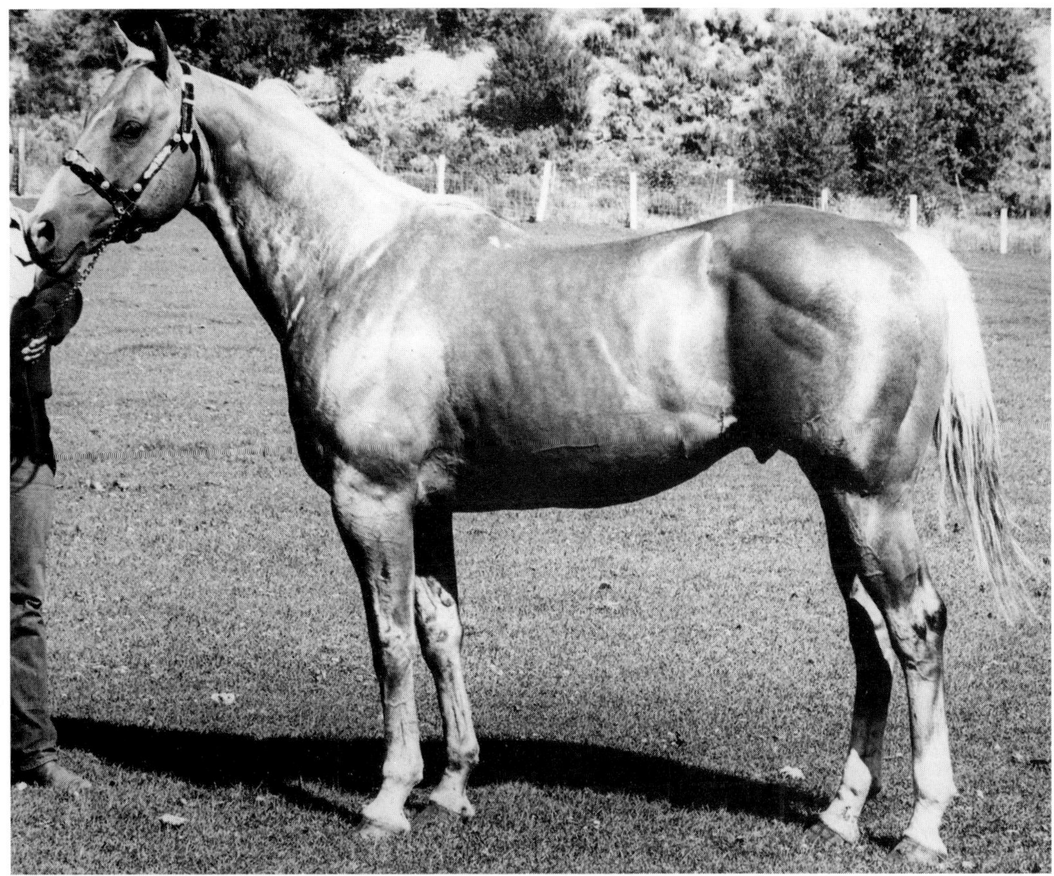

Skip's Pride, a son of Skipador, was out of Shorty's Blonde, by Shorty Bill. An AQHA Champion, he was a close descendant of both Barney Owens and Cheri Mac.

Photo by Darol Dickinson, Courtesy of *The Quarter Horse Journal*

mares sired by A.D. Reed, a son of Peter McCue. A.D. Reed had achieved fame early in his life as a sire in southwestern Oklahoma and eventually wound up in northeastern New Mexico under the ownership of Filiburto Gallegos.

"I didn't have room here at the home place to keep 92 more horses," continues Hank. "So I rented the stockyards across the tracks and put 'em there. I bought three burros and used them to break those horses to lead. I'd tie one to each burro. In 3 days I'd turn 'em loose and get three more. Eventually I got 'em all gentled down and broke to lead and that sure made 'em easier to peddle."

In time, Wiescamp sold or traded off most of the Baca horses. He held on to the 10 or 15 best young mares, breeding them to the stallions that he had at that time, who included Booger, a son of Booger named Lucky, and Clark Gable, a son of the Remount Thoroughbred Captain Alcock.

At around this same time Hank also acquired a top Quarter Horse stallion named Barney Owens.

Barney Owens was bred by W.J. Francis, Floyd, N.M., and foaled in 1929. He was reportedly a son of Jack McCue, by Peter McCue, and was out of Maud, by Shorty.

As is the case with a number of foundation Quarter Horses, there is some controversy surrounding Barney Owens' pedigree. While his AQHA-recognized pedigree is as stated above, volume 2 of the AQHA stud books shows him as being sired by a horse named Schlechle II.

This name was probably a misspelling of Shillelagh II. Shillelagh II was a remount Thoroughbred who stood during the late 1920s and early 1930s at the ranch of J.A. Black, Santa Rosa, New Mexico. Given Barney Owens' birthdate and place, it is entirely possible that he was sired by Shillelagh II and not Jack McCue.

Although Hank purchased him from a local Alamosa horseman, Barney Owens

Skip Nurse, sired by Skipper W and out of Night Nurse, was a winning halter and race mare, and a top producer. Kenneth Gann is holding her in this win photo, after a victory at La Mesa Park in Raton, New Mexico.

had been previously owned by Jesus Baca of Santa Fe, and had, in fact, been used extensively on the Baca mares during the years just prior to their purchase by Hank.

As a result, Wiescamp had the living proof right in his corrals of how Barney Owens crossed on the Baca mares, and it was good enough, in his opinion, to purchase the stallion when he came up for sale.

"I thought Barney Owens was a model kind of a horse," remembers Hank. "He was by Jack McCue, but he didn't look like most of the Jack McCues I ever saw. Most of them weren't too good-headed, but this little horse was keen-headed. He was a dark chestnut and he only stood about 14.2, but I'll guarantee you he could run a hole in the wind. He was a match-race horse and a good one."

Hank used Barney Owens as a herd sire for 7 years. During that time he sired several notable show champions including the gelding Nye's Barney Google, an AQHA Champion who stood grand at halter at the 1956 Denver National Western.

While owned by Wiescamp, Barney Owens also sired the Register of Merit race horses Bank Roll and Joe M. His greatest contribution to Hank's early horse breeding program, however, was as the sire of a number of excellent broodmares.

Barney Owens was initially bred to the Baca mares and then, later on, to the Old Fred-bred mares Hank assembled.

Lucille M., a 1941 mare by Barney Owens and out of Lona Lee, by A.D. Reed, was purchased by Guy Corpe, Sacramento, Calif., from Hank in 1945. She was in foal to Nick Shoemaker. The resulting foal, a smutty-colored palomino colt named Shorty Bill, went on to become a top show horse and sire on the West Coast. One of his get, a 1957 palomino stallion by the name of Toppereno, earned honors as the AQHA Honor Roll western riding horse of 1963, 1964, 1965, and 1967.

Shorty Bill was indicative of the kind of smooth, athletic horse the daughters

Here is Skip Barta, an AQHA Champion son of Skipper's King, out of Cherry Barta, who was by Bart B.S. and out of Cheri Mac.

Photo by Roger Wilson, Courtesy of *The Quarter Horse Journal*

of Barney Owens consistently produced. Hank thought enough of Shorty Bill as an individual to go to California and purchase a daughter of his named Shorty's Blonde. When bred to Skipador, she produced Skip's Pride, a 1960 palomino who went on to earn his AQHA Championship in 1965.

Red Bottom, a bay mare foaled in 1946, was sired by Barney Owens and was out of Sunkist, by Plaudit. Sold by Hank as a young mare to Guy Corpe, Red Bottom was bred to Joe Less, by Joe Moore, in 1954 and produced the legendary running mare No Butt in 1955.

Racing during a time of small purses, No Butt went to the post 103 times, winning 29 races and $63,882. In 1961 she was named the AQHA World Champion 3-Year-Old Filly, and the following year she came back to earn the racing titles of AQHA World Champion Aged Mare, World Champion Mare, and World Champion Quarter Running Horse.

Among the other Barney Owens mares who went on to become solid producers for Wiescamp were Loraine S., Skit Skat, Slip On, Spanish Charm, Silk Hat, Slip Over, and Sailor's Girl.

In 1948, Hank parted company with Barney Owens, selling him to Dr. C.H. Hall, of Casper, Wyo., who, in turn, sold him to Hugh Bennett, of Falcon, Colorado.

"Barney Owens was a good horse," Hank concludes. "My decision to sell him when I did was based more on the increased interest that I had developed in the Old Fred line of horses than it was on any great dissatisfaction with him.

"I had made up my mind to line-breed the Old Freds and that made Barney Owens more or less excess baggage. So I sold him and went on."

5 THE COKE ROBERDS CONNECTION

This horse, known today as Old Fred, is the one individual in the Coke Roberds program who has had the most profound affect on . . . the breeding program of Hank Wiescamp.

During the course of his travels throughout southern Colorado and northern New Mexico in the late 1920s and early 1930s, Hank Wiescamp was drawn more and more to a family of horses that had been popularized by Coke Roberds, who ranched near Hayden, Colorado.

Roberds had been born in Texas in 1870. He moved with his family to a ranch about 20 miles east of Trinidad, Colo., a decade or so later. The ranch was soon well-stocked with horses and cattle, and Coke, who loved ranch life, was seldom out of the saddle. He

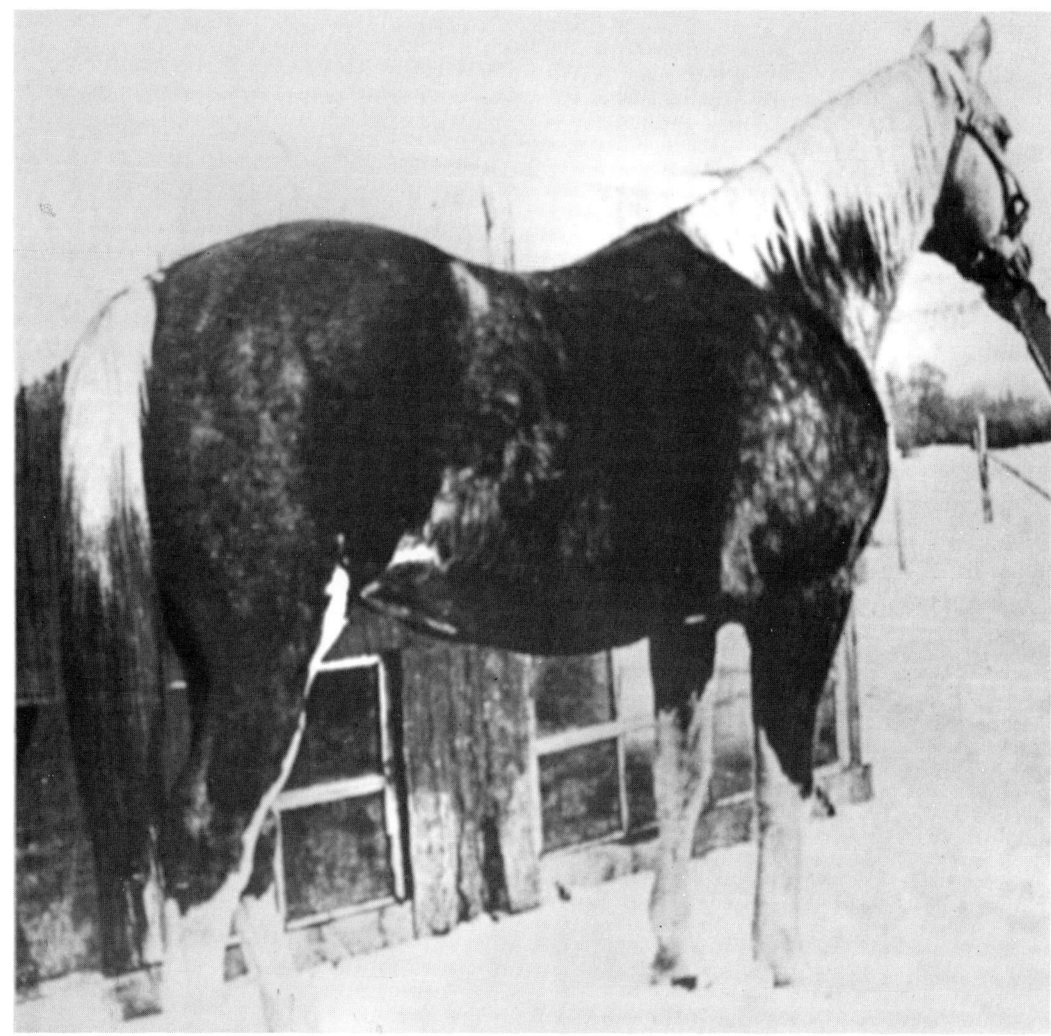

Descendants of the legendary palomino stallion Old Fred (1894-1915) served as the cornerstone for the family of Quarter Horses that Hank Wiescamp began developing in the early 1940s.

became a top hand at an early age.

Even though he was better educated than most ranch boys of the time, having been sent to college back east, Coke never wanted to pursue any vocation other than ranching.

During the late 1890s, he began working for the Holland and Easley Ranch, north of the XIT in west Texas. It was there that he met his future wife, Beulah. They wed in 1898.

Shortly after the turn of the century, when farming began to creep into west Texas, Coke moved to the "no man's land" of the Oklahoma panhandle, hiring on with the A-11 Ranch.

Just prior to his move to Oklahoma, Coke had purchased eight or nine Steeldust mares from a cowboy who had stopped at his place with the horses in tow. Around this same time, he had also acquired a mare of running blood. He bred this mare to a stallion known as the Circus Horse, who belonged to a circus that wintered in Trinidad. The result of this breeding was a flashy stallion that Coke called Arab.

Roberds used Arab as both his ranch and buggy horse. He also bred him to his Steeldust mares for the next several years, initially for no other reason than to produce good ranch horses for his own use.

Eventually, Coke needed a second stallion to cross on the daughters of Arab. After an extensive search, he settled on a blazed-face, stocking-legged horse named Primero, whom he purchased from Senator Casimiro Borilla of Trinidad.

In 1908, after visiting Si Dawson, a boyhood friend who owned a ranch in north-central Colorado, Coke decided to move once more. This resulted in the purchase of a ranch near Hayden, which had become available when the previous owner was sent to the Colorado penitentiary in Canon City after shooting a neighboring rancher in a dispute over water rights.

The Roberds family shipped all of their belongings, including Primero and his broodmare band, to Wolcott, Colo., on the Rio Grande railroad. From there they were to be freighted over the mountains, through the Yampa Valley, to Hayden. En route to Wolcott, the train wrecked, killing Primero.

Coke Roberds, pioneer horse breeder and one-time owner of Old Fred, in a photo taken during the 1950s. Roberds' development of a superior family of ranch and race horses in northern Colorado greatly influenced Wiescamp's early horse breeding goals.

Once more, Coke needed a herd sire. This time it didn't take him long to find one.

During his initial trip from Wolcott to Hayden, Coke saw a number of horses who made a favorable impression on him. On one occasion, a banker drove by in a buggy pulled by two fine-looking mares. Upon inquiring how they were bred, Coke found out that they were sired by "a horse around here called Fred."

A short while later, Roberds happened upon a cowboy riding a "crackin' good horse" and asked if he was for sale. The rider refused because his horse was by a stallion called Fred.

On a subsequent trip back to Wolcott, Coke and his wife came across a freighter heading for Oak Creek. Roberds spotted a palomino horse on the wheel, and figured it was the Fred horse he had been looking for.

The freighter was in a hurry and would

Squaw, by Peter McCue and out of an Old Fred mare, is an excellent example of the type of horse that Coke Roberds was breeding in the 1920s. Squaw was a top race mare, winning 49 of her 50 starts. **Photo Courtesy of Emmett Roberds**

Billy Whiskers, the Coke Roberds-bred gelding who is at least partially responsible for Hank Wiescamp's decision to use the Old Fred family of horses in his breeding program. Note Billy's high withers and strong top line—features that Roberds stressed in his horses.

barely consent to stop long enough to talk to the rancher, but Roberds persisted and stood in the road that day until he had traded for the stallion.

This horse, known today as Old Fred, is the one individual in the Coke Roberds program who has had the most profound affect on, not only the breeding program of Hank Wiescamp, but also those of a host of other early Quarter Horse, Palomino, Appaloosa, and Paint breeders.

Old Fred was foaled in Missouri in 1894. The most commonly accepted pedigree information on him lists his sire as Black Ball, by Missouri Rondo, and his dam as a palomino mare by John Crowder by Old Billy.

In size, Fred was a big horse, standing 16 hands and weighing more than 1,400 pounds. Those statistics, especially the weight, might seem hefty by today's standards, but Old Fred was born into, and prospered in, a far different horse world than the one that we know.

Ninety years ago, horses were bred to be worked all week long—under saddle, between buggy shafts, and in front of horse-drawn machinery. On the weekends and at fair time, more than a few of them were raced for fun and profit.

Old Fred and his descendants excelled in all of these fields. As Coke put it, "You could breed Old Fred to a draft mare and get the best work horse you ever hitched; or you could breed him to a race mare and get yourself a race horse."

In color, Old Fred was a deep gold, with snow white mane and tail. He had a full-blazed face and white lower lip. On his front legs were two high stockings, extending a considerable distance above his knees. Both hind legs were white to the hocks, with the right hind having a white strip stretching up to the stifle. He was also reported to have had a white spot on his left side.

Old Fred headed the Roberds breeding program for a number of years before being sold to the Watson Brothers of Eagle, Colo., where he died in 1915. After Old Fred, Roberds used a number of other great stallions, including Peter McCue (see *Legends, Vol. 2*), the cavalry Remount Thoroughbreds Dundee and Dancing Master, Brown Dick, Prince (Coke T), Smokey T, Ute Chief, Champagne, Buddy Nile, and Fred M.

Nick S., by Sheik P-11 and out of Sylvia, by Bob H, was bred by Marshall Peavy of Clark, Colorado. The blood of Nick, primarily through his son Nick Shoemaker, and daughter Leche, had a major impact on Wiescamp's horse program. "Leche," by the way, is the Spanish word for milk.

Photo Courtesy of *The Quarter Horse Journal*

"So we made a trip to Hayden and, once I got a look at Coke's breeding stock, I got plumb horse-foundered."

Coke was an active horse breeder for almost 60 years—from before the turn of the century until the middle 1950s. His efforts as a pioneer Quarter Horse breeder were sufficient to see him enshrined in the AQHA Hall of Fame in 1986.

Probably the easiest way to put Coke Roberds in proper perspective as a early-day horse breeder is to note that his program served as a basis for the creation of such great successive operations as those of Marshall Peavy, Dan Casement, Warren Shoemaker, and Hank Wiescamp. All of these men have also been inducted into the AQHA Hall of Fame.

Hank Wiescamp remembers very clearly the first Coke Roberds-bred horse that he ever saw, and the impression it made on him.

"Frank Burns and I were at a race meet in Canon City in the late 1930s," he recalls. "I saw a gelding there who was one of the nicest horses I had ever seen. He was a bay with four stocking legs and a blaze face. His name was Billy Whiskers, and he was

Here's a photo of Plaudit taken on the Philmont Ranch in the mid to late 1930s. The influence of Plaudit, through his daughters and granddaughters, on the Wiescamp program in its formative years was profound.

Photo Courtesy of Philmont Museum/ Seton Memorial Library, Cimarron, New Mexico

owned by the Wallace brothers from Alamosa.

"Frankie and I went over to the Wallace boys and inquired about the horse. We found out that he had been bred by Coke Roberds. He was sired by a horse named Brown Dick, and out of a Peter McCue-Old Fred-bred mare.

"I remember I asked them why they had ever gelded a horse as good as him? They told me there was no sense in leaving him a stud because he wasn't registerable (as a Thoroughbred). I said, 'What difference does that make, you can't ride or breed papers!'

"Anyway, Frank knew Coke Roberds and had been to his place. He told me that if I was so crazy about Billy Whiskers, he could take me to where he came from and show me a ranch full of horses just like him.

"So we made a trip to Hayden and, once I got a look at Coke's breeding stock, I got plumb horse-foundered. I had never seen horses as good as the ones Coke was raising. They were line-bred Peter McCue-Old Freds with just the right amount of Remount Thoroughbred thrown in. They were big, elegant horses, standing 15.2 or 15.3. They had the best heads and necks that I'd ever seen on a set of horses and their toplines were absolutely perfect—high withers, strong backs and loins, and big hips.

"They weren't excessively muscled, but what they did have was the right kind—long, functional muscle that tied in the way that it was supposed to. And, because

Question Mark, by Plaudit and out of Pepito, was another Philmont-bred stallion whose daughters were utilized by Wiescamp in his early breeding program.

Photo Courtesy of *The Quarter Horse Journal*

of their Old Fred breeding, they were colorful—sorrels, palominos, and duns with a lot of chrome. I made up my mind right then and there that these were the kind of horses that I was going to raise."

Hank returned to southern Colorado and immediately set out to locate some good stock of Coke Roberds breeding to add to his program.

When Wiescamp began his search, there were two definitive "pockets" of Old Fred-bred horses in northern New Mexico. The first was near Watrous.

It was to this area that Jack Hauskins had relocated from northern Colorado in 1931. He brought with him about 15 head of select Old Fred-bred horses. Among them were a 4-year-old palomino stallion named Nick S., and a yearling colt named Plaudit.

Hauskins got into financial trouble within a year after moving to New Mexico and, as a result, had to sell his horses. Most of them wound up in the hands of his neighbor, Warren Shoemaker. Nick S., who had been bred by Marshall Peavy of Clark, Colo., literally put Shoemaker in the horse business. The yearling stallion Plaudit went on to become a foundation sire of the Quarter Horse breed (see *Legends, Vol. 1*).

The second pocket of Old Fred horses arrived in New Mexico via a rather circuitous route.

Coke Roberd's older brother, Emmett, worked most of his life for the famed Matador Ranch, which had its headquarters at Channing, Texas. In 1916, the Matador sent him to Brazil to work on one of its ranches there.

Emmett was convinced that the only way to be assured of having good ranch horses to ride in South America was to

The blood of the Philmont-bred Gold Mount, by Brush Mount and out of Miss Helen by Plaudit, also had a positive impact on the early Wiescamp program. Gold Mount's son Showboat and his daughters Joy Ann, Question Mount, and Scotch Lady all made key contributions to the program. **Photo by John Stryker**

take his own breeding stallion with him to cross on native stock. Naturally, he sought out a colt of his brother's breeding.

The horse he wound up with was a Si Dawson-bred yearling buckskin stallion named Fred Litz, who was sired by Old Fred and was out of the registered Thoroughbred mare Queen Litz. Fred Litz was a full brother to Marshall Peavy's famed stallion Bob H.

Upon arriving at the port of Galveston, Tex., with Fred Litz, Roberds was told that the only way the colt could be transported would be as a gelding. Feeling that he was too good to geld, Roberds chose, instead, to give him to his younger brother, Hardy, who lived near Trinchera, Colorado.

Hardy, in turn, leased Fred Litz to Gibb George of Raton, N.M., on several occasions. George was a race horse man, and he raised two full brothers sired by Fred Litz and out of a running mare named April Fool. They were the buckskin gelding Yellow Gold, whose racing exploits in southern Colorado and northern New Mexico are legendary, and Jiggs, a palomino stallion whose influence would eventually be felt in almost every large-scale horse breeding program in north-central New Mexico. The CS, Philmont, Moore, WS, and Vermejo Park ranches are just a few outfits that benefited, at one time or another, from the blood of Jiggs.

The blood of Nick, Plaudit, and Jiggs would also have a profound effect on the early Old Fred breeding program of Hank Wiescamp.

Hank's initial search for Old Fred horses took him in 1942 to the ranch of John Leatherwood, near Watrous. Leatherwood had recently purchased a typey buckskin stallion and several mares from Shoemaker.

"I had heard that Leatherwood had some Old Fred-bred horses," recalls Wiescamp. "So I hunted him up. I got him to price the stud and mares and I wound up buying 'em all and loading 'em up on the spot. I remember that it was dark by the time I got home with 'em, so I put the lights on in the sale barn and unloaded them into the sale ring.

"I had the stud partitioned off in the front of the truck, so I unloaded the mares first. Charley Wheeler, who worked for me for a long time as my weigh man in the sale barn, was helping me. We got the mares unloaded and I went and got the stud. I brought him into the sale ring and tied him up.

"Ol' Charley wasn't too talkative. In fact, he wouldn't say 10 words in a day if you didn't ask him a question. He stepped around behind the stud and stared at him for a while.

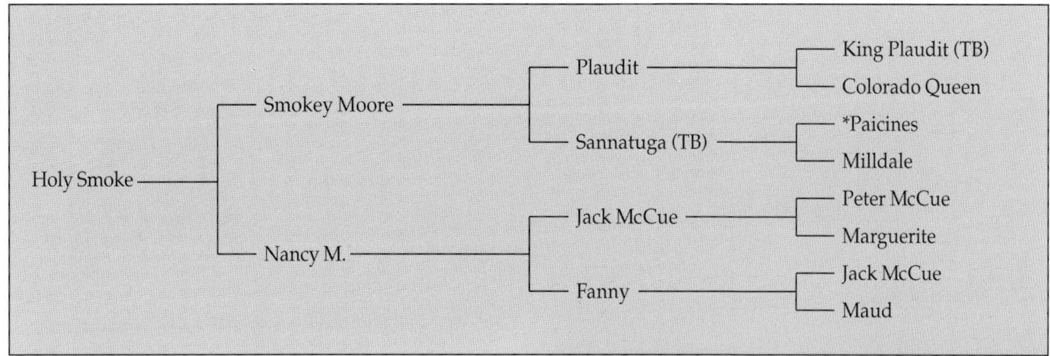

"Now that stud was a model kind of horse, with the biggest hind leg of any horse I'd ever seen up to that time. Anyway, Charley stood there and looked for a while, and finally he said, 'Ho-o-o-ly Smoke.'

"So I thought, 'Gee, that's a pretty good name for the horse. It's quite an expression, and he's quite a horse, and he is smoky colored.' So I just named that stud Holy Smoke."

Holy Smoke was bred by Warren Shoemaker and was foaled in 1940. He was sired by Smokey Moore, by Plaudit, and was out of Nancy M. by Jack McCue.

The big stallion was one of the first Quarter Horses to be shown by Wiescamp, and he did well. In 1945, he became the first of a long line of Wiescamp stallions to stand grand at the Denver National Western Stock Show. He also stood champion at the Colorado State Fair in 1944 and the New Mexico State Fair in 1945.

As a breeding horse, however, Holy Smoke did not live up to the high expectations that Wiescamp had for him.

"Although I did get a few mares from Holy Smoke who went on to be good producers," notes Hank, "by and large, he just did not sire foals who were as good as he was.

"There were just too many holes in his pedigree. His sire, Smokey Moore, was a decent enough horse, but his (Smokey's) mother, Sannatuga, was just a weedy little Thoroughbred mare. And Holy Smoke's mother, Nancy M., although she was a helluva race horse, was not a very good-headed mare. And, once you get a line of bad-headed horses in your breeding program, you'll play hell getting it out.

"If you don't believe that, just look at the heads on two of Nancy M.'s daughters—Shue Fly and Shu Baby S. Heads

Holy Smoke, by Smokey Moore and out of Nancy M., was, in Wiescamp's opinion, "a model horse." He stood grand champion at some of the largest Quarter Horse shows of his day and is shown here at the Colorado State Fair in 1944.

G-Fern Gold Smoke was one of the few get of Holy Smoke to be shown. He was a champion in both Quarter Horse and Palomino competition. This shot of him was taken at a California show in the early 1950s.

Sage Scooter, by Scooter W. and out of Sage Bird by Holy Smoke, was a top halter and performance point-earner in the Rocky Mountain region during the late 1950s and early 1960s.

Photo by Darol Dickinson, Courtesy of *The Quarter Horse Journal*

Skipper's Smoke, by Skipper W and out of Silver Leche by Holy Smoke, was one of the most dominant show horses in the Rocky Mountain region in the early 1960s. Unfortunately he, like his maternal grandsire, did not prove out as a breeding horse.

Photo by Darol Dickinson

breed true down through the years—whether they're good or bad."

(Note: Shue Fly was registered with the AQHA as being sired by Cowboy P-12, and out of Lady Luck. However, most of the people who were personally acquainted with the famed race mare's origins, including Hank Wiescamp, maintain that she was sired by Erskine Dale (TB), and was out of Nancy M. For more on Shue Fly, see *Legends Vol. 1.*)

Few of Holy Smoke's offspring were ever shown, and only one accumulated any points in AQHA-approved events. That was Casper, a 1950 bay stallion out of Hussy B, by Sobre. He earned 13 halter and 8 performance points, and a Register of Merit in performance.

G-Fern Gold Smoke, a 1948 palomino stallion out of Golden Slippers by Golddust Shoemaker, was a halter winner in both Quarter Horse and Palomino shows on the West Coast, but he has no official AQHA show record.

Holy Smoke did fare a little better as a broodmare sire. All told, his daughters produced five AQHA Champions, three Superior halter horses, three Superior performance horses, twelve performance ROMs, and three racing ROMs. They earned a total of 569 open halter, 551 open performance, 156 youth halter, and 501 youth performance points.

Silver Leche, by Holy Smoke, was the dam of three AQHA Champions: Sir Teddy, Skipper's Smoke, and Silver Son. Together, these palomino stallions earned an impressive 294 halter and 277.5 performance points. Silver Leche was also the dam of Skip's Castle, who earned 16 halter points.

Sage Bird, by Holy Smoke and out of Sagey by Golddust Shoemaker, was the dam of four point-earners including Sage Scooter, who netted a total of 39.5 halter and performance points.

HJ Smoke Along, by Holy Smoke and out of Brushalong by Brushmount, was the dam of Skip Boss, who accumulated 11 halter and 4 performance points, and Skip Thrush, who earned 154 open halter points, 77 open performance points, 152 youth halter points, and 232 youth performance points.

Holy Sage, another Holy Smoke daughter out of Sagey, was the dam of Baca Sage, who earned 10 halter and 38.5 performance points. Holy Sage also produced Bar Sagey, who earned a speed index of 95 in racing. Nola Smoke, by Holy Smoke and out of Taffy C. by Pay Check, produced the AQHA Champion Dinky Doll Cash.

Hank Wiescamp used Holy Smoke in his breeding program for 10 years, from 1942 through 1951, before selling him to Dr. C.H. Hall of Casper, Wyoming. However, Wiescamp never used the buckskin stallion very heavily.

In the final analysis, Holy Smoke proved to be an above-average individual, conformation-wise, who simply did not pan out as a sire.

"When I got Holy Smoke," relates Wiescamp, "I had high hopes for him as a breeding horse. He never lived up to my expectations, so as soon as I got other stallions who proved they could out-sire him, he had to go."

Skip Thrush, by Skipador and out of HJ Smoke Along by Holy Smoke. Shown during the late 1960s and early 1970s, Skip Thrush was both an open and youth AQHA Champion. He also earned dual Superiors in halter and western pleasure, and was the 1972 AQHA High-Point Youth Halter Gelding.

Photo by Alfred Janssen III, Courtesy of *The Quarter Horse Journal*

6 Philmont and Ghost Ranch Mares

BY THE EARLY 1930s, Hank was aware of two tremendous sets of Old Fred-bred mares in northern New Mexico. The first, and largest, group was on the Philmont Ranch, near Cimarron.

The Philmont, owned by Oklahoma oilman Waite Phillips, ran 3,000 Hereford cattle and 9,000 sheep on its 130,000 acres. It also maintained an ambitious horse breeding program, designed to produce both top-notch ranch horses and polo ponies.

Among the ranch's broodmare band, which numbered over 100, were a number of mares sired by the famous palomino Plaudit.

Plaudit was a son of the Remount Thoroughbred King Plaudit, and was out of Colorado Queen, a Coke Roberds-bred mare by Old Nick, by Old Fred. Bred by Tom Mills of Meeker, Colo., Plaudit was purchased as a weanling by Coke Roberds for the then-substantial price of $250. Roberds, in turn, sold him as a yearling to Jack Hauskins.

As was noted earlier, Plaudit eventually wound up in the hands of Warren Shoemaker.

In 1933, Shoemaker traded the then-3-year-old stallion to Waite Phillips for $300 in cash and six mares. It was at the Philmont that Plaudit made some of his most lasting contributions to the fledgling Quarter Horse breed. Crossed on the daughters of Little Joe (of New Mexico) and Little Joe Springer, two top stallions owned by the CS Ranch, he sired a set of mares who, by the late 1930s and

In 1941, Wiescamp purchased the entire broodmare band, numbering over 100, of the famed Philmont Ranch in northern New Mexico. This transaction did much to establish the Colorado horseman as both a businessman and a horse breeder. Here is a panoramic view of some of the Philmont mares about the time of their purchase by Hank.

Photo Courtesy of the Philmont Scout Ranch Museum

Plaudit, by King Plaudit (TB), and out of Colorado Queen by Old Nick, is shown here as a young horse on the Philmont. The palomino stallion had a profound effect on Wiescamp's early breeding program. For more information on Plaudit, see Legends, Vol. 2.

Photo Courtesy of the Philmont Scout Ranch Museum

early 1940s, were the envy of all who saw them.

In addition to the Plaudit mares, the Philmont Ranch broodmare band of this era also included a number of top mares sired by Lani Chief (TB), Brush Mount, Fred Litz, and Jiggs.

Hank was introduced to the Philmont and its horses by Frank Burns.

"Frankie Burns was first and foremost a race horse man," Hank says. "But he also traded a lot in polo ponies, and when he got hold of a horse who couldn't quite make it on the track, he'd train him for polo. When he got a few horses together he thought could make the grade as polo prospects, he'd head on down to Cimarron and trade 'em for a race prospect or two.

"You know, in those years that Cimarron area was just like a little Kentucky. Ranches like the Philmont, the CS, and Vermejo Park all had top breeding programs. And they all had the resources to go back east and bring back the best Thoroughbred blood available to upgrade their stock."

During the early '30s, Hank accompanied Burns on one of his trips to the Philmont. Hank was so impressed with the quality and numbers of the ranch's stallion battery and broodmare band

Lani Chief (TB) was another stallion who was used extensively by the Philmont Ranch. As the maternal grandsire of Nick Shoemaker, Showboat, and Scooter W., he had a positive impact on the Wiescamp program as well.

Photo Courtesy of the Philmont Scout Ranch Museum

Wiescamp in front of the old International truck in which he hauled the Philmont mares, six at a time, from Cimarron, N.M., to Alamosa.

that he promptly dealt for a young, crippled mare himself.

This transaction set the stage for what would become a 10-year pattern for Wiescamp—buying a horse or two from the Philmont whenever he could put together a little extra cash, taking them home to Alamosa, trading them off, and returning to the ranch to buy one or two better ones.

Throughout this decade of trading, Hank got very few horses who remained with him for any length of time. He did, however, establish a working relationship with the horsemen who ran the ranch. That, in time, paid a bigger dividend than he could have ever imagined.

In 1941, Phillips donated most of his ranch to the Boy Scouts of America. As a result, the ranch's entire broodmare band was put on the market.

"I had tried for a number of years to get just a few of the top-end Philmont mares," he relates, "but I just hadn't experienced any success to speak of. Then, out of the blue, the entire set came up for sale."

In 1941, Phillips donated most of his ranch to the Boy Scouts of America. As a result, the ranch's entire broodmare band was put on the market. Wiescamp, as soon as he learned of the situation, was quick to take advantage of it.

"I was down in Cimarron in 1941 over the 4th of July, with our bucking string," he recalls, "when I heard that the Philmont Ranch had been given away and all the horses put up for sale. I remember telling the ranch's foreman that I thought they'd gotten it a little backwards. They should've given the livestock away and put the ranch up for sale.

"Anyway, I made a deal with Waite Phillips to buy all 117 of those mares with the understanding that I'd pay for them, and pick them up, 6 at a time. I had an old International truck at the time, and that's all I could fit in it. I bought the entire broodmare band and I gave $50 apiece for them—a lot of money in those days. During the Depression, a good-broke ranch horse would only bring $35 or so and breeding stock maybe half of that.

"I'm sure that one of the main reasons that Mr. Phillips ever agreed to the deal was the fact that we had been doing business with each other for 10 years or so. I just don't think that he would have agreed to that kind of a deal with someone who had just walked in out of the blue.

"Well, I graded those Philmont mares from top to bottom, and set aside the 25 best. They were the ones that I meant to pick up last, and they were the ones that I meant to keep.

"I'd make a trip to Cimarron," Wiescamp continued, "load a half-dozen mares, and then give the ranch foreman a check that wasn't worth the paper it was

Santa Maria, by Plaudit and out of Four Roses, was probably the best of the mares from the Philmont. She proved to be an exceptional producer and was the dam of Skipperette, Skipper's King, Skipper's Prince, Show Lady, Show Maria, Nicka Maria, and Skipper Queen.

Photo Courtesy of the American Quarter Horse Museum & Heritage Center, Amarillo, Texas

Mexicala Rose was another of the top Philmont mares. By Plaudit and out of Blossom Time, she produced Spanish Rose, Spanish Nick, and H.J. Skippit.

Photo Courtesy of the American Quarter Horse Museum & Heritage Center, Amarillo, Texas

Cimarroncita, by Plaudit and out of Valley Queen, was yet another Philmont mare who had a positive impact on Wiescamp's breeding program. Among the top horses she produced were Nick W, Sailor Maid, Skip Hi, and Sanda Rita.

Photo Courtesy of the American Quarter Horse Museum & Heritage Center, Amarillo, Texas

Sanda Rita, by Handy Britches and out of Cimarroncita, was sold by Wiescamp to Jack Kyle, then of Santa Rosa, New Mexico. Kyle showed the typey dun mare to her AQHA Championship, and she went on to produce his first AQHA World Champion, Skip's Fancy Pants. This picture was taken in 1959 at Santa Fe.

***Western Horseman* Photo**

printed on. In those days, it took a check 10 days to 2 weeks to clear, and I knew that I'd have time to get home, resell those mares, and make that check good, provided that my old International didn't break down.

"I told my banker what I was doing, and I also told him, 'If I break down on the way home with a load of mares, and don't make it back before the check does, you cover that check and I'll make it right with you.'

"Well, I never did break down, and within 3 months or so, I got all those Philmont mares bought and resold, except for the ones I had set aside to keep. Included among those keepers were Santa Maria, the dam of Skipper's King and Skipperette; Miss Helen, the dam of Skipper's Lad and Skipadoo; Mexicala Rose, who produced Spanish Rose and Spanish Nick; Cimarroncita, the mother of Nick W; Saucy Sue, Scooter W.'s mama; Colorado Queen II; and Summit. Those Philmont mares sure did a lot to put me in the horse business.

"It's funny how some things stick in your mind, even after 60 years," Hank continues. "When I was going through all of those mares, evaluating them, one little roan filly stuck out like a rose among thorns.

"While I was looking her over, I said to her, 'Honey, I don't know who you are, but you're coming home with me, and you're never going to leave.' I named her Santa Maria, after a name that I had read on an inscription on a shrine that sets alongside the highway between Alamosa and Denver."

Santa Maria did in fact spend her entire life on the Wiescamp Ranch, where she had as great an impact on the overall Wiescamp breeding program as any other single mare.

In the years to come, when the Philmont mares began producing champion after champion for him, Wiescamp took great delight in relating to ranch visitors one of the more amusing aspects of their acquisition.

"All of those good mares had mule colts by their side when I bought them," he relates. "The ranch had bred all the mares to a jack to raise pack mules for the Boy Scouts.

"Later on, when people would come to

At the time he acquired the Philmont Ranch and Ghost Ranch mares, Wiescamp did not own much land. For several years, he leased grass in the San Juan Mountains west of Alamosa for his cattle and horses. Here are two rare photos, taken during the mid-1940s, of mares and foals on their summer range.

the ranch and start in bragging on this horse or that horse, I'd thank 'em and say, 'and that's not all—he had a helluva good jackass for a brother!'"

The Ghost Ranch Mares

Shortly after Wiescamp acquired the Philmont mares, yet another, smaller set of outstanding mares came up for sale. They were located on the Ghost Ranch, north of Abiquiu, New Mexico.

"The Ghost Ranch was owned by Arthur Pack, a New York philanthropist," says Wiescamp. "He was a multimillionaire who used the ranch to get away from it all."

A lover of palomino horses, Pack had bought a stud named Brujo, which means witch in Spanish, and a half-dozen Nick fillies from Warren Shoemaker in the early 1930s. Brujo was a deep-golden palomino by Plaudit and out of an Old Fred-bred mare. Nick, a Marshall Peavy-bred palomino, also carried close-up Coke Roberds-Old Fred breeding through both his sire and dam.

"I don't think that Warren really wanted to sell that set of horses," Wiescamp noted. "I think they were the ones he had set aside to go on with. But he was putting together the money to buy the ranch at Watrous at the time and, the way I heard it, Mr. Pack offered him $1,500 for Brujo and $1,000 apiece for the fillies. It was just so much money that he couldn't turn it down."

During the course of his travels in northern New Mexico, Hank became acquainted with Arthur Pack and his

Colorado Queen II, by Plaudit and out of Pretty Baby, was one of the few palomino mares that Wiescamp got from the Philmont. Although there was a strong palomino influence within the Philmont herd, the golden foals produced were sold by the ranch almost immediately as parade and saddle horse prospects.

Photo Courtesy of the American Quarter Horse Museum & Heritage Center, Amarillo, Texas

Hired Girl, by Cowboy P-12 and out of Leche, was a Ghost Ranch mare whose influence on the Wiescamp program, primarily through her son Skipper W, was monumental. She was also the dam of two other sons, Skipity Scoot and Shawnee Sheik, and four top-producing daughters: Sailor's Girl, Spotless Penny, Skip's Sis, and Senator's Maid. Hired Girl is shown here with Hank in 1960, at the age of 22.

This photo has a unique historical flavor. In addition to the mares and foals that Hank Wiescamp got from the Ghost Ranch, there was a top gelding by the name of Sailor. Here he is, photographed sometime in the 1940s behind the Alamosa Sale Barn, with Kit Carson II in the saddle. Kit, who was an Alamosa resident, is attired in his famous father's buckskins. Standing in front of Sailor is Kit II's son, Billy, holding his grandfather's pistol and holster.

Here is Coin, a full sister to South Wind. Among others, Coin produced Southern Maid, a halter-winning daughter of Nick Shoemaker.

Photo Courtesy of the American Quarter Horse Museum & Heritage Center, Amarillo, Texas

golden horses. As was the case with the Philmont mares, all initial attempts by the Colorado horseman to acquire one or two of the typey mares met with failure.

Then, in a move that bore a striking similarity to the one made by Waite Phillips, Pack donated a major portion of the Ghost Ranch to the Presbyterian Church, complete with livestock. The church promptly put the cattle and horses up for sale.

"I had a man by the name of Omar Coons traveling around that part of the country at the time, buying cattle for me to run through my sale barn," remarks Wiescamp. "One day he called me and said, 'Hank, I've bought a bunch of cattle from the Presbyterian Church, but I had to take a set of old, starved horses with them. I had to give $50 apiece for them. Would you give me my money back, plus $5 a head or so for my time?'

"Well, I got so excited that I just about had a stroke! I knew who those horses were, and I knew how much Mr. Pack had paid for them, so I hollered back at him, 'I'll damn sure give you what you're asking—don't you show those horses to anybody else!'

"Now Mr. Pack used to baby his horses, and they always looked like they had just stepped out of the show ring. It turned out that, after the church had taken over the ranch, the mares had been kicked out on poor pasture, with their foals still nursin' 'em. According to Coons, they'd gone downhill something terrible.

"But I knew what they had looked like, and I couldn't wait to set eyes on them again, so Freda and I and another couple

"Well, those mares and foals got fat, and they got well, and most of them wound up becoming great producers and living out their lives in Alamosa."

South Wind, by Brujo and out of Leche, was another of the great Ghost Ranch mares. She was the dam of the great Wiescamp show mare School Mama, and the top-producing mares H.J. Showstar and Skipity. This photo of South Wind was taken at Honnen's Quincy Farms, Denver, Colo., when she was 24.

Photo by Darol Dickinson, Courtesy of Valerie Covalt Furman

jumped in my car and headed for the stockyards at Taos, which is where Omar had driven all the livestock.

"When we got there, we all got out of the car and went over to the pens where the mares and foals were. I have to admit that they were a pretty sorry lot, but I knew that there was nothing wrong with them that a little good feed wouldn't fix.

"I made arrangements with the owner of the stockyards to start feeding them up, a little at first, then building to where they were getting all that they could stand. I told him that I'd be back to pick them up in 6 weeks or so, and we all piled back in the car and headed home.

"Well, for a half-hour or so, no one said a word. Finally Freda said, 'Hank, I've seen you fall into the sewer more than once making deals that I thought weren't too bright, and you've always come out smelling like a rose. But this is one deal you've made where I think you're going to come out smelling like a sewer!'

"'You might be right,' I replied. 'We'll just have to wait and see.'

"Well, those mares and foals got fat, and they got well, and most of them wound up becoming great producers and living out their lives in Alamosa. They included mares like South Wind, the dam of School Mama; Southern Queen, the dam of Spot Cash; Leche, Shampoo, Coin, Skipaway, and Penny.

"Brujo was also in the bunch," continued Hank. "You know, at one time or another, I saw most of the sons of Plaudit. I even owned a pretty good one named Scooter W. In my opinion, Brujo was the best one of them all.

"And he would have probably wound up being the best-known son of Plaudit, if

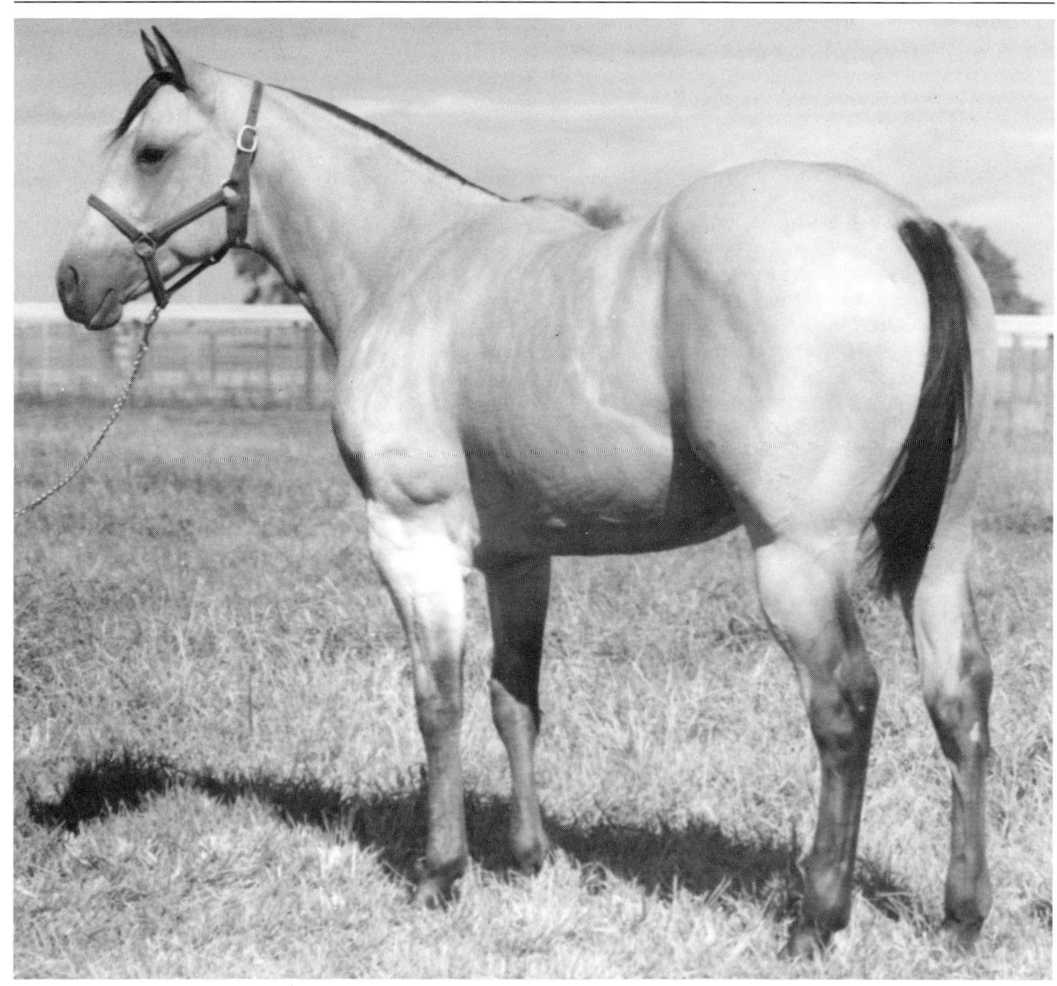

he wouldn't have gotten sick with distemper at the Ghost Ranch. He survived the illness, but it left him sterile. I tried for several years to get mares in foal to him after I got him, but I never could.

"I finally sold him to George Hineman, who had the big horse and mule barn at Dighton, Kansas. George had a son who was a veterinarian, and they thought they could get the horse breeding again. As far as I know, they never did.

"When Brujo contracted distemper, the Ghost Ranch leased Cowboy P-12 to use on their mares. Of course he wasn't known as Cowboy then. That was before he was registered, and they called him Cowpuncher.

"Anyway, when I got the Ghost Ranch mares, there were several young daughters of Cowboy in the bunch. One of 'em was a a smutty-colored palomino out of Leche who I registered as Hired Girl. She was the dam of Skipper W.

"I'll take a bath in that kind of a sewer any day."

After she was sold to Ed Honnen, South Wind produced Quincy Bars (top) and Quincy Bars II (bottom). Both of these stallions were sired by Good Bars, by Three Bars (TB), and both were AQHA Champions. James Cathey took the photo of Quincy Bars.

Photos Courtesy of *The Quarter Horse Journal*

7 NICK SHOEMAKER

"When I first laid eyes on Nick Shoemaker, I knew that I'd found the horse I'd been looking for."

AFTER HIS acquisition of the Philmont Ranch and Ghost Ranch mares, Hank Wiescamp began the search for a new stallion to put on them. Both Barney Owens and Holy Smoke were still in residence at the ranch but, as was noted earlier, neither totally suited Hank.

He felt that he needed a better horse to put on his new mares—a horse who was better headed and necked, with more size and substance, and preferably a palomino of Old Fred breeding.

"I had been looking for a new stud for several years before I got the Philmont Ranch and Ghost Ranch mares," says Wiescamp. "I hadn't found one to suit me. I guess I was looking for a horse who hadn't been born yet."

One fall day in 1942, Hank and Freda made a trip to Warren Shoemaker's to

Nick Shoemaker, the cornerstone stallion of the Wiescamp Old Fred-bred Quarter Horse breeding program.

Photo Courtesy of *The Quarter Horse Journal*, Amarillo, Texas

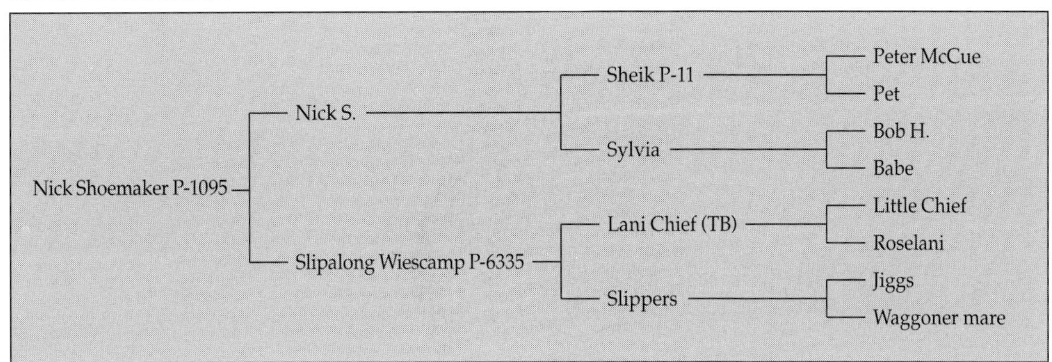

see if he had any stud prospects. On their arrival, the couple noticed three palomino stallions in a corral. Hank approached Shoemaker, who was working on a piece of horse-drawn machinery near the corral, and asked whether any of the horses might be for sale. Shoemaker's reply was that two of the three were, and he invited Wiescamp to take a closer look at them.

"Both Nick Shoemaker and Golddust Shoemaker were in that corral," recollects Wiescamp, "and also a son of Plaudit. When I first laid eyes on Nick Shoemaker, I knew that I'd found the horse I'd been looking for. He came with everything I wanted on a stud horse—a beautiful head with a big eye and little fox-ears, long slender neck, short back, long underline, long hip, deep-forked chest with a well-defined forearm, and a lot of stifle and hind leg.

"And he had the right kind of breeding too. He was sired by Nick S., and out of a mare by Lani Chief (TB). His maternal granddam was a daughter of Jiggs. So, on top of everything else that he had to offer, Nick Shoemaker was sure bred the way that I wanted.

"There was only one thing wrong. After I'd looked all three studs over, from top to bottom, I said to Freda, 'Well, I've finally found the horse I've been looking for, but I'll guarantee you he's not for sale.' I thought for sure that he'd be the one that Warren would keep for himself.

"Warren came on over about then, so I asked him which one of the three was not for sale. He motioned toward Golddust Shoemaker and said, 'He's the one I'm gonna keep. You can have either of the other two.'

"Now, Golddust Shoemaker was a

Spanish Nick (above), Nick W, and Skipper W were the three sons of Nick Shoemaker who wound up having the most influence on the Hank Wiescamp breeding program. Here are head studies of the famous trio.

"Well, I didn't have $1,500 to spend on a stud horse, and Warren wouldn't budge off that price, so I left Watrous without Nick Shoemaker."

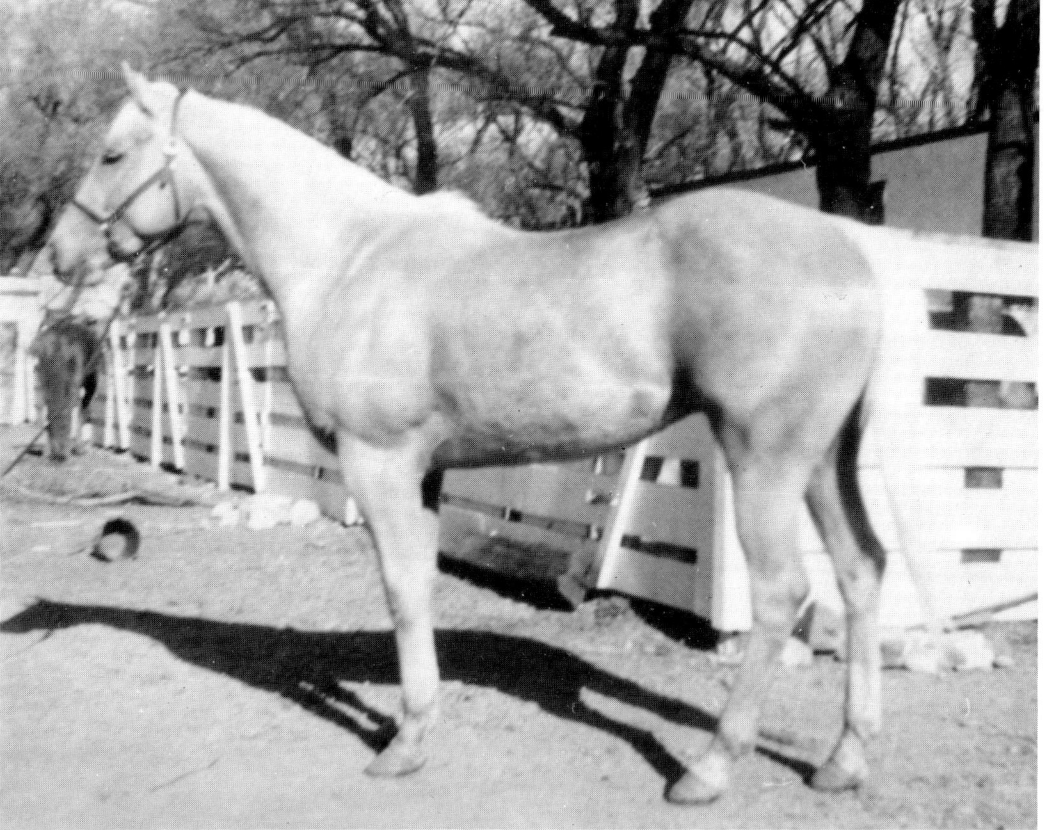

Here are two shots of a younger Nick Shoemaker, taken at the time of his registration with AQHA.

Photos Courtesy of The American Quarter Horse Heritage Center & Museum, Amarillo, Texas

pretty good horse, and I could see why Warren would be a little partial to him, because he was out of the old race mare, Nancy M. But Golddust had a little bit too much of his mama's bad head, which she got from her daddy, Jack McCue, to suit me. On the other hand, Nick Shoemaker's head was absolutely perfect!

"So I thought I was home free, and I said to Warren, 'What'll you take for the others?' 'I'll take $500 for the son of Plaudit,' he said, 'and $1,500 for Nick Shoemaker.'

"Well, that may sound cheap today, but it wasn't so cheap then. I still owed $1,500 on my sale barn and was paying it off at $100 a month. At the time, you could buy cows and calves for $15 or $20 a pair. You could buy a brand new Buick for $1,500 or a Model T for $900. That's how much money it was.

"Well, I didn't have $1,500 to spend on a stud horse, and Warren wouldn't budge

Nick Shoemaker and Clyde Swift won the calf roping at the Ski Hi Stampede in Monte Vista, Colo., 2 years in a row. Clyde recalls that he had only been roping off "Golddigger," as he called the stallion, for a couple of weeks prior to the 1946 Stampede. As a result, he had to stop Nick with the reins more than he did later on, when the big horse knew what was expected of him.

off that price, so I left Watrous without Nick Shoemaker."

Later that winter, however, Wiescamp received a call from Shoemaker that reopened the door on a possible deal.

"Warren called me the following February and asked me if I was still interested in Nick Shoemaker," remembers Hank. "I told him I was, but I was no closer to having $1,500 to spend on him than I had been in the fall. He said, 'Well, he won't cost you $1,500—you can have him for $500 if you pick him up by this coming Sunday. If you don't, I'm going to geld him on Monday because he's turning into one of the best riding horses I've ever been on.'

"Now this was on a Friday," continues Wiescamp. "I told Warren that I had to cry my Saturday sale, but that I'd be down on Sunday to get the horse.

"I still had my old International truck, and it could be a bear to start on cold winter mornings. On Saturday night, I was so afraid that the truck wouldn't start in the morning that I set the alarm to ring every 2 hours or so. I'd hop out of bed, get dressed, and run out and start the truck and let it warm up.

"At about 3 in the morning, Freda looked over at me and said, 'Hank, you're about to freeze me to death, hopping in and out of the bed! Why don't you just get in the truck and go down there and get that horse?' So I did."

There was still one small hitch connected with the acquisition of Nick Shoemaker.

Here's another shot of Nick Shoemaker and Clyde Swift in action, getting in a little practice behind the show barn on the Wiescamp ranch.

Photo Courtesy of Clyde Swift

"When I wrote Warren the $500 check to pay for Nick," says Wiescamp, "I only had around $30 in the bank. I knew that I had to have him though, and I also knew that I'd figure out how to cover the check by the time it got back to the bank.

"When I got back to Alamosa, I asked Freda how much cash she had on hand and she answered, '$30.' I said, 'Loan it to me—I need it to help pay for my new stud!'

"Now, during the Depression, a lot of folks, myself included, had developed a

Joker W. emerged as one of the superstars from Nick Shoemaker's first full foal crop for Hank Wiescamp. A foal of 1944, he won the Rocky Mountain Quarter Horse Futurity in 1946. He is shown here after winning a race in September of 1947 at La Mesa Park, Raton, New Mexico.

"Now, if I'd sold Nick Shoemaker for $3,500, he wouldn't have built this house, he wouldn't have built this yellow garage, he wouldn't have built anything."

little distrust in banks. There'd been too many of them fail and too many folks had lost everything they'd had.

"I'd gotten in the habit of setting aside all of the silver dollars that I took in during my auction sales, and I'd toss 'em into a sack I kept hid in an old butter churn that was buried in our bedroom closet floor. I reached down in that churn and grabbed out the sack of silver dollars and headed for the bank. Mr. Hiller was the head clerk at the bank. He was the same man I had dealt with when I bought the Philmont mares, and he also clerked all of the farm sales I was having at the time.

"Well, I walked into the bank, went over to his desk, sat down and said, 'Mr. Hiller, I bought myself a stud horse.' And he said, 'Hank, that's good—you needed a stud to put on those new mares of yours. What'd he cost you?'

"'They was asking $1,500 for him,' I stated. 'Good Lord, Hank,' he sputtered, 'what's he made out of—gold?'

"'That he is. He's the prettiest shade of gold that you've ever seen. But I didn't give $1,500 for him, I gave $500. But you know, Mr. Hiller, I've got to have some money.'

"'Hank, you know I can't loan any money on a horse.'

"'I know, but there's more than one way to do these things.'

"'How much do you need,' he finally asked.

"'Oh, I don't know,' I replied, and I poured all those silver dollars out of the Gooch's Flour sack, all over his desk.

"Those ol' bankers could rake off $5 silver dollars with one hand just as fast as you could count 'em, and Mr. Hiller counted out 170 double eagles in about the time it took me to blink my eyes.

'We've got about half of it,' he announced. 'Now what are we going to do?'

"'I don't know,' I said. 'You're clerking

Joker W. also became a successful cutting horse. Here he is in action with Jack Kyle aboard, circa 1950.

my farm sales, and I'm havin' one about every day. I'd look awful funny havin' to go to jail every night and being handcuffed to you every day workin' those sales.'

"I tried to get a little humor into him, but he wasn't very amused.

"'Well, I haven't paid you for any of those sales for the last 10 days, and that comes to another $130,' he said.

"Times were still pretty tough in the valley, and folks were going broke every day. I was making a 2 percent commission selling those sales, but an average sale would only bring $500, and that was if they had a team of horses.

"We was up to $360 or so by this time. It was my turn to ask, 'Now what'll we do?'"

"By this time he was a-sweatin', but he answered, 'I'll loan you my personal money. I'll put a little note down in this box here.' He was getting up in years, so he added, 'Hank, if anything ever happens to me, you dig down in this drawer and get this note and pay whatever you still owe on it to my widow.' I told him that I would, and that's how I came to get Nick Shoemaker."

Not long after getting his new stallion home, Wiescamp had a chance to sell him for considerably more than he'd paid for him.

"Mike Levis from Denver came down to look at my horses," recalls Wiescamp. "Mike was heir to a glass company, so he wasn't hurtin' for money, and he also

Spanish Cash, by Spot Cash and out of Spanish Money by Joker W., was owned by well-known horseman Leonard Lightizer of Hayden, Colorado. Spanish Cash is shown here standing grand at the 1957 Laramie, Wyo., Quarter Horse show.
Photo by James Cathey

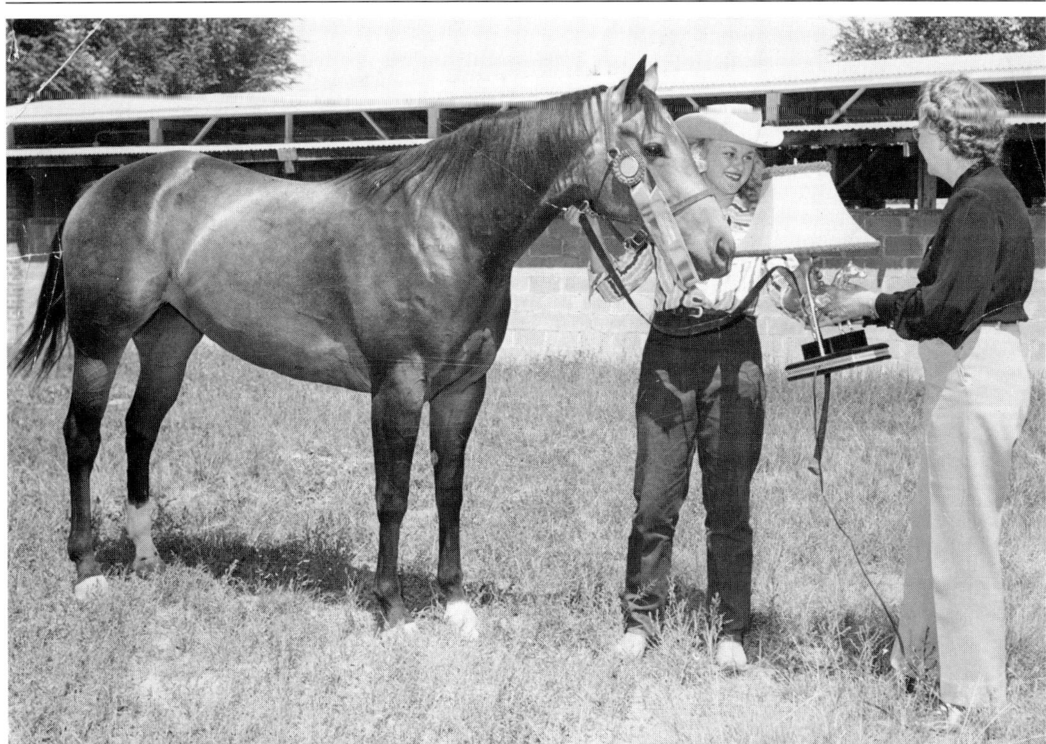

Spanish Rose was the epitome of the type of Quarter Horse that Hank Wiescamp set out to breed when he put Nick Shoemaker on the Plaudit-bred mares. The mare had looks, speed, and athletic ability. One day at the 1947 Colorado State Fair, Spanish Rose was named the grand champion halter mare in the morning, won the RMQHA race futurity in the afternoon, and the reining class in the evening.

She is shown in the top photo after her halter win, with Loretta Wiescamp receiving the trophy from Mrs. Van Grundy, wife of RMQHA Secretary Martin Van Grundy. In the bottom photo, she stands in the futurity winner's circle, with Hank at her head, Billy Brite in the irons, and Mrs. Van Grundy presenting the garland of roses.

knew a good horse when he saw one. Mike took one look at Nick Shoemaker and told me, 'Hank, I'm gonna' buy this horse from you. I'll give you $3,000 for him.'

"Now this was a pretty tempting offer, but I had been looking for a horse like Nick Shoemaker for a long time and I hadn't even gotten a chance to see what he could do on those Philmont and Ghost Ranch mares, so I turned Levis' offer down.

"'Okay, then, I'll give you $3,500 for him,' he said.

"Now this was starting to get serious. If I gave in and sold Nick Shoemaker, I'd get back all of the money I had put into him; I could pay off the sale barn; and I'd still have $1,500 left to go hunt for a new stud.

"But I just couldn't do it—I turned him down again.

"After he left, I went in to the house, sat down, and said to Freda, 'You know, you didn't marry the smartest man in the world. I've just turned down seven times what I paid for that yellow stud.

"We were still living in the apartment in the sale barn at this time—had been for 10 years. We were wanting to build a house real bad.

"Freda looked at me and said, 'Hank, you've never told me how to run my business, and I've never told you how to run yours. You've looked for a horse like Nick Shoemaker for a long time and you've finally found him. You just go ahead and keep that yellow horse and someday he'll build us a yellow house.'"

A short time later, fortune smiled on Wiescamp and relieved a little of his financial pressures.

"About a week after I'd turned down all that money for Nick Shoemaker, the Army called me from Camp Carson in Colorado Springs, wanting to buy some cavalry horses. I had quite a few of the right kind of geldings at that time, so Captain Fudge from the Remount Service came down, looked them over, and bought 10 for officers' mounts. They all went to the military institute at Roswell, N. M., and I got $175 apiece for them.

"So I got my check, stuck it into my shirt pocket, and went to see Mr. Hiller at the bank.

"'Mr. Hiller,' I announced, 'I've come to pay you the money I owe you on Nick Shoemaker, and I want to pay off the

Son O Nick was another halter-class-winning son of Nick Shoemaker. With George Mueller showing him, he was named the grand champion Palomino stock horse stallion at the 1949 New Mexico State Fair in Albuquerque. He was later gelded to make a riding horse for Freda Wiescamp.

Sir Hank, a 1947 gelding by Nick Shoemaker, out of Flamette, served as a riding horse and cutting mount for both Loretta and Charlotte Wiescamp. Loretta is shown up in this photo.

Silver Son, an AQHA Champion sired by Senator, by Nick Shoemaker, was one of the most durable of all of the Wiescamp show horses. Campaigned during the 1960s, he accumulated 176 halter and 201 performance points.

Photo by Darol Dickinson

note on the sale barn too.'

"'How on earth are you going to do that, Hank?'

"'With this $1,750 check that I've got right here in my shirt pocket,'

"Hiller stated, 'Hank there ain't no one in this part of the country that can write a $1,750 check and make it good.'

"'This someone can,' I countered, and laid that check, written against the Treasury of the United States, down on his desk. He took one look at the check and conceded, 'Well, I guess no one could write a better one.'

"So I paid off Nick Shoemaker, and I paid off the sale barn. That was the last time that I ever borrowed money in my life."

Several years later, Freda's prophesy about Nick Shoemaker and the yellow house proved accurate.

"In 1945, a fellow by the name of Grey came in from California, looking for palomino horses," he recalls. "He had a customer in California, a doctor, whose wife liked palominos, and he was looking for an extra good one for her.

"I had a super 2-year-old palomino colt by Nick Shoemaker, out of Flamette, who I called Fort Knox. Grey looked him over, from top to bottom, and said, 'This colt'll do—what will you take for him?'

"Now, I didn't really want to sell the colt so I said, 'I want $15,000 cash for him, and that's as a gelding.' Well, I knew I'd blown him clear off the face of the earth, but he went into the house, called up the doctor and talked to him for a little while, then came back out and announced, 'I guess we'll just buy your horse.'

"A few weeks later, Loren Glaser from Halleck, Nev., called me and wanted a yellow stud, and I sold him a young horse named Little Nick—a son of Nick Shoemaker, out of one of the Ghost Ranch mares—for $10,000. Then I sold another palomino son of his, out of a grade mare, for $1,000.

"Inside of 2 or 3 weeks, I sold $26,000 worth of colts, all sired by Nick Shoemaker. I took that money and used it to build the yellow brick house that I still live in. It cost me $25,800 and I paid cash for it.

"Now, if I'd sold Nick Shoemaker for $3,500, he wouldn't have built this yellow house, he wouldn't have built this yellow garage, he wouldn't have built anything."

When Wiescamp first got Nick Shoemaker, the bulldog-type Quarter Horse was in vogue in many parts of the country. Although the palomino stallion, at 15.1 and 1,300 pounds, would look small compared to some of today's halter horses, for that time he was considered by many horsemen to be too large.

"Not long after I got him home, Hugh Bennett came by to inspect some mares for AQHA registration. He looked Nick Shoemaker over from one end to the other and finally asked me, 'What are you going to do with this big ol' plow horse?' 'I'm gonna plow a bunch of those little ol' ponies under,' I shot back. And that's just what I did for quite a while.

"Nick Shoemaker might have been a little bigger than most people were used to in those days, but his size and his muscling fit together right. He had a lot of muscle, but it was the right kind of muscle; it was long muscle that tied in right; it was functional muscle.

"And Nick was a great riding horse. In fact, he was probably one of the smoothest riding horses that we have ever had around here. We rode him all the time. If we had to go out and bring the mares in, we wouldn't go get a gelding—we'd just saddle him up. He was also a heckuva rope horse. Clyde Swift won two good ropings off of him. There wasn't a calf anywhere that could outrun him and, when he set his brakes, he could stand the stoutest of 'em straight up.

Spanish Nick, who was both a halter and performance champion and a top broodmare sire, is shown here in a photo taken at the Wiescamp ranch in the early 1960s.
Photo By Darol Dickinson

"But the nicest thing about Nick Shoemaker was not his conformation, or his athletic ability, or his speed. The nicest thing about him was his disposition. Everything you asked him to do, he did willingly. He wanted to please you. He was just a nice horse to be around.

"And one more thing—he was the horse that I needed to put on those Plaudit and Nick S. mares. They were lightly made mares; beautifully headed and necked mares with all the refinement that you

Here are two outstanding maternal grandsons of Nick Shoemaker, both out of Stepaway. Sure Cash, by Spot Cash, is shown on the left, held by Ron Wiescamp, after winning his yearling Quarter Horse class at the 1955 New Mexico State Fair. Scooter's Lad, by Scooter W., is on the right with George Mueller at the halter, after winning the 2-year-old Quarter Horse stallion class at the same show in 1954.

could ever want, but, for the most part, they were not heavily muscled. He crossed well with them."

From Nick Shoemaker's first full foal crop, which hit the ground in 1944, Joker W. emerged as an all-around star. This stallion, who was out of Hollyhock W. by Reighlock (TB), won the RMQHA futurity in 1946 and became one of Wiescamp's first notable cutting horses, ridden by Jack Kyle and Loretta Wiescamp.

Fourteen Nick Shoemaker foals were born in 1945, and they included Skipper W, Spanish Rose, Southern Maid, and Senator.

Skipper W, of course, went on to become one of the best-known sires in the annals of the Quarter Horse breed. He is discussed in detail in the following chapter.

Spanish Rose, out of Mexicala Rose, became a three-way star for Wiescamp, winning at halter, racing, and arena performance. She remains a favorite of her breeder to this day.

"We took Spanish Rose to the Colorado State Fair in 1947," recalls Wiescamp. "We had her paid up in the race futurity and we also entered her in halter and reining. She won the futurity, stood grand at halter, and won the reining.

"She also stood grand at the Denver National Western Stock Show and the New Mexico State Fair, and she was a great producer. I wished that I could have raised a hundred more just like her, but her kind doesn't come along every day, so all you can do when you finally get one like her is just appreciate it."

Southern Maid, a sorrel mare out of Coin, by Brujo, was sold to Edith Lieuallen of Athena, Oregon. She became a champion show mare and an excellent producer.

Senator was kept by Wiescamp and used sparingly at stud. Although he did not qualify as one of the better sons of Nick Shoemaker in his breeder's eyes, he did make a significant contribution to Hank's program as the sire of the well-known halter and performance stallion, Silver Son.

Nick W, a dun stallion out of Cimarroncita, by Plaudit, was foaled in 1946 and would have to be considered the cream of that year's crop. Renowned for his classic head and neck, Nick W made significant contributions to the Wiescamp breeding program. He is also discussed in more

Hank Wiescamp's yellow brick house, which was built and paid for in 1948 with the proceeds from the sales of three sons of Nick Shoemaker. Hank still lives in the house today.

detail in a subsequent chapter.

Nick Shoemaker's 1947 foal crop numbered only eight. Nuevo Boyero, a palomino stallion out of Shampoo, by Brujo, was sold to Bob Schafer, of Boyero, Colo., and became well-known as a sire throughout the eastern section of the state.

There were just six foals in the 1948 foal crop, but they included three of Nick Shoemaker's best-known get.

Spanish Nick, a palomino son out of Mexicala Rose, proved to be one of the most successful Wiescamp show horses of his era, standing grand at halter several times in both Palomino and Quarter Horse shows and winning in performance. He earned an AQHA Championship in 1954 and went on to become a great sire for Wiescamp.

Son O Nick, a palomino stallion out of Sunkist by Plaudit, was also a show horse of note for Wiescamp, standing grand as a palomino at the 1946 New Mexico State Fair. He was ultimately gelded to make a riding horse for Freda Wiescamp.

Stepaway, a palomino daughter out of Scarlett Oaks, by Clark Gable by Captain Alcock, was yet another champion Nick Shoemaker offspring from the class of '48.

A consistent threat at both halter and performance, Stepaway once stood grand at the Colorado State Fair in both the Palomino and Quarter Horse divisions and also won the junior reining in both.

In the spring of 1947, at the age of 8, Nick Shoemaker was playing in his corral when he slipped on the ice, fell hard against some fence poles, and broke his neck.

"Losing Nick Shoemaker that early in his life was a blow to me," Wiescamp relates. "He was a great horse and a great sire. And even though I only had the use of him for a short while, I still had those good Philmont and Ghost Ranch mares. And I had managed to keep ahold of his best sons and daughters.

"So I just kept right after it—I didn't slow down or miss a beat. But sometimes I get to thinking—what if Nick Shoemaker had lived a full life and I'd had the use of him for another 10 or 12 years. What if I had another full set or two of horses like Skipper W, Nick W, Spanish Nick, Spanish Rose, Joker W., and Stepaway?

"I've always said that Nick Shoemaker built an empire. If he'd lived a full life, he could've built three."

8 SKIPPER W

. . . more than any other stallion Hank had at the time, Skipper W had the kind of conformation that Hank felt would complement the Plaudit mares.

THE SUDDEN death of Nick Shoemaker, occurring just prior to the 1947 breeding season, left Hank with little time to decide who was going to replace the big palomino as his main herd sire.

Barney Owens and Holy Smoke were still in residence at the ranch, but for reasons already documented, they were not acceptable to Hank. Showboat and Scooter W., both 2-year-olds at the time, were also considered and passed over by Hank.

Showboat, who was by Gold Mount and out of Slipalong Wiescamp, was a good-looking horse and a top athlete, but he was a palomino. Therefore he could not have been used on many of the mares due to their buckskin, palomino, and cream coloring. Breeding a palomino to these colors can lead to

This photo of Skipper W was taken in 1947 when he was a 2-year-old. It clearly shows the strong hindquarter muscling that led Hank to choose him as Nick Shoemaker's replacement.

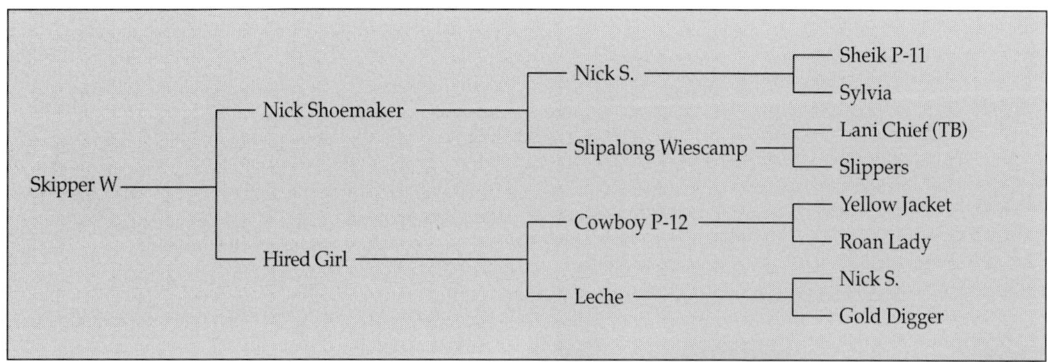

albinoism.

Scooter W., by Plaudit and out of Saucy Sue by Lani Chief (TB), was a sorrel, so he was the right color to go on the mares. But he was too lightly muscled and too closely related to most of the Philmont mares to suit Hank.

Nick Shoemaker had crossed so well with the Plaudit-bred mares that Hank felt his best bet was to go with one of Nick Shoemaker's sons. This narrowed his choice to Nick W, Joker W., or Skipper W.

Nick W, who was out of Cimmaroncita by Plaudit, was a yearling in 1947, so even if Hank had chosen to elevate him to the No. 1 spot, he would have had to wait at least a year to do it. And Nick W did reflect the conformation of Plaudit in his appearance. He was beautifully headed and necked, but lightly muscled. And he was a buckskin, which, again, would have limited his use.

Joker W., out of Hollyhock W. by Reighlock (TB), was a 3-year-old and a proven race and cutting champion. Like Nick W, however, he was lightly muscled and a buckskin.

Skipper W was a chestnut, and Hank liked the bottom side of his pedigree; he was out of Hired Girl by Cowboy P-12. Finally, and more than any other stallion Hank had at the time, Skipper W had the kind of conformation that Hank felt would complement the Plaudit mares. For these reasons, the nod went to him.

Much has been written over the years about the influence Skipper W had, not only on the Wiescamp breeding program, but on the entire Quarter Horse breed. To say that he has become a legend is an understatement. His breeder and lifetime owner, however, has a slightly dif-

Here is a never-before-published photo of Skipper W as a yearling.

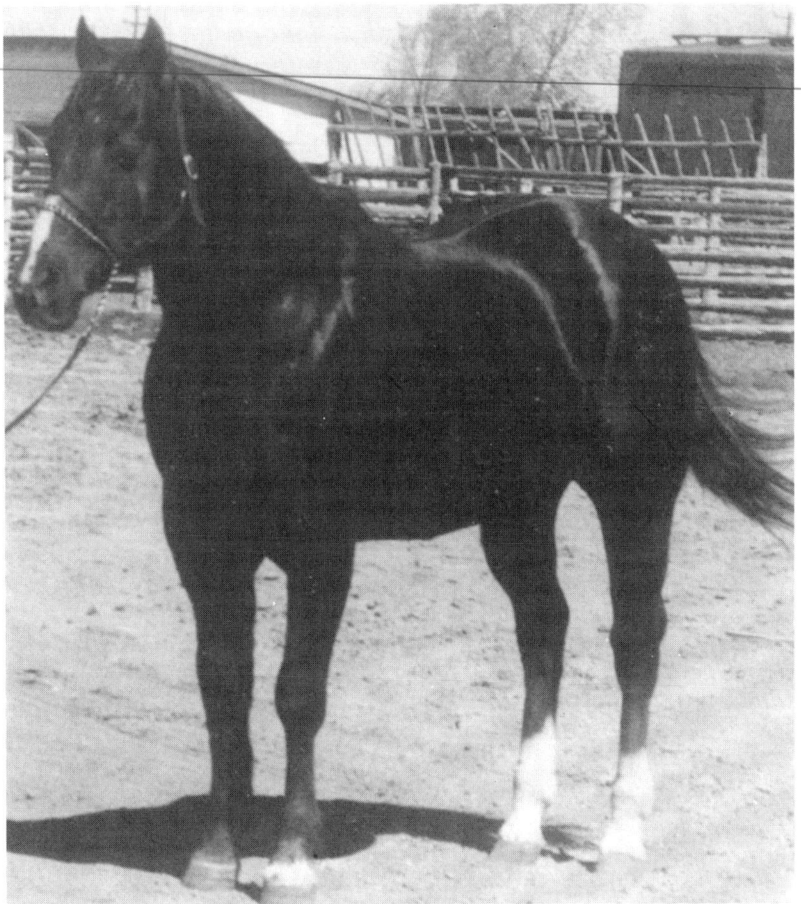

A good three-quarter-front view of Skipper W taken in Alamosa in the early 1960s.
Photo by Darol Dickinson

ferent opinion of Skipper W than does the general public.

"Skipper was a good horse, and I'm sure not trying to take anything away from him," comments Hank. "But he was not a great horse. If I could have, I would have changed him in a number of ways.

"His head never did suit me. Nick Shoemaker had a better head than Skipper, and, for that matter, so did Nick W and Joker W. But Skipper had the shortest fox ears that you've ever seen, and he had a good, long neck that just got better as he matured. He also had a tremendous hip, stifle, and hind leg. He was strong where the Philmont and Ghost Ranch mares were weak, so I went with him and it turned out to be the right thing to do."

(Note: Skipper W's life story can be found in *Legends 2*.)

"At the time I chose Skipper W to replace Nick Shoemaker," continues Wiescamp, "I had seen how well Nick S. and the Plaudit-bred mares had crossed. I felt that Skipper and those same mares would cross just as well. After all, he had his daddy's blood on top and he had another shot of Nick S. blood through his maternal granddam, Leche.

"Leche was a tremendous mare. She was without a doubt the best Nick S. mare I ever saw. Her dam was a Waggoner Ranch mare named Gold Digger, by Yellow Wolf. Besides Hired Girl, Leche produced Southwind, and Southwind produced School Mama, so you see, it was a great mare line that just kept on producing."

As was documented in *Legends 2*, Skipper W was almost sold several times before he reached maturity. For one reason or another, the deals all fell through, so he remained in Alamosa.

Skipper W was broke to ride as a 2-year-old by long-time Wiescamp ranch hand, George Mueller, and he proved to be a willing and athletic mount. So athletic, in fact, that Mueller wanted to rope calves competitively. But Hank wanted Skipper W conditioned for halter competition instead, so that's the direction his show career went.

Skipper W was shown at halter only three times—at the Denver National Western Stock Show, the Colorado State Fair, and the New Mexico State Fair. He stood grand at all three.

Then, the unexpected death of Nick Shoemaker put an end to Skipper W's show and riding career and cast him instead in the role as the senior sire in the Wiescamp breeding program. Skipper W's record as a sire has been well-documented over the years. From a total of only 132 registered foals, he sired 58 halter point-earners and 27 performance point-earners. They earned a total of 1,392 points in halter and 586.5 points in performance.

Thirteen of Skipper W's offspring earned AQHA Championships, seven became Superior halter horses, and one earned a Superior in performance. Eighteen of his get earned their performance Registers of Merit, and four earned the same honor in racing.

But the real worth of Skipper W as a sire

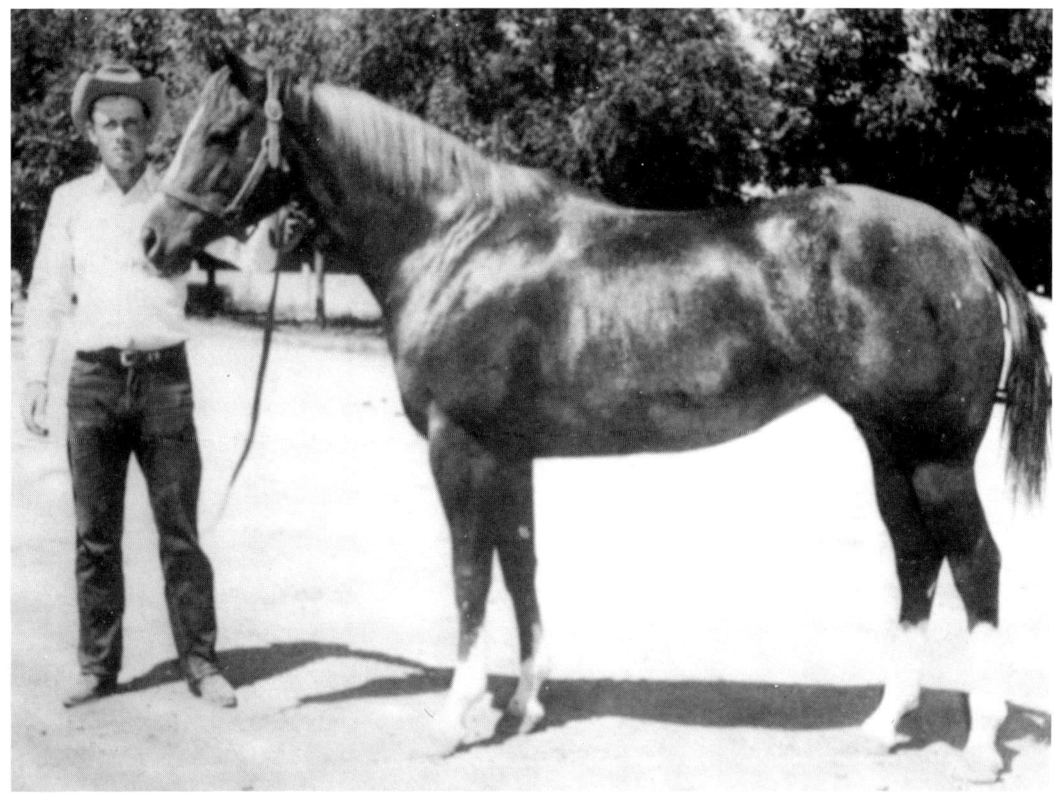

Skipperette, foaled in 1950, by Skipper W and out of Santa Maria. Like her sire, she stood grand at the Denver National Western Stock Show, Colorado State Fair, and New Mexico State Fair. Heavily muscled and yet totally feminine, she went on to become a great broodmare for Hank. The handler is Larry Walker.

Photo by Clarence Coil/Stewart's Photo

Skipper's King, foaled in 1954, was a full brother to Skipperette. This sorrel stallion, who also stood grand at the "big three," stood 15.3 hands and weighed 1,400 pounds in show shape. Although not shown extensively in performance, Skipper's King was reportedly a great athlete. He also gained fame as a superior broodmare sire.

Photo by Darol Dickinson

Here is the classically headed Skip's Reward, by Skipper W and out of Show Lady. Shown here as a 2-year-old, Reward was a grand champion halter horse and a top broodmare sire.

Photo by Harvey Caplin, Courtesy of Abby Caplin

"When Skip's Reward came along, I thought he was one of the greatest-headed colts I had ever raised."

does not lie solely in the show and racing records of his get.

Skipper W's most lasting legacy as a breeding stallion lay in the fact that he consistently sired *both* sons and daughters who were better than he was, and who went on to become top sires and producers in their own right.

"Skipper W flat outproduced himself," comments Hank. "I don't know any other way to put it. When I bred him to a mare, he consistently sired a foal who was better than both he and the mare.

"He was also a sire of sires, and a broodmare sire. Often times, a breeding stallion will prove to be predominantly a sire of sons who go on to become good sires, or daughters who go on to become good producers. Three Bars (TB), for instance, was a sire of sires, and Leo was a broodmare sire. Well, Skipper was a sire of both, and as such, he was a rarity."

Of the many top sons that Skipper W sired, Skipper's King and Skip's Reward stand out because of their impact on the Wiescamp program.

Skipper's King, foaled in 1954, was out of Santa Maria. In the eyes of Wiescamp, this massive sorrel stallion was the top son of Skipper W. Both his show and sire record bear this out, and they will be discussed in detail in a subsequent chapter.

Skip's Reward, foaled in 1958, was out

This side view of Skip's Reward, taken at Alamosa in the early 1960s, shows his superior shoulder, heart girth, and top line.

Photo by Darol Dickinson

of Show Lady by Show Boat. Show Lady's dam was the great producer Santa Maria.

"When Skip's Reward came along," notes Hank, "I thought he was one of the greatest-headed colts I had ever raised. I named him Reward because that's just what I thought he was.

"Unlike Skipper W and Skipper's King though, Reward was primarily a sire of mares. He did sire one son, Skip's Supreme, who made a pretty good breeding horse; but, by and large, his sons weren't as good as his daughters."

Another top son of Skipper W who left his mark on the Wiescamp program was Sailalong.

"Sailalong was a different kind of horse than Skipper's King and Skip's Reward," recalls Hank. "They were heavily muscled and quiet-natured. He was lighter made and a little spooky as far as his personality went.

"But he came by his disposition honestly. His dam, Brushalong, was a Philmont mare by Brush Mount, out of Colorado Queen II by Plaudit. Now those Brush Mount horses could get a little warm when you went to riding 'em, and those Plaudits were the same way. And sometimes, when you crossed the Brush Mounts and the Plaudits, what you got could get a little hot.

"Sailalong's mama was that way and so was he. But he was a great athlete. He was a reining horse deluxe. He sired

Sailalong, by Skipper W and out of Brushalong. A foal of 1956, Sailalong was one of the toughest reining horses in the Rocky Mountain region in the early to mid-1960s, shown by Jack Kyle and Leroy Webb. **Photo by H.D. Dolcater**

Here is the elegant Skip Twin Bar, a 1961 mare sired by Skipper W and out of Twin Bar (TB) by Three Bars. Skip Twin Bar was both a halter champion and top producer for Hank. **Photo by Darol Dickinson**

some good show horses for me and some good broodmares."

Skipper's Lad, who was out of Miss Helen, and Skipador, who was out of Cheri Mac, were two sons of Skipper W Hank used in his program for a while and then sold. Both stallions made positive contributions to the Wiescamp program.

Still other sons of Skipper W who Hank used at one time or another were Spot Cash, Sirlette, Sir Skip, Skip Sir Bar, and Skip Fare.

And then there were the daughters.

Skipper W sired only 68 mares. Hank kept a tight hold on them, though, and very few of them ever left Alamosa while in their prime.

AQHA records show that the daughters of Skipper W produced a total of 94 performers. Ten of these earned their AQHA Championships, and twenty-two garnered performance Registers of Merit. Five more earned Superiors in either halter or performance. On the racetrack, four maternal grandget of Skipper W earned their Registers of Merit.

Skipperette, foaled in 1950 and a full sister to Skipper's King, is considered by Hank to be the top daughter of Skipper W. Like her sire, Skipperette stood grand at the Denver National Western Stock Show, Colorado State Fair, and New Mexico State Fair. She was considered the mare to beat in any halter competition she entered.

"Skipperette was a timeless kind of mare," remembers Hank. "She defied the terms 'old-fashioned' and 'modern.' She was just plain good. And another thing about her: She was a broodmare. She raised four sons who were good enough for me to use as breeding stallions. Very few of my show mares have ever done that for me.

"People seem to think that just because a mare stands grand at a show, or wins a race or a cutting contest, she'll automatically be a good producer. It doesn't always work out that way. Some of my greatest show mares were never able to reproduce themselves. On the other hand, some of my mares who never saw a show ring or racetrack just kept on producing champions for me, year after year. Skipperette was the exception though. She did it all."

Close behind Skipperette on the list of the top daughters of Skipper W is Skipadoo. Foaled in 1949, this palomino mare was out of Miss Helen.

"Skipadoo wasn't a very big mare," recalls Hank, "but she was a good one. She was heavily muscled and yet very feminine. We showed her all over, in Quarter Horse and Palomino competition, and she was tough to beat. She wasn't

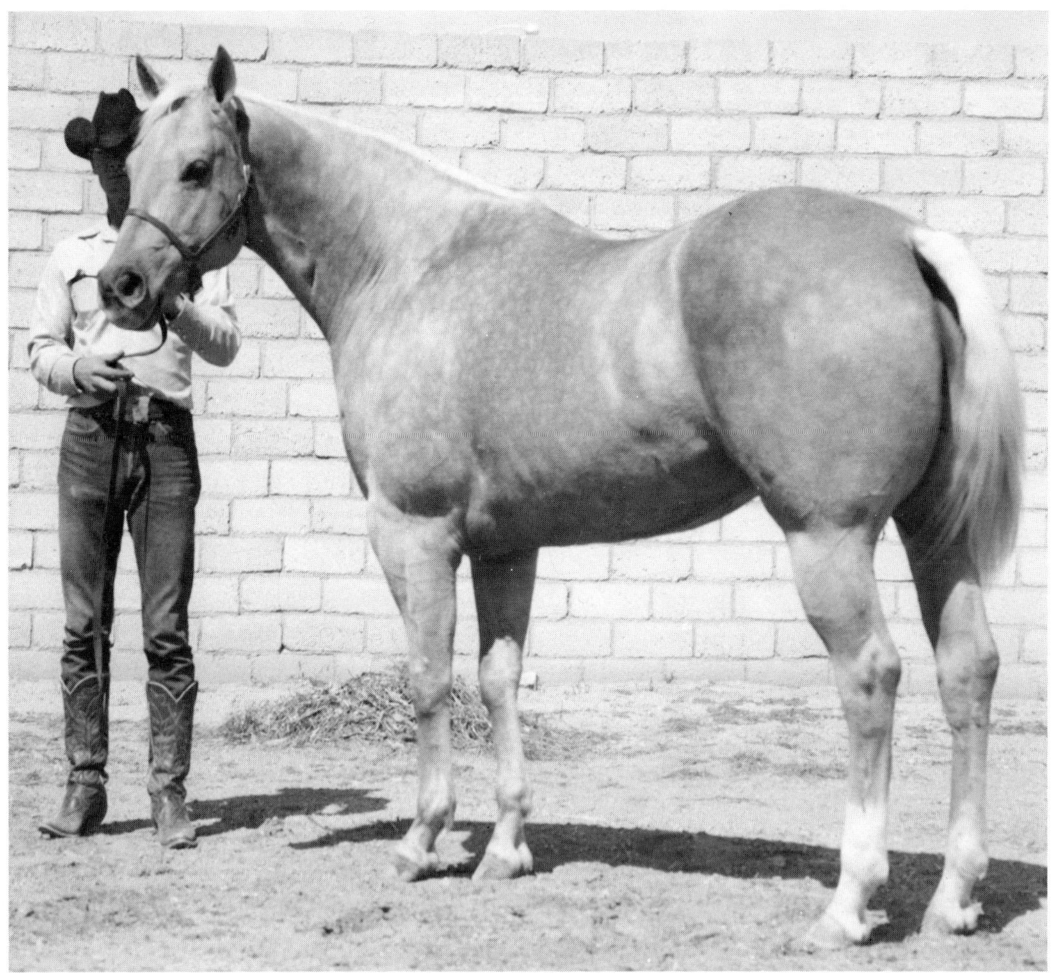

Skipadoo, by Skipper W and out of Miss Helen, was her sire's first superstar. Shown in both Quarter Horse and Palomino competition during the mid- to late 1950s, Skipadoo often championed both divisions. Jack Kyle is shown with the palomino mare in this photo taken at the 1958 New Mexico State Fair.

quite as good a broodmare as Skipperette was, but she did produce a couple of good sons I wound up selling, and several top daughters I kept."

Two other daughters of Skipper W who proved to be excellent producers were H.J. Skippa, out of Question Mount, and H.J. Skippit, out of Mexicala Rose.

H.J. Skippa, a Register of Merit race horse, was the dam of Skippa String, SI 95; Skip The Bar, SI 95; and Scooter's Maid, race winner.

H.J. Skippit produced Skip's Princess, AQHA Champion; Skip Cash, AQHA Champion; Sheik's Image, earner of 21.5 performance and 8 halter points; and Scooterette, earner of 13 halter points.

Other daughters of Skipper W who produced either AQHA Champions or AAA runners were Skip Hi, Skip Too, Skip Queen, Skipper's Maid, Sea Skipper, and Skip's Aid.

And there were still other Skipper W daughters who lived out most of their lives in Alamosa, quietly producing top sons and daughters. These were mares such as Skiparado, Skipover, Skip Lady,

Skip On, by Skipper W and out of Scoot On, was a highly successful show horse for Hank and earned an AQHA Championship in 1961. Shortly thereafter, he was retired to stud with high expectations, but died after siring only one registered foal.

Skip's Dilly, foaled in 1963, was the final AQHA Champion sired by Skipper W. Out of Sassy Nick, she earned both her AQHA Championship and a Superior in western pleasure in 1966. She was also the open high-point western pleasure mare that year. The handler is Walter Hughes.

Photo Courtesy of *The Quarter Horse Journal*

Sea Skipper, by Skipper W and out of Whisper W, was foaled in 1956. In addition to being a top halter mare, Sea Skipper was a multiple AQHA Champion-producer. She is shown here with Ted Waldhauser after standing grand at the 1959 Roswell, N.M., Quarter Horse show. **Photo by Harvey Caplin**

Southern Babe, Skip Bird, Skip's Choice, Skipper's Bustle, and Sassy Skip. Although they might not have been in the limelight as much as some of the others, all had a positive impact on the overall Wiescamp program.

"Skipper W happened along at just the right time to make the kind of an impact that he did," reflects Hank. "I had that good set of Philmont and Ghost Ranch mares and I kept adding mares to the mix.

"Skipper was a great sire, I'll grant you that. But where would he have been without mares like Santa Maria and Mexicala Rose? How would he have done if I hadn't added mares to his broodmare band like Joy Ann, Question Mount, Scotch Lady, Barbara Star, and Twin Bar?

"People like to give all the credit to the studs. I guess that's all right. But you show me any successful horse breeding program that has endured over the years, and I'll show you a program that is built around broodmares. Not mares—*broodmares.*

"I've always put it this way: A good mare is 60 to 70 percent responsible for what her foals are, and a bad mare is 100 percent.

"If I had to point to one single thing that was most responsible for Skipper W's success as a sire, it would have to be the set of mares that I put him on.

"Skipper W did a good job for me, but he didn't do it by himself. He had a little help."

Skipette was one of Skipper W's most durable show ring stars. Foaled in 1959, out of Sis Nick, Skipette earned 113 halter and 61 performance points. She was an AQHA Champion, and earned a Superior in halter. She was also the 1964 open high-point calf roping mare.

Photo by Darol Dickinson

9 THE OTHER SIRES

"Each one of these horses had qualities that I liked, so I bred mares to them, too."

EVEN THOUGH Hank Wiescamp had decided in 1947 that Skipper W was going to be his main herd sire, that did not mean that he planned to ignore the other stallions he owned at that time.

"I've never believed in putting all my eggs in one basket," remarks Hank. "I don't do that now and I didn't do it then. At the time that I decided to use Skipper W on the bulk of the Plaudit-bred mares, I also owned Scooter W. and Show Boat. The following year I bought Brush Mount. Each one of those horses had qualities that I liked, so I bred mares to them, too."

Brush Mount was a product of the CS Ranch of Cimarron, New Mexico. Foaled in 1938, he was sired by Chimney Sweep (TB) and was out of Hula Dancer by Jiggs. After using him for several

Scooter W., by Plaudit and out of Saucy Sue by Lani Chief (TB), had a positive influence on the early Wiescamp breeding program. The 1948 Champion Running Stallion, he's shown here after winning a 300-yard race at La Mesa Park, Raton, New Mexico. Trainer Jim Phillips is at Scooter's head and Billy Brite is in the irons.

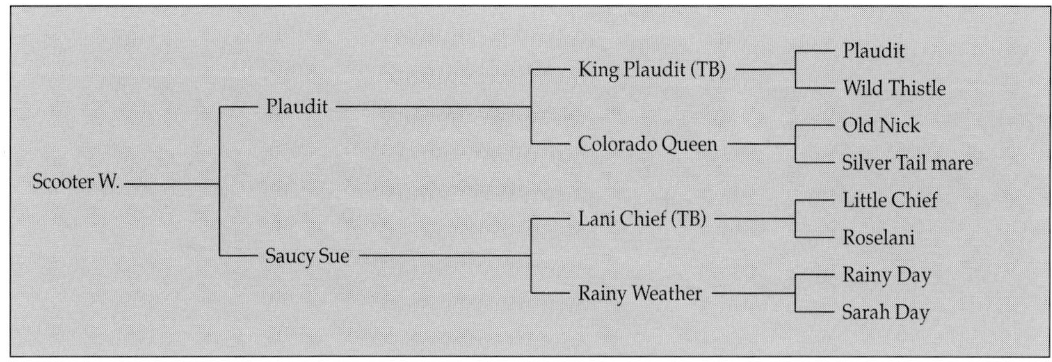

years, the CS sold Brush Mount to a man in Mexico. Hank, in turn, purchased him from that man.

"Brush Mount's daddy, Chimney Sweep, was one of the best-looking Thoroughbreds I ever saw," recalls Hank. "He was right up there with Maple Prince and Lani Chief as far as looks went.

"The CS got him from the same place I got Maple Prince—the Fort Robinson Remount Depot. One of the main reasons that he was in the Remount program was because those race horse people back East couldn't ride his foals. They were too salty.

"I had known about Chimney Sweep for a number of years before I bought Brush Mount. In fact I was there, right north of Cimarron, on the day they unloaded him from the train to take him to the CS.

"He was a good horse and once I've laid eyes on a good horse I never forget when and where I saw him. So, 6 or 7 years after I first saw Chimney Sweep, I decided to pay a visit to the CS to see if they had any young horses by him for sale.

"On my way to the ranch headquarters I came upon a CS cowboy, so I stopped him and asked where the foreman was. He just looked up toward the sky and never said anything.

"'Well, where is he,' I said, 'up in an airplane or something?' 'Nope,' he replied, 'the boss and a couple of the boys took off a while ago riding some Chimney Sweep geldings. When they're doin' that, there's usually a couple of 'em in the air—either goin' up or comin' down.'

"Brush Mount was like that," continues Hank. "He was a good-looking horse, a colorful horse with a beautiful head and neck. But his foals had a lot of buck in 'em. He didn't cross too well with my Plaudit mares. So, after a couple of years, I sold him to Kelly Moore at Raton. He got along all right with him."

Although he was used by Hank very sparingly, Brush Mount did have a positive impact on the Wiescamp program.

"The CS Ranch and the Philmont Ranch bordered each other," says Hank. "They did some swappin' back and forth with their studs, so when I got the Philmont mares there were several daughters of Brush Mount among 'em.

"Colorado Queen II, one of the daughters of Plaudit, had a palomino Brush Mount filly at her side when I bought the mares. I named her Brushalong and she was one of the good ones."

Bred to Skipper W, Brushalong produced Sailalong, an AQHA Champion; Skipato, a halter-point earner; and Skip Brush, a performance point-earner. In addition, two of her daughters, H.J.

The influence of Brush Mount in the Wiescamp breeding program was also felt through his top son, Gold Mount, and his grandson, Show Boat.

Skipity Scoot was one of the most durable halter and performance horses of his era. The good-looking palomino was often shown by Casey Darnell at halter, in reining, and in cutting at the same show. Here's a good action shot of Casey and Skipity Scoot in the cutting arena.

Photo Courtesy of *The Quarter Horse Journal*

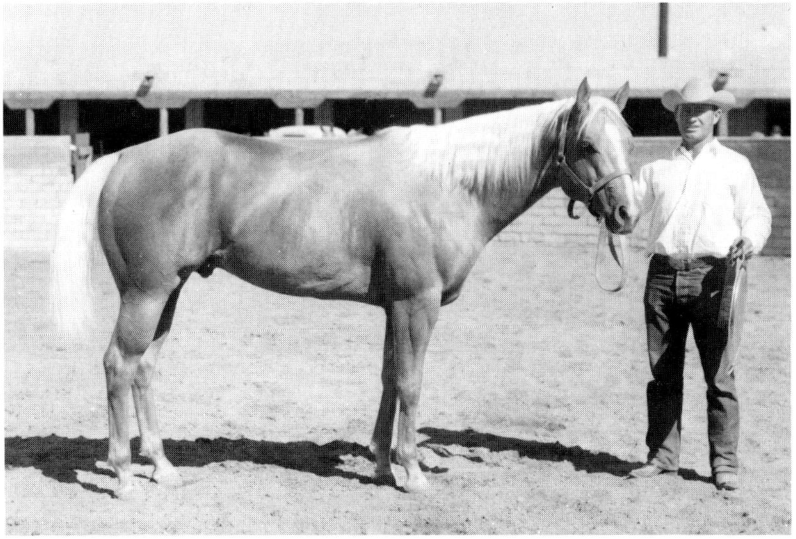

Skipity Scoot, by Scooter W. and out of Hired Girl, was shown in both Palomino and Quarter Horse competition. Here he is after winning the Quarter Horse stallion championship at the 1956 New Mexico State Fair.

Photo Courtesy of *The Quarter Horse Journal*

Smoke Along and Brushette, were also AQHA Champion producers.

Two other daughters of Brush Mount, both foaled in 1949, also proved to be superior producers when placed in the broodmare band.

H.J. Silver Finn, out of Finn by Nick Shoemaker, was the dam of three full brothers by Skipper W: Silver Skip, an AQHA Champion; Skipper's Image, the earner of 188 halter points; and Stagehand, who earned 18 halter points. All three of these stallions also went on to sire AQHA Champions themselves.

Spanish Flower, out of Spanish Rose by Nick Shoemaker, was the dam of two show point-earners and one Register of Merit runner. She was also the dam of Shawnee Gal and Skipper's Rose, top producers in their own right.

The influence of Brush Mount in the Wiescamp breeding program was also felt through two of his top sons: Gold Mount and Show Boat.

"I came close to owning Gold Mount when he was just a colt," remembers Hank. "Freda and I were down at Cimarron for the Fourth of July rodeo in 1940,

Chimney Sweep (TB) was a Remount stallion whose blood was incorporated by Wiescamp into his program. Foaled in 1927, Chimney Sweep was by Whisk Broom II and out of Polly Flinders by Burgomaster.

Photo Courtesy of the Nebraska State Historical Society

"I bred Scooter W. to be a race horse and that's what he turned out to be."

and as we were driving by a part of the Philmont Ranch, I spied this good-looking palomino mare with a palomino foal by her side. I pulled off on the side of the road, got out, and looked both of 'em over.

"When I got back in the car I told Freda, 'I don't know who that colt is, or how he's bred, but I'll guarantee you one thing: By the time the sun sets today, I'm gonna own him.'

"I hunted up the ranch foreman and told him that I'd spotted a palomino colt I'd sure like to own. He said, 'You're a day late, Hank. Warren Shoemaker bought him yesterday.'

"Warren registered that colt as Gold Mount, and I might have just missed out on the chance to buy him, but I didn't forget about him.

"After I bought Nick Shoemaker from Warren, I went back and bought his mother and grandmother too. You see, when Warren sold Plaudit to the Philmont, he took some of his payment in cash and some of it in mares. Nick Shoemaker's mother and grandmother were two of the mares he took in on trade.

"Anyway, I went down to Watrous and bought 'em both. They weren't registered at the time. I never did register the old mare, Slippers, but I registered her daughter as Slipalong Wiescamp. She was in foal to Gold Mount when I bought her, and Show Boat was the resulting foal."

Show Boat, a palomino stallion foaled in 1945, went on to become a top halter, reining, and cutting horse for Hank, and a good broodmare sire.

"I showed Show Boat in a lot of Palomino shows during the late 1940s and early 1950s," recalls Hank, "and he did his share of winning. He stood grand one year at the Denver National Western Palomino show and won the Quarter Horse reining at the New Mexico State Fair the following fall."

Among the top-producing daughters of Show Boat who made their presence felt in

A photo of Brush Mount taken in the mid-1950s with his owners Landon K. and Mary Moore of Raton, New Mexico. Although this is not a flattering picture of Brush Mount, Hank said the horse favored his sire, Chimney Sweep (TB) in conformation as well as disposition. Used sparingly by Hank, Brush Mount still left his mark on the Wiescamp program through several top-producing daughters.

Photo by Cecil Hellbusch, Courtesy of Alice Moore

the Wiescamp broodmare band were H.J. Show Star and Show Lady.

H.J. Show Star, foaled in 1950 out of South Wind, was sold as a young mare to Floyd and Esther Covalt of Broadwater, Nebraska. She was shown by them and earned 11 halter points and an arena Register of Merit. She also went on to become a great broodmare for the Covalts and was the dam of Dollars Cash, Gypsy Cash, and Mr Show Bars.

Leased by Hank from the Covalts and bred to Skipper W, H.J. Show Star produced the Superior halter mare Skip's Glory.

Show Lady, by Show Boat and out of Santa Maria, was never shown, but made her impact on the Wiescamp program solely as a broodmare. Bred to Skipper W, she produced Skip's Reward, Skip Lady, Skip's Choice, Show A Skip, and Skip's Review.

Skip's Reward, as was mentioned earlier, made an excellent show horse and sire for Wiescamp. Among his noted show offspring were the AQHA Champions Skip Trama, Skip Relic, and Skip's Mark. Skip Trama was also a Superior halter horse, as were Skip's Barred and Skip Barba.

Skip Lady, Skip's Choice, Skip's Review, and Show A Skip all turned out to be tremendous producers for Hank. The first three were the dams of multiple halter and performance point-earners, and all four mares produced both sons and daughters who were good enough to

A 1962 photo of Stagehand, when he stood grand at the 1962 Farmington, N.M., Quarter Horse Show. By Skipper W and out of H.J. Silver Finn by Brush Mount, Stagehand earned 18 halter points and sired several top show horses including Fancy's Little Bit, an open and youth AQHA Champion who amassed 864 points.

Photo by Alexander

be made part of the Wiescamp breeding program.

Show Boat was also the sire of H.J. Sandman.

"The Sandman story is kind of a funny one," says Hank. "Frank Vessels of Los Alamitos, Calif., called me one time in the early 1950s, looking for a lead pony for his race horses.

"He wanted a palomino with a long tail. I told him I had a good one by Show Boat and out of a Plaudit mare. He said he'd come and look at him. Well, right before it was time for Frank to arrive, I told the boys to clean the colt up extra special for him. When I stopped by a little later to see how they were doing, I almost had a stroke!

"They'd trimmed that colt's tail off plumb up to the hocks! They'd made a stock horse out of him. I didn't think Vessels would take him, but he did. And then, when he got him out to California, he realized that the horse had a little speed. He started working him against those Clabber II race colts of his, and Sandman just ran off and left 'em in the dust.

"So Frank made a race horse out of

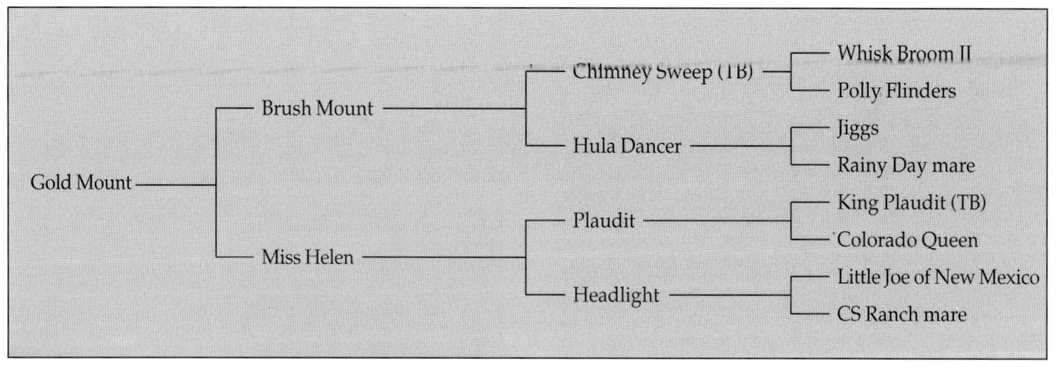

This photo of Gold Mount was taken when he was registered by Warren Shoemaker with the AQHA. Hank narrowly missed the chance to buy this great son of Brush Mount as a foal, but made liberal use of his blood at a later date.
Photo Courtesy of the American Quarter Horse Museum & Heritage Center, Amarillo, Texas

him and he was a good one for a number of years. Good enough to run AAA and stay sound."

Hank also incorporated the blood of Gold Mount into his breeding program by adding several of the noted stallion's best daughters to his broodmare band.

"In 1949, I went down to Warren's looking to buy a good Gold Mount mare," recalls Hank. "I wound up getting Scotch Lady, a palomino full-sister to Music Mount. She made a pretty good broodmare for me and was the dam of Great Chance, Scotch Nick, Scotch Maid, and Beau Chance."

"I wanted some more Gold Mount mares though, so I hunted around until I found three that Warren had sold to a man in southwestern Kansas. They were all full sisters, by Gold Mount and out of Red Bird Shoemaker, who was by Nick and out of Plaudette, the mother of the great race mare Bright Eyes.

"I had to buy that man's whole mare band to get those three mares, but it was worth it because two of 'em, Joy Ann and Question Mount, sure turned out to be great producers.

"Joy Ann was a sorrel mare, and I'm here to tell you she was a good one. She stood out in my broodmare band in 1950, and she'd look just as good in it today. And she never produced a foal for me who wasn't a good one."

After she was purchased by Wiescamp, Joy Ann had 14 foals. Of the 14, 9 were shown and accumulated 174 halter, 33 performance, and 3 racing points. Skipity Skip, by Skipper W, and Skip's Admiral, by Skipper's King, earned AQHA Championships. Skip's Champ, by Skipper's King, earned a Superior in halter with 73 points, and Skipper's Joy, by Skipper W, stood grand at the Denver National Western Stock Show.

Three more of Joy Ann's offspring: Shirley Nick, by Nick W; Skipem, by Skipper W; and Senor Skip, by Skipper W, were halter point-earners, and at least eight of her daughters went on to become top producers in their own right. One of these, the famed Spanish Joy, will be discussed in detail in a subsequent chapter.

Joy Ann's full sister, Question Mount, was a totally different mare from her in looks and disposition, but she made her contributions to the program none the less.

"Joy Ann was a show type of mare," says Hank, "Question Mount was more of a race type. And Joy Ann threw back to the Nick side of her pedigree, so she was pretty quiet-natured. Question Mount threw back to the Brush Mount and Plaudit side. She was a little hot.

"In fact, Question Mount was a 4-year-old when I got her and she wasn't halter-broke. I never did break her to lead—just put a stud in with her every spring, and the next year she'd have me a good foal."

The first stallion that Hank turned in with Question Mount was Skipper W. Bred to him in 1949, she produced H.J. Skippa the following year.

"I raced H.J. Skippa the fall of her 3-year-old year, at Centennial Race Track in Denver," recalls Hank. "She qualified for her Register of Merit up there running against some top horses. But they wanted to hang more weight on her than I thought a 3-year-old filly should carry, so I brought her home and put the boys to riding her in a stock saddle.

"We took her to the Denver Stock Show the next January, and she won day money in roping there. Then I put her in the broodmare band and she had Skippa String, Skip The Bar, Scooter's Maid, and Scooter's Charm for me."

Skippa String, by Rukin String, earned his AAA rating on the racetrack and was a multiple stakes winner. Retired to stud, he went on to found one of Wiescamp's top male lines. Skip The Bar, by St Bar D (TB), also earned his AAA race rating, and Scooter's Maid and Scooter's Charm went on to become top producers.

In addition to H.J. Skippa, Question Mount was also the dam of another son, Bar Mount, and two daughters, Sassy Nick and Some Question, who made significant contributions to the Wiescamp breeding program.

Scooter W., by Plaudit and out of Saucy Sue by Lani Chief (TB), was yet another stallion bred by Hank who made solid contributions to the Wiescamp program during this time period.

"Frank Burns owned Plaudit for a while," says Hank. "I had a chance to buy him myself, and a lot of folks have asked me why I didn't. My answer to them has always been, 'Why would I want to?' I

The daughters of Gold Mount proved to be excellent producers when crossed on Hank's Skipper W line. Great Chance (above), was by Skipper W and out of Scotch Lady. He is shown with R.Q. Sutherland after being named grand champion stallion at the 1957 Denver National Western Stock Show. Skipper's Joy (below), by Skipper W and out of Joy Ann, is shown after championing the mare division at the same show the following year. ***Western Horseman* Photos**

Show Boat was a son of Gold Mount and Slipalong Wiescamp. This keen-headed stallion was both a halter and performance champion and also sired a number of top broodmares. Show Boat is shown with Walt Alsbaugh after winning the Quarter Horse reining at the 1949 New Mexico State Fair. **Photo by Windom Studio**

already had his best daughters. I already had his best granddaughters. I could have bought him and bred mares to him until doomsday and never got any better mares than I already had.

"But I liked Plaudit. He was a great individual. So I bred Saucy Sue, one of the good Philmont mares, to him when he was in this country, and that's how I got Scooter W."

Scooter W. was foaled in 1945, the same year as Skipper W and Show Boat. While Hank made show horses out of the latter two, he had other plans for Scooter.

"I bred Scooter W. to be a race horse and that's what he turned out to be," notes Hank. "He was a nice-looking horse, just like his daddy. He had a good head and neck, and a nice topline. But he didn't have a lot of muscle. He could run though."

Raced lightly by Wiescamp as a 2- and 3-year-old, Scooter W. proved adept at distances ranging from 300 to 440 yards. In the fall of his 3-year-old year, he won the 440-yard Stallion Stakes held during the New Mexico State Fair, placed second by a nose to Miss Banks in a 300-yard event, and third behind Stella Moore and Leota W. in the 440-yard New Mexico Championship.

In the latter race, he covered the 440 yards in 22.5, equaling both the 3-year-old colt and the stallion records of the day. Based on his performances in these three races he was voted the Champion Quarter Running Stallion of 1948.

"Again, because Scooter W. did not have the kind of rear-end muscling that I was striving to put on my horses, I did not use him very heavily as a breeding stallion," notes Hank. "He did sire some good horses for me though."

Skipity Scoot was without a doubt the top show horse sired by Scooter W. A foal of 1952, this palomino stallion was out of Hired Girl. Wiescamp started Skipity Scoot on his way toward a stellar career as a true all-around performance horse, and then sold him to J.P. Davidson of Albuquerque.

From this point on, Skipity Scoot was handled by the noted New Mexico trainer Casey Darnell, and they proved to be formidable competition in halter, cutting, reining, and working cowhorse competition for a number of years. Skipity Scoot was the AQHA 1957 Honor Roll Working Cowhorse and an AQHA

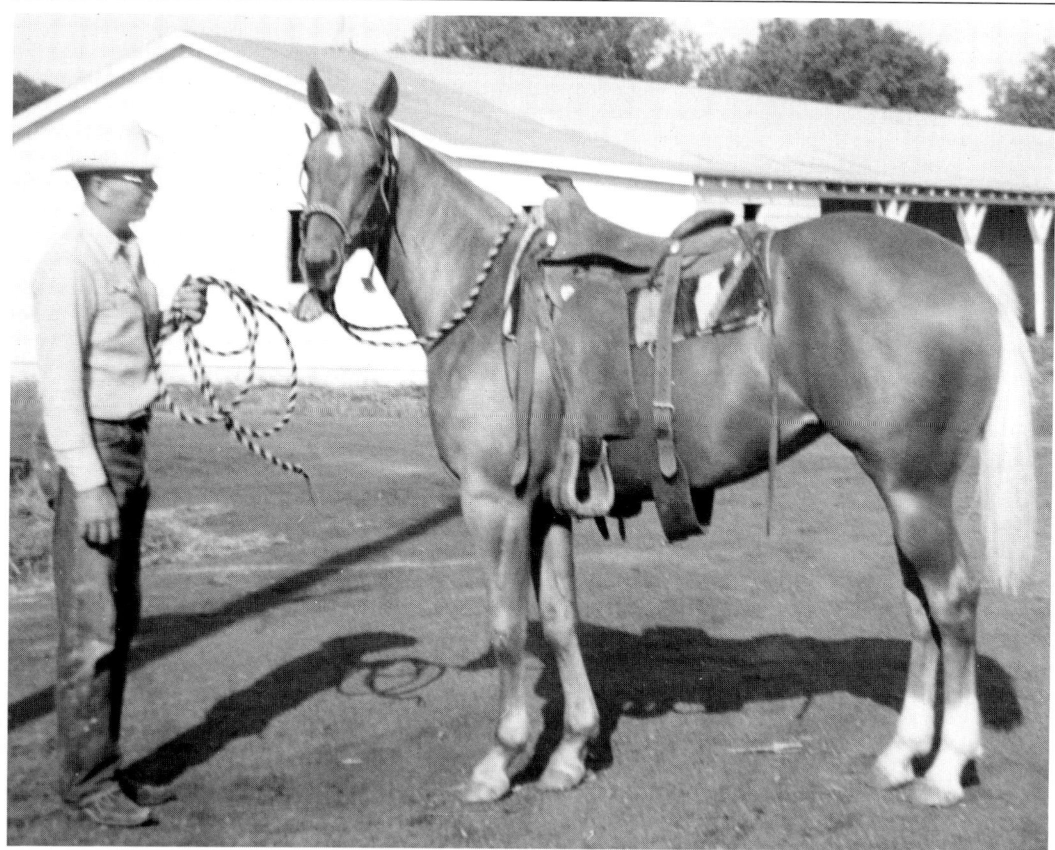

H.J. Show Star was sold by Hank as a young mare to Floyd and Esther Covalt of Broadwater, Nebraska. Hank leased her back several years later to breed to Skipper W. Skip's Glory, a Superior halter mare, was the resulting foal. In this photo, Floyd Covalt and the 3-year-old Show Star are shown at the Ak-Sar-Ben Livestock & Horse Show in Omaha.

Photo Courtesy of Valerie Covalt Furman

Champion, earning a total of 23 halter and 87 performance points.

Other top show horses by Scooter W. included Scooterette, out of H.J. Skippit, earner of 13 halter points; and Scooter Lad, out of Stepaway, earner of 10 halter points.

Among the top producing daughters that Scooter W. sired for Hank were H.J. Scootaway, Scoot On, Scooter's Charm, and Spanish Rita.

In any final analysis, the influences that Brush Mount, Gold Mount, Show Boat, and Scooter W. had on the Wiescamp program during its formative years would have to be put on a plane somewhere below that of Skipper W and the line he founded.

Each of the four did make key contributions to the program, however, and they deserve to have those contributions recognized.

10 Nick W and Spanish Nick

"And most people don't know it, but Nick W could run too. In fact, he could outrun Scooter W."

THE FINAL two stallions who made significant contributions to Hank Wiescamp's breeding program during the era immediately following Nick Shoemaker's death were Nick W and Spanish Nick.

Both were sired by Nick Shoemaker. Nick W was out of Cimarroncita by Plaudit, and Spanish Nick was out of Mexicala Rose by Plaudit.

"Nick W was a son of Nick Shoemaker," observes Hank, "but he favored his dam's family more than his sire's.

"Cimarroncita was a bay mare. She could run a hole in the wind. And most people don't know it, but Nick W could run too. In fact, he could outrun Scooter W.

"We trained Nick W as a rope horse, so we knew he had a little gas. When we were getting Scooter W. ready for the Stallion Stakes in Albuquerque, we worked the two of them against each other twice. Nick W won both times.

"So we decided to take Nick W to Raton too. We got up at the crack of dawn every

Nick W's buckskin coat and light muscling limited his use on the similarly colored and built Wiescamp mares. He still went on to become a top all-around sire whose foals excelled at halter, in performance, and on the racetrack.

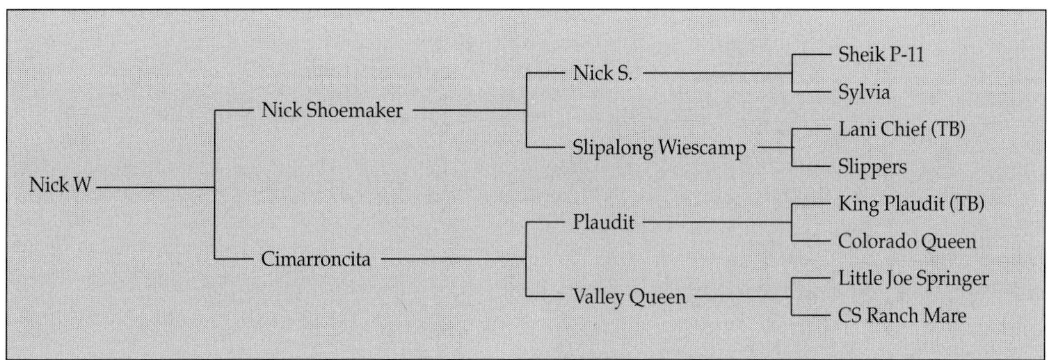

morning and worked him on the back side of the track. We were going to enter him in the Stallion Stakes. Everybody knew Scooter W., but nobody knew Nick W.

"We were going to enter him, bet a lot of money on him, and fill our sacks. But when we started working him out of the gate we ran into all sorts of trouble.

"When we sprung the starting gates, Nick just sat on the tailboard. He froze! There was no barrier to pop, and no calf to chase. He didn't know what we wanted him to do!

"So we waited a few days and tried it again. We popped the gates open, and Nick just sat on the tailboard again. Jack Phillips, who was my race trainer at that time, said, 'There ain't but one thing to do. Let's shut the gates, pop 'em open again, and I'll hit him a little bit with a hot shot. He'll either come out of the gate a-flyin', or he'll come out backwards.'

"And that's just what he did. When Jack hit him with that hot shot, Nick flipped! He came out of that gate backwards! Well, we tried for a couple more days after that, but we just didn't have time enough to retrain him, so we took him home. But I'll tell you one thing: Nick W could fly!"

As was alluded to earlier, Nick W's buckskin coat and light muscling limited his use as a breeding stallion in the Wiescamp program. This fact notwith-

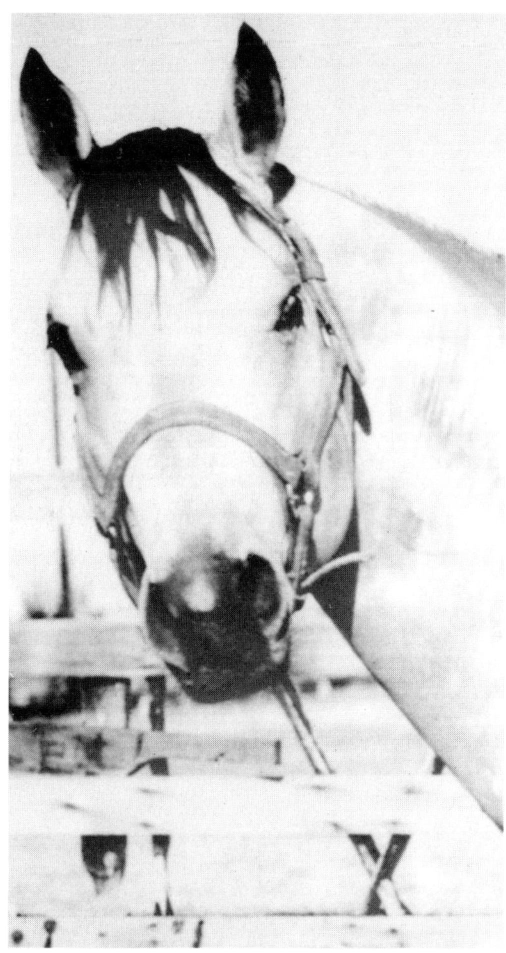

Nick W was renowned for his beautiful head, a trait that he consistently passed on.

"Nick W's foals could halter, they could run, and they could work cattle."

School Mama, by Nick W and out of South Wind by Plaudit, was an excellent example of the type of horse that Hank was raising in the early 1950s. One of the top halter mares of her day, School Mama is pictured here with George Mueller after standing grand at the 1954 Pikes Peak Roundup in Colorado Springs.

Photo by Clarence Coil/Stewart's Photography

Scotch Maid, by Nick W and out of Scotch Lady by Gold Mount, proved to be a champion both in the show ring and broodmare band. Here she is, held by Ron Wiescamp, after winning the 3-year-old mare class at the 1955 New Mexico State Fair.

Photo by Cecil Hellbusch, Courtesy of *The Quarter Horse Journal*

standing, he proved to be a great all-around sire.

"Nick W's foals could halter," observes Hank, "they could run, and they could work cattle. And his daughters made great broodmares, especially when I put them on some of my heavier-muscled studs, such as Skipper W and Skipper's King."

School Mama was one of Nick W's first get to enter the show ring. Foaled in 1950, out of South Wind by Brujo, this powerful buckskin mare was campaigned in the same show string as Skipperette and Skipadoo. She held her own against both of them and the rest of the competition as well.

"I knew I was on the right track when I bred School Mama," says Hank. "I took that lightly muscled Nick W, bred him to South Wind, one of the heavier-muscled Plaudit-bred mares that I owned, and hit the jackpot.

"School Mama had one of the biggest butts ever put on a mare. We championed both the Colorado and New Mexico State Fairs with her, and also the Pikes Peak show. Those were three of the toughest shows of that era. And then School Mama made a pretty good broodmare for me too. But why wouldn't she; she had it on both sides of her pedigree."

Among the other top halter point-earners by Nick W were Roanwood Nick, a Superior halter horse with 64 points, Second Nick, Nicka Maria, Scotch Nick, and Scotch Maid.

Speedster, a 1952 dark dun gelding by Nick W and out of Hollyhock W., was also a halter point-earner. He was far better known, however, for his ability as a cutting horse. With 250 AQHA cutting points, he more than qualified for a Superior award in that event. He also fared well in open competition and was a member of the NCHA top 10 in 1962.

The top son of Nick W, as far as overall impact on the Wiescamp program is concerned, would have to be Scottish.

Scottish was a 1953 foal out of Sagey by

Scottish was a halter, performance, and race winner. He also had a far-reaching impact on the Wiescamp breeding program as a top broodmare sire.

Photo by Darol Dickinson

After achieving his AAA rating on the racetrack, Scottish was turned into a cutting horse. Here he is in action, ridden by Jack Kyle.

Photo by Harvey Caplin

Roanwood Nick, by Nick W and out of Soppy's Question by Soppy, was a Superior halter horse with 64 points. He is shown here at the 1966 Denver National Western Stock Show, where he was the grand champion gelding. He was owned by the Elmwood Ranch of Broomfield, Colorado.

Photo by Darol Dickinson, Courtesy of *The Quarter Horse Journal*

Golddust Shoemaker. Hank rates his purchase of Sagey as one of the shrewdest bargains he ever made.

"I went down to Warren Shoemaker's in 1943," recalls the venerable horseman, "and bought several weanling fillies, including Sagey, for $50 each. Sagey was by Golddust Shoemaker and out of Red Allen, who was by Nick S.

"She was just kind of an average mare as far as looks go, but she produced five AAA running horses, sired by five different stallions, so she was probably worth the $50 I gave for her.

"Scottie (Scottish) took after Nick W and Cimarroncita in build and disposition. He could get a little snorty. We raced him as a 2-, 3-, and 4-year-old and he was a solid AAA runner. Then we showed him at halter a little and Jack Kyle started cutting off him. He just did everything we ever asked him to.

"And Scottie was a great broodmare sire. You can look around this ranch today and see his influence in a lot of the mares. They have really crossed well with my Skipper-bred studs over the years."

Two more Nick W stallions who proved themselves as show horses and broodmare sires were Shawnee Sheik and his son, Sheik's Image. Shawnee Sheik, a bay foaled in 1953, was out of Hired Girl. The buckskin Sheik's Image was foaled in 1959 and was out of H.J. Skippit.

Shawnee Sheik was another Nick W son who proved himself in the show ring and at stud. The bay stallion, foaled in 1953, was out of Hired Girl. He is shown with Loretta Wiescamp after standing grand at the 1955 Colorado State Fair.

***Western Horseman* Photo**

"Outside of their color, Shawnee Sheik and Sheik's Image were a lot alike," notes Hank. "They were both real good-headed, but kind of small. I had to watch the way I crossed them so that I didn't lose too much size."

Nick W sired a total of only 117 registered foals. Of these, 25 were shown, and they accumulated 216 halter and 293.5 performance points. H.J. Sir Nick, Scotch Nick, Speedster, Nick Lagrone, Roanwood Nick, and Elm's Fast Time earned performance Registers of Merit. In addition, Roanwood Nick was a Superior halter horse and Speedster earned a Superior in cutting.

Far more profound than the mark he made as a sire, however, was Nick W's record as a broodmare sire. The daughters of Nick W produced 88 foals who had show records. They amassed 1,319.5 halter and 834.5 performance points. Twenty-one earned performance Registers of Merit and four were AQHA Champions. In addition, four were Superior halter horses and four earned their Superiors in performance.

Some of the most renowned early show horses in the Wiescamp family were out of Nick W daughters. Some of those show horses included Skip's Dilly, Skipette, Bar Criada, Skip Sister, Skipa Maria, Dido

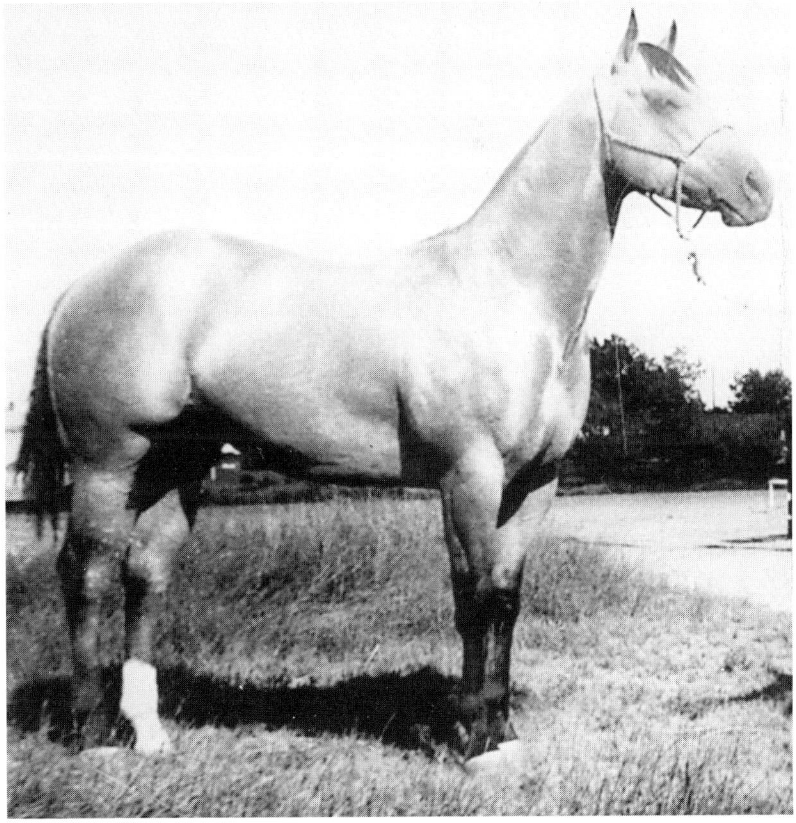

Sheik's Image, by Shawnee Sheik and out of H.J. Skippit by Skipper W, carried on the Nick W family tradition by becoming a halter and performance champion, and a top broodmare sire. This photo was taken in the mid-1960s behind the Wiescamp show barn.

The daughters of Nick W crossed well with Hank's other stallions, resulting in top show horses such as Bar Criada, a 1966 mare by Bar Mount and out of Spanish Waitress by Nick W. Shown here with Bobby Goodwin at the halter, Bar Criada was a Superior halter horse with 91 open points.

Photo Courtesy of *The Quarter Horse Journal*

This is Shawnee Skip, a 1958 stallion by Shawnee Sheik and out of Skip Too by Skipper W. Billy Allen, who showed the sorrel to his AQHA championship in 1962, is aboard in this photo taken at the New Mexico State Fairgrounds in Albuquerque.

Photo by Darol Dickinson, Courtesy of *The Quarter Horse Journal*

Cash, and Skip's Waiter.

When crossed on the Skipper W male line within the family, the Nick W mares also produced a number of top sires, including Silver Cash, Sir Raleigh, Skip Shi, Sir Skip, and Skip School.

And, as evidenced by the popular world champion halter horses Emotions and Impressive Poise, the potency of Nick W's blood has carried down into the modern horse show world as well.

"Back in the mid-1960s, I leased Nick W to W.G. Brown, of Lake Village, Ark.," notes Hank. "He raised several mares by him who went on to become top producers."

Two of these mares, Buddy's Nick and Baby Nicky, were eventually bred to The Intimidator, whose dam was of Skipper W-Nick W breeding. From these matings came Emotions, a four-time world champion halter mare, and Impressive Poise, the 1982 World Champion 3-Year-Old Stallion.

In reflecting back on Nick W, both as an individual and as a breeding stallion, Hank sums it up like this:

"Nick W had one of the greatest heads of any of the studs I'd raised up to that time. And he had a lot of speed and ath-

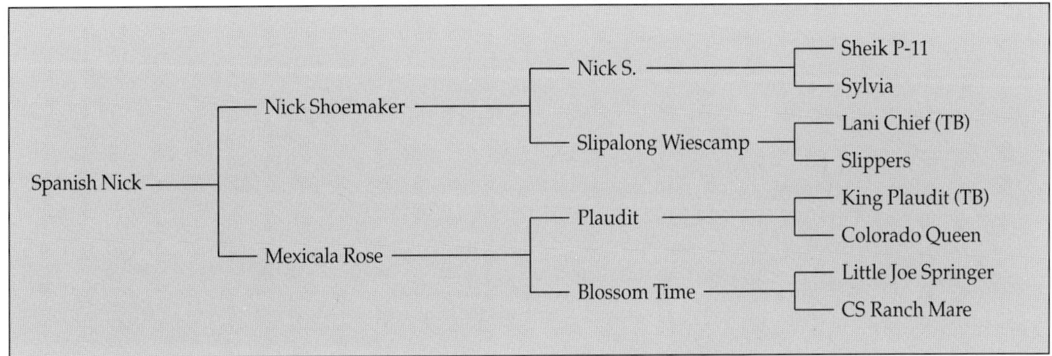

letic ability. But he was 2 inches too long in the back; 2 inches too short in the hip; and 2 inches too shallow in the heart. He was just 2 inches off everywhere.

"But I was careful with the mares I bred him to. I hand-picked the ones who were strong where he was weak. By the time it was all said and done, Nick W made his mark on my program. He didn't hurt it none."

Spanish Nick

The final son of Nick Shoemaker to have a significant impact on the Wiescamp program was Spanish Nick. This palomino was foaled in 1948.

"Spanish Nick was a top show horse," notes Hank. "Like a lot of our other horses, we showed him in both Quarter Horse and Palomino competition. At one time or another, he was either the champion Quarter Horse or Palomino stud at the Denver National Western Stock Show, the Colorado State Fair, the New Mexico State Fair, and the Pikes Peak Roundup."

Spanish Nick was also a top performance horse, earning his AQHA Championship in 1954. Retired to stud shortly thereafter, he was often overlooked when breeding season rolled around.

"You know, they say you're too soon old and too late smart," says Hank. "That hits the nail right on the head as far as Spanish Nick goes.

"It was hard for me to pass Skipper W by and breed a mare to Spanish Nick. And, later on, when Skipper's King and

Spanish Nick is acknowledged by Hank as being one of the top broodmare sires in the history of the Wiescamp program. A foal of 1948, Spanish Nick is shown here in the early 1960s on stud row at the Wiescamp Ranch. **Photo by Darol Dickinson**

As was the case with Nick W, Spanish Nick sired a number of mares who crossed well with Hank's Skipper W-bred stallions. Here is String's Nick, the result of one of those crosses. By Skippa String and out of Spanish Miss by Spanish Nick, String's Nick was the earner of 23 halter and 14 performance points. He is shown here after winning his halter class at the 1966 Wyoming State Fair, at Douglas.

Photo by Darol Dickinson, Courtesy of *The Quarter Horse Journal*

"Like the Plaudit-bred Philmont and Ghost Ranch mares, Nick W and Spanish Nick made monumental contributions to the program through their maternal descendants."

Skip's Reward came along, it got even harder. Spanish Nick just wasn't as good an individual as those other horses. And he never did set the world on fire as a sire of show horses.

"But I'll tell you one thing that I came to realize about him in time: He was as good a sire of broodmares as has ever come out of this program. As it turned out, I didn't use him enough. If I had it to do over, I'd do it different. But that's just the way it goes.

"You know, if this horse breeding business was easy to figure out, if it was some sort of exact science, the rich people would own all the good ones, and you and I couldn't afford to own any of 'em.

"Trying to figure out how to make the crosses—how to produce an individual who's an improvement over both of his parents—has kept me in the horse breeding business for over 60 years. And it'll keep me in it until the day I die."

Spanish Nick was indeed used sparingly. In 12 seasons at stud, he sired only 50 registered foals. Two of these, Spanish Ruler and Spanish Prince, were AQHA Champions. Sixteen more were either halter- or performance point-earners. All told, the sons and daughters of Spanish Nick accumulated 253 halter and 75 performance points.

As a broodmare sire, however, his record was a bit more impressive. There were 29 daughters of Spanish Nick who produced 51 foals who amassed 536 halter and 417.5 performance points in AQHA-sanctioned competition. They earned 28 performance Register of Merits, 8 racing Register of Merits, 1 Superior Halter award, 2 Superior Performance awards, 8 AQHA Championships, and 2 Supreme Championships.

At the head of the list of top-producing daughters of Spanish Nick would have to be Spanish Joy.

Foaled in 1954, out of Joy Ann, this

Spanish Nick also sired several top show geldings. Spanish Prince, shown above with Jack Kyle in the saddle, was an AQHA Champion and earned 98 halter and 40 performance points. Spanish Skipper (below) earned 46 halter points and stood grand at the Denver National Western Stock Show, and Colorado and New Mexico state fairs. He is shown here after being named grand champion at the 1962 Pikes Peak Quarter Horse Show in Colorado Springs. Also shown (from left): Charlene Hammond Morgan, Bobbi Jo Spencer, Marilyn Higby, and Terry Hendricks. Terry showed Spanish Skipper for the Elmwood Ranch.

Photo by Darol Dickinson

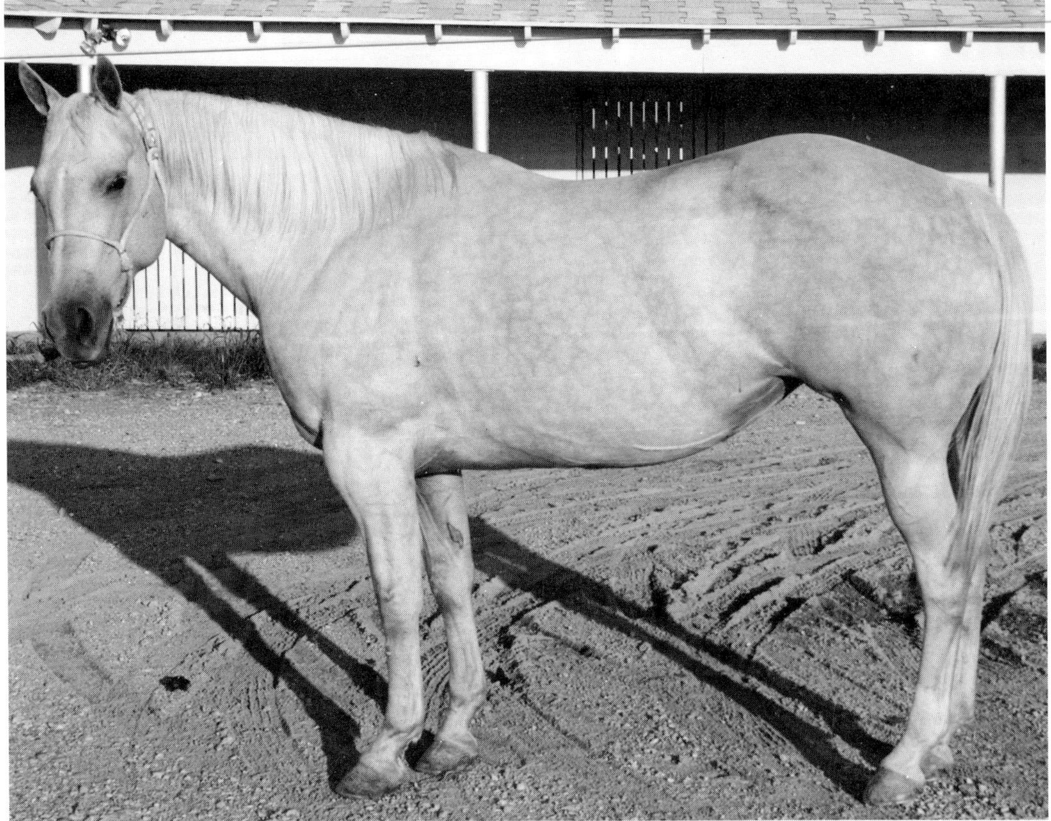

Spanish Joy was one of the Quarter Horse breed's premier producers. By Spanish Nick and out of Joy Ann by Gold Mount, she was the dam of two Supreme Champions, five AQHA Champions, and five AAA-rated race horses.

Photo Courtesy of *The Quarter Horse Journal*

Mach I, by Junior Reed, was the first of Spanish Joy's Supreme Champions. He qualified for the prestigious award in 1970 with 19 racing, 41 halter, 8 reining, 5.5 western pleasure, 5 heading, and 5 heeling points.

Photo Courtesy of *The Quarter Horse Journal*

palomino mare was the dam of Mach I, Supreme Champion; Goldseeker Bars, Supreme Champion; Leo Spanish, AAA AQHA Champion; Mr Spanish Lee, AAA AQHA Champion; Rochester's Star, AA AQHA Champion; Baby Joy Jet, SI 92; Jet Spanish, SI 88; and Bar None Spanish, SI 85.

As the leading dam of Supreme Champions and AAA AQHA Champions, Spanish Joy is truly in a league by herself as one of the top producing Quarter Horse mares of all time.

"Spanish Joy was not one of the better mares I ever raised," notes Hank. "She had too many little things wrong with her conformation for me to keep, so I sold her to Elna McKee of Norwood, Colorado.

"But, like I've always said, 'It's usually not the beauty queens who make the best mothers.' Spanish Joy wasn't a show mare, but she sure turned out to be a great producer. You can't take that away from her."

In addition to Spanish Joy, Spanish Nick sired a number of other solid producers, including Spanish Bird, Spanish Dancer, Skipperetta, Spanish Shasta, Spanish Bustle, Skipalita, Spanish Gown, Elm's Slipcover, Spanish Miss, Spanish Sister, Spanish Scoot, Spanish Fury, Spanish Spy, Spanish Kit Bar, Spanish Way, and Spanish Parade.

In both color and conformation, Nick W and Spanish Nick reflected their Plaudit heritage. This limited their use in the breeding program that Hank Wiescamp had conceived in his mind's eye.

But, like the Plaudit-bred Philmont and Ghost Ranch mares, Nick W and Spanish Nick made monumental contributions to the program through their maternal descendants. Like all of the Plaudit-bred horses that Hank placed in his breeding program, they bred true and they left their mark.

Mr Spanish Lee, by Leo, was one of five sons of Spanish Joy to be named an AQHA Champion. Also AAA-rated on the racetrack, the good-looking sorrel earned 46 halter and 19 performance points.

Photo by Orren Mixer, Courtesy of *The Quarter Horse Journal*

11 Two of a Kind

"The greatest accomplishment that Skipper W ever made, in my opinion, was that he sired Skipper's King and Skipperette."

AS HAS BEEN chronicled earlier, Skipper W had a tremendous impact on both the Wiescamp breeding program and the Quarter Horse breed. He was the sire of some of the greatest halter and performance Quarter Horses of the 1950s and 1960s, and he founded a tremendously potent family of breeding horses.

In Hank Wiescamp's opinion, however, one thing that Skipper W did overshadowed all of his other accomplishments.

"Skipper W did a lot of good, in a lot of

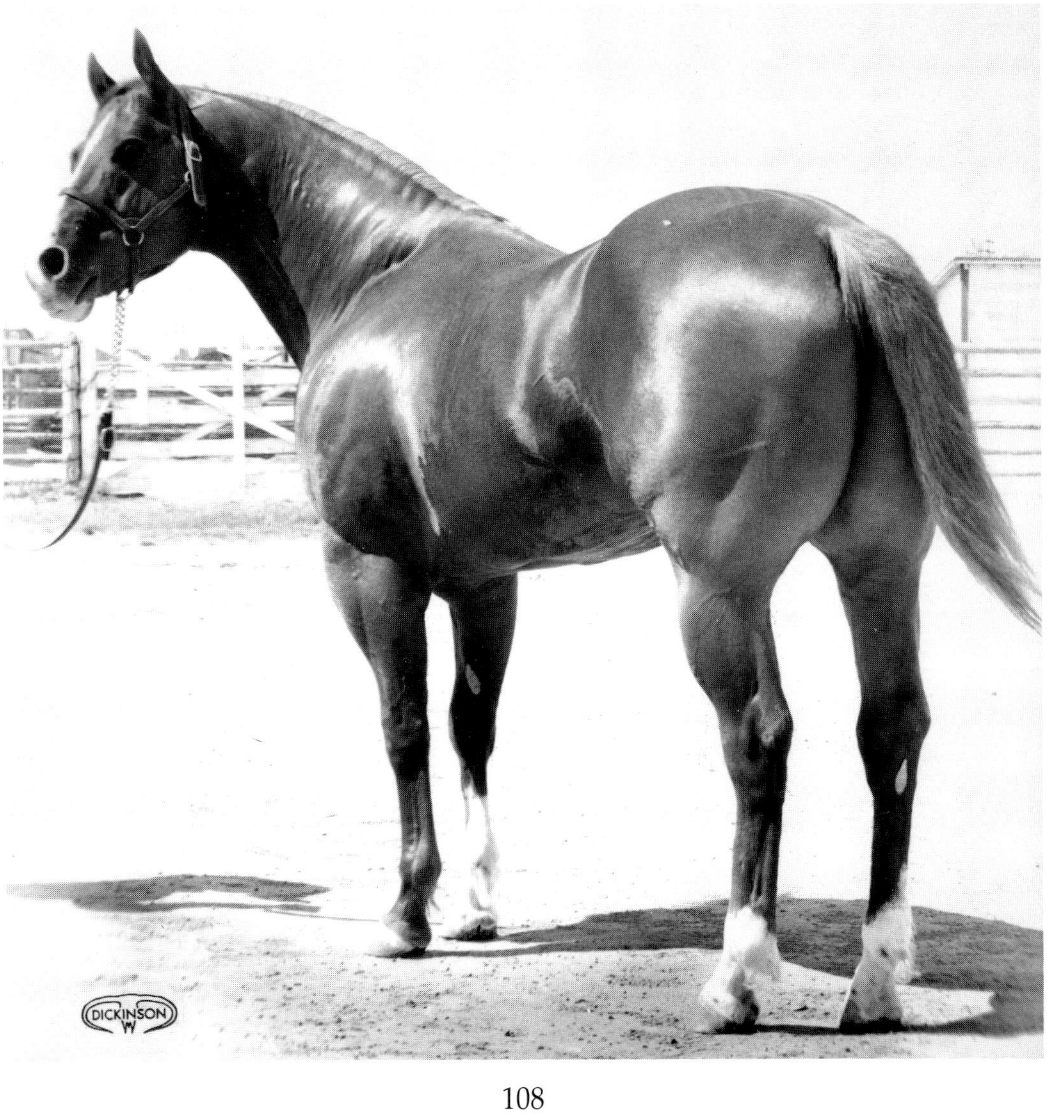

Skipper's King was considered by Hank to be the top son of Skipper W. His arrival on the scene in 1954 marked the beginning of a new era for the Wiescamp Quarter Horse program.

Photo by Darol Dickinson

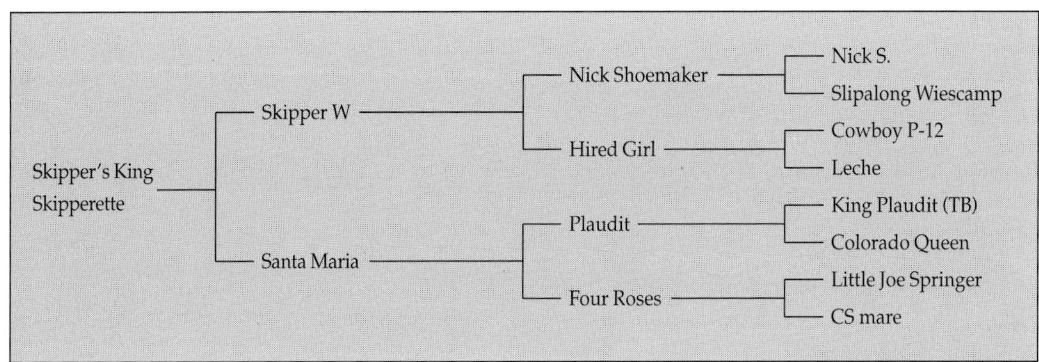

different ways," reflects Hank, "but, if I had to point to one thing that he did that stands out above all the rest, there's no doubt about what that would be.

"The greatest accomplishment that Skipper W ever made, in my opinion, was that he sired Skipperette and Skipper's King."

Skipperette and Skipper's King were full sister and brother, out of Santa Maria by Plaudit. Skipperette was the older of the two, foaled in 1950. Skipper's King was born in 1954.

"When I got the Philmont mares," recalls Hank, "Santa Maria was a weaner. Her dam, Four Roses, was an old mare at that time.

"Years earlier, the Philmont had bought a bunch of broodmares from the CS to breed to Plaudit. They were daughters of Little Joe (of New Mexico) and Little Joe Springer. Four Roses was one of those mares. There were still a few of them left when I bought the bunch. They all had a big CS branded on their right shoulder, with a vent, or line, through it. That's what the Philmont had to do after they bought 'em.

"Anyway, Four Roses and the other CS mares were old when I got 'em. I did bring most of 'em home, but I traded or gave 'em away. Four Roses never had another foal after I got her."

Santa Maria was first bred to Nick Shoemaker. From that cross, she produced Copper Nick, a palomino stallion foaled in 1943, and Senator, a sorrel stallion foaled in 1945. Hank then bred Santa Maria to Show Boat. Show Lady, a palomino mare foaled in 1948, was the result of that mating.

In 1949, Skipper W was the horse that Hank chose to put on Santa Maria. The following spring, a sorrel filly with a strip in her face, four stockings, and a lot of roan on her body was born.

Skipperette was 4 years older than her full brother, Skipper's King. By the time he was born, she had already notched up an impressive string of championships in the show ring. Here she is with George Mueller after standing grand at the 1954 New Mexico State Fair. ***Western Horseman* Photo**

"I've raised hundreds of mares over the last 60 years that are dead and gone," notes Hank. "If I could have just one of 'em back today, it would be Skipperette.

"Skipperette was everything that I ever looked for in a mare. She was the right

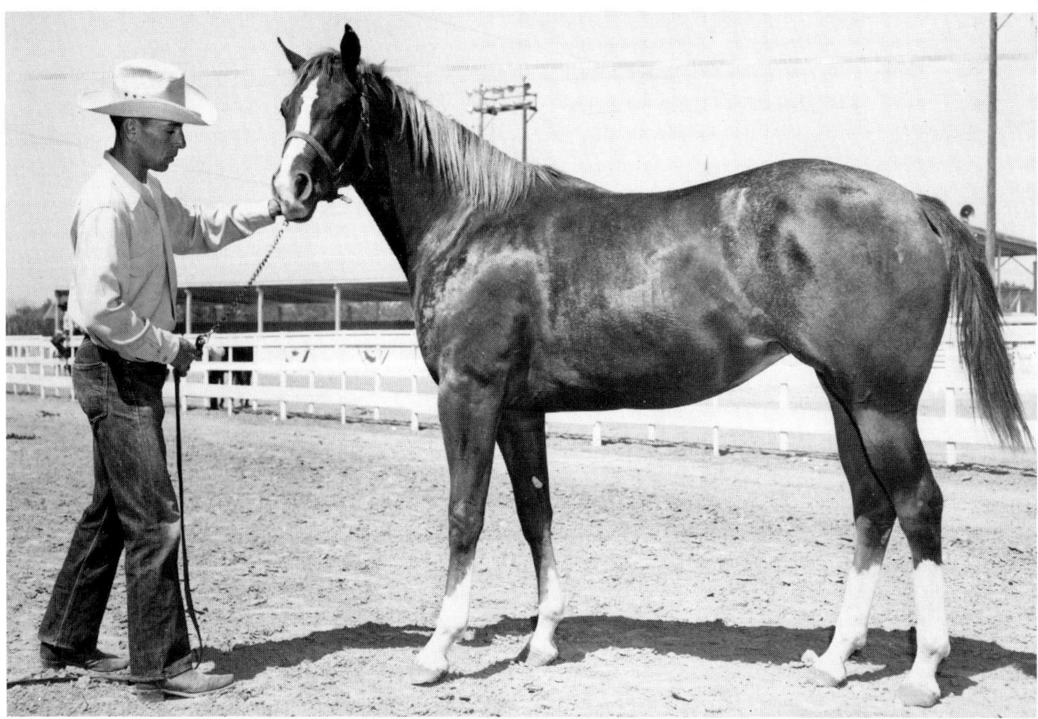

Even as a young mare, Skipperette showed the conformation that would make her a consistent halter champion in the years to come. Walt Alsbaugh holds the 2-year-old filly here after she had won her class at the 1952 Colorado State Fair.

Photo by Clarence Coil/Stewart's Photography

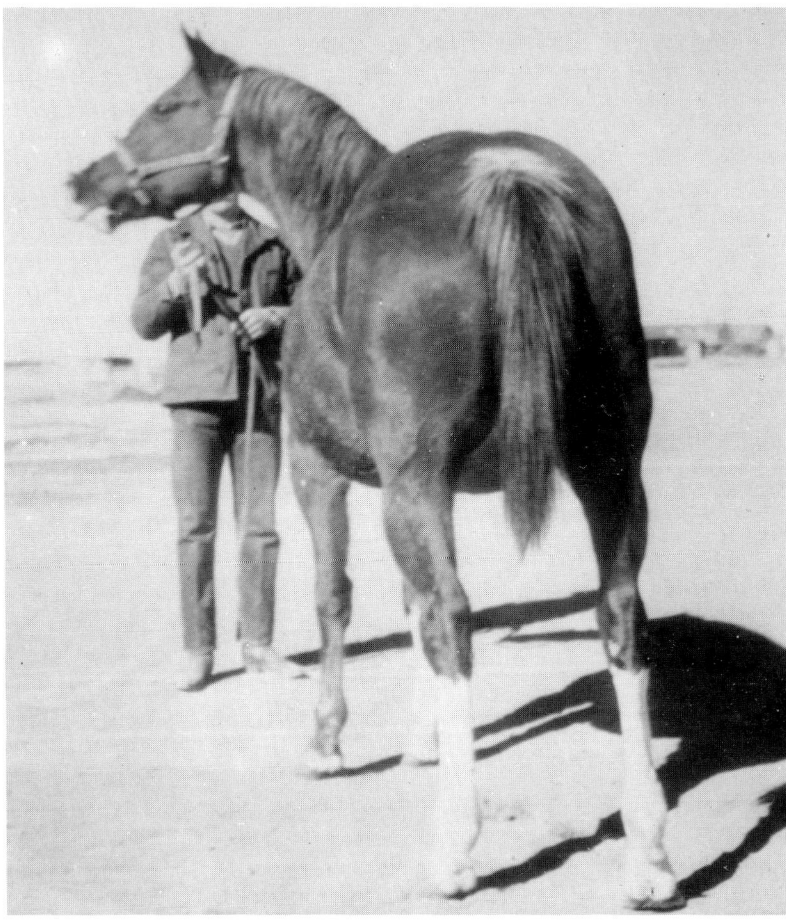

Santa Maria, who is also pictured in Chapter 6, was in the large band of mares that Hank purchased from the Philmont Ranch in 1938. By Plaudit and out of Four Roses by Little Joe Springer, Santa Maria was the dam of Skipperette and Skipper's King.

Photo Courtesy of the American Quarter Horse Heritage Center & Museum, Amarillo, Texas

size—a scant 15 hands and 1,250 pounds; she was the right color—sorrel with flaxen mane and tail and a lot of roan through her body; she had the chrome I like; and she had the conformation.

"Skipperette was a heavy-muscled mare, but she never lost that feminine look. A lot of the top show mares that I see pictures of today are massive all right, but they don't look female; they look male. Skipperette wasn't like that. She was a lady.

"We showed Skipperette at halter at the bigger shows," Hank continues. "In those days (mid-1950s), there weren't as many shows to go to as there are today. Denver, Pueblo, Albuquerque, Colorado Springs, and Santa Fe—that was about it. Skipperette stood grand at about every one of those shows. They couldn't hardly beat her."

Official AQHA records for Skipperette credit her with 39 halter points. Hank could have easily campaigned the typey roan mare to her Superior in halter, but he chose instead to retire her to the broodmare band in 1956.

"The years have taught me that the best show mares don't always make the best broodmares," says Hank. "Just because a mare has won a lot at the shows, that doesn't mean she can reproduce herself. Very few of my top show mares went on to be top producers. Skipperette was an exception to the rule. She was every bit as great a producer as she was a show horse."

Skipperette produced 10 foals for Hank.

As a produce-of-dam entry, Skipperette and Skipper's King were rarely defeated. A.E. Bonnarens is at Skipperette's halter and Kenneth Gann holds Skipper's King in this photo taken after the pair had won the produce-of-dam class at the 1958 Denver National Western Stock Show. Produce-of-dam and get-of-sire classes were very popular in that era.

Photo by Ralph Morgan, Courtesy of Morgan-Gerard Studio

Only four of these were ever shown. Skipperita, a 1957 bay mare by Rukin String, earned her racing Register of Merit in 1959. Skip 3 Bar, a 1960 roan stallion by Bar Mount, earned an AQHA Championship and Superior at halter in 1964. His two full brothers—Skip's Martial, foaled in 1964, and Skip's Chant, foaled in 1968—were also halter point-earners.

Skipperette's most important contribution to the Wiescamp program was not as a producer of show horses, however, but rather as a producer of breeding horses. Four of her sons were retained by Hank as breeding horses, and three daughters found their way into the Wiescamp broodmare band.

"The fact that I used four sons of Skipperette—Skip 3 Bar, Skip Barette, Skip's Cadet, and Skip's Chant—as herd sires says a little bit about what I thought of her. Skip 3 Bar and Skip Barette were both by Bar Mount. Skip's Cadet and Skip's Chant were by Skippa String. They were all a little different in looks and breeding ability, but they all left me with some good show and breeding horses.

"Skipperette's three daughters also proved themselves as producers. Skipperetta and Skipalita, the first two, were by Spanish Nick. Skipperita was by Rukin String. They all did a real good job for me over the years as broodmares.

"Skipperette was foaled in 1950. I ran an ad in one of the horse magazines in 1968 with her picture in it. I said she was a 1950

Skip 3 Bar, a 1960 roan stallion by Bar Mount and out of Skipperette, was an AQHA Champion, a Superior halter horse, and a winner at halter, reining, and calf roping. Here he is with Leroy Webb up at the Colorado State Fair in the mid-1960s.

Photo by Darol Dickinson

Skip's Princess, a 1958 palomino mare by Skipper's King and out of H.J. Skippit by Skipper W, not only looked good, but rode too. In a 3-year show career, she earned 71 halter and 64 performance points. She was an AQHA Champion, with Superiors in halter and reining. In 1962 she was the High-Point All-Around Horse for the Rocky Mountain Quarter Horse Association. Above, she's pictured as a young mare at the Wiescamp ranch. Below, she competes in calf roping with Leroy Webb aboard.

Photos by Darol Dickinson

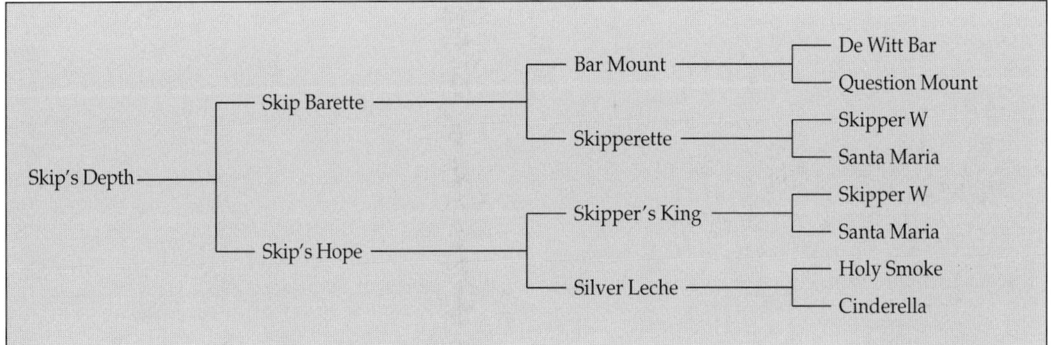

model who was also a 1968 model. I could run that same ad today and use her to illustrate the type of horse that I'm trying to breed today.

"People have said that Skipperette was 30 years ahead of her time. Maybe she was. I know that if I had her today, she'd fit right in to my program the same as she did in 1950. She was timeless."

After Skipperette was foaled, Hank bred Santa Maria to Nick W. Sunstep, a 1951 roan mare, was the result. Bred again to Nick W in 1952, Santa Maria produced the buckskin mare Nicka Maria the following year.

In 1953, Hank decided to try the Skipper W-Santa Maria cross once more. Skipper's King was the result.

"Skipper's King was in a class by himself," states Hank. "He was better than his daddy. He was better than his mama. He was better than any of his ancestors I'd seen.

"I raised three more foals out of Santa Maria after she had Skipper's King. Skipper Queen, a 1955 sorrel mare, and Skipper's Prince, a 1956 chestnut stallion, were by Skipper W. Skip's Major, a 1962 sorrel stallion, was by Skipador.

"Skipper's Prince was a pretty good horse. I sold him to Rose Fulton of Dragoon, Ariz., and she made him an AQHA Champion. For all practical purposes though, I could've quit on Santa Maria after she had Skipper's King. She'd done all for me that she was ever gonna do.

"When we took him to the Denver stock show in 1958, they only had those tie stalls in the old cattle barn to put him in. He stood 15.3 and weighed 1,350 to 1,400. He

Hank got excellent results when he bred the sons of Skipperette to the daughters of Skipper's King. Skip's Depth, a 1967 sorrel stallion by Skip Barette and out of Skip's Hope, was the result of just such a cross. One of the top show horses in the Rocky Mountain region in the early 1970s, Skip's Depth was an AQHA Champion and a Superior halter horse.

Photo by Darol Dickinson

Skip's Alibi, by Skipper's King and out of Elm's Slipcover by Spanish Nick, was an AQHA Champion with Superiors in halter and steer roping. He was also the AQHA Honor Roll roping stallion in 1972 and 1974.

Photo by Ted Hill

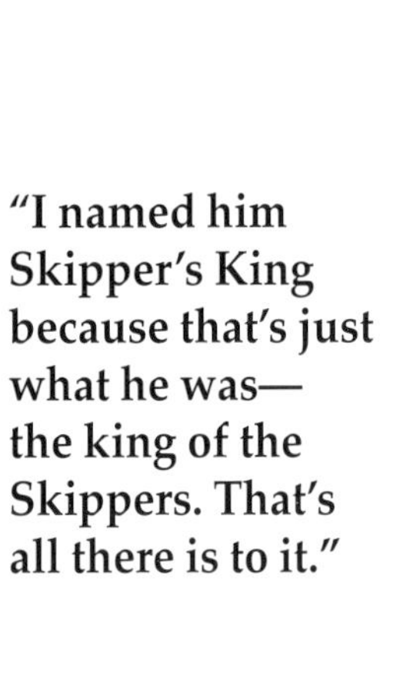

"I named him Skipper's King because that's just what he was— the king of the Skippers. That's all there is to it."

flat filled that tie stall. But he wasn't coarse, or heavy-boned. He was as breedy as you could make one.

"And those folks up there had never seen one like him up to that time. The judge for the show that year was Tim Bernard, from Loomis, Washington. After he made Skipper's King grand, you should have seen the crowd gather around his stall."

Like his sire, Skipper's King was almost sold by Hank as a baby.

"Over the years, I've priced some of my horses for sale that I probably shouldn't have," says Hank. "That happens sometimes, when you're breeding horses for a living."

In the fall of 1958, the Hankins brothers—Jess, Lowell, and J.O.—were looking for a young stallion to breed their King P-234 mares to. They contacted Hank and made arrangements to travel from south Texas to Colorado to look at what he had for sale.

"After they'd looked at all my colts," remembers Hank, "they wanted me to pick 'em out one. I didn't want to, but they kept after me so finally I chose Skipper's King. I priced him to them at $750.

"Man, you'd have thought that I'd asked for the moon and stars the way they carried on. 'My God, Hank,' one of 'em said, 'You'd ask $750 for a weaner?'

"This was on a Friday night—the night before my sale. It was in November. I replied, 'I'll tell you what fellas, if you've never sold one of those sons of King for $750, if you'll wait until this sale is over with, I'll go home with you and show you how!'

"By that time I was beginning to think I'd made a mistake in offering the colt for sale. I wanted to get out of there, so I excused myself. I said I had to go call up my cow buyers to tell them what I had in the sale, and that was the truth.

"I got back to the house and said to Freda, 'If anyone knocks at that front door, I'm not home. If that phone rings, I'm not here.' She asked, 'What's the matter?'

"'Four fools just met,' I answered, 'and I'm the biggest fool of them all. I just priced the best colt I've ever raised, and I'm afraid they're gonna take me up on it.'

"Well, they left without him, and I've been glad about that ever since."

At the time of the Hankins brothers' visit, Skipper's King was unnamed.

"People started spreading a rumor years later that I'd named Skipper's King the way I did just to show the Hankins brothers that they didn't have the only king in the country," reflects Hank. "That wasn't the way it was at all.

"I named him Skipper's King because that's just what he was—the king of the Skippers. That's all there was to it."

Like his older sister, Skipperette, Skipper's King was groomed for a halter career. And, like her, he stood grand at the Denver National Western Stock Show, the Colorado State Fair, and the New Mexico State Fair.

After being retired from the show ring in 1958, Skipper's King was brought back out in 1964 to compete in both halter and performance.

"Skipper's King was a tremendous athlete," notes Hank. "We started roping and cutting off of him and decided to make him an AQHA Champion.

"We showed him in February of 1964 at El Paso. He was first out of 15 in aged stallions, grand champion stallion, first out of 14 in the calf roping, and second out of 11 in the reining.

Skip's Admiral was another of the AQHA Champion get of Skipper's King. A sorrel stallion foaled in 1961 out of Joy Ann by Gold Mount, Skip's Admiral earned 35 halter and 12 performance points. **Photo by Darol Dickinson**

"Shortly after we got him home from that show, the boys hurt one of his hocks, cutting some cattle. After he healed, I put Jack Kyle on him. Jack told me that he was one of the greatest athletes that he'd ever ridden, but he didn't think he could keep him sound. Jack said he just had too much heart and try in him. So we retired him to stud."

AQHA records show that Skipper's King accumulated 18 halter and 3 performance points in his injury-shortened show career. Like so many of his relatives, however, the big sorrel stallion's greatest accomplish-

Skipabank was one of the latter-day Skipper's King show ring stars. Foaled in 1972 out of Skip's Chipeta by Silver Son, this sorrel mare earned 87 points and a Superior at halter. **Photo Courtesy of *The Quarter Horse Journal***

Skip's Count, a 1965 palomino son of Skipper's King, out of Skip's Sis by Sir Duster, was also a Superior halter horse with 65 halter and 24 performance points.

Photo by Darol Dickinson

ments were not destined to be in the show ring, but as a sire.

Skip's Princess, a 1958 palomino mare out of H.J. Skippit by Skipper W, was the first of the Skipper's Kings to make a splash on the show circuit. Shown during the early 1960s, she was an AQHA Champion with Superiors in halter and reining. In 1962, she was the all-around champion of the Rocky Mountain Quarter Horse Association, and earned high-point honors that year in halter, junior calf roping, and junior reining.

Skip's Alibi, a 1967 bay stallion out of Elm's Slipcover by Spanish Nick, was another top show horse sired by Skipper's King. Shown during the early 1970s, Alibi was an AQHA Champion with Superiors in halter and steer roping. He was also the 1972 and 1974 Honor Roll Steer Roping Stallion.

Other AQHA Champions by Skipper's King include Copperelm Queen, Skip A Barb, Skip Barta, Skip's Admiral, Skip's B Day, and Skip School Day.

Skipper's King sired four Superior halter horses in addition to Skip's Princess and Skip's Alibi. They were Skip's Champ, Skip Flash, Skip's Count, and Skipabank.

Rounding out his list of top show ring achievers were Skip Whiskers, Skip's Call, Skip Beware, Skip Shirley, Spanish Dove, Skip Balladier, Skip's Bartender, Skipatip, and Slip N Skip, all of whom earned double-digit points in either halter or performance.

AQHA records show that Skipper's King sired 180 registered foals over a span of 22 years. They earned 816 halter and 389.5 performance points. Eight were AQHA Champions and fourteen earned performance Registers of Merit. Led by Skipabank, with 87 points, six were Superior halter horses.

As a broodmare sire, Skipper's King had an even greater impact on Hank's breeding program.

"Skipper's King was a tremendous broodmare sire," notes Hank. "People found out early on that trying to get one of his daughters from me while she was in her prime was next to impossible. At one time, I had over 70 Skipper's King mares in my broodmare band."

The daughters of Skipper's King produced 82 foals who were entered in AQHA-sanctioned competition. They accumulated a total of 1,752 open, amateur, and youth points. Two were AQHA

Champions, two were Superior performance horses, and eighteen earned performance Registers of Merit. In addition, six were Superior halter horses.

The sons of Skipper's King also made their mark on both the Wiescamp program and the Quarter Horse breed as a whole.

"You know, I kept a lot more daughters of Skipper's King than I did sons," observes Hank. "I did keep Skip's Bid though. He was out of Spanish Shasta, one of the great producing daughters of Spanish Nick. He was a great broodmare sire, just like his daddy was."

A number of the sons of Skipper's King who were sold went on to become excellent sires for their new owners. Included among them were Skip A Barb, Skip Shi, Skip's Call, Skip Beware, Skip Flash, Skip's Agent, Skip's Count, Skip's Alibi, Spanish Admiral, Skip One Skip, Skip School Day, and Skips Retreat.

Of these, Skip A Barb was the most successful.

"Jack Kyle liked Skipper's King so much that he really wanted a good son of his to head his own breeding program," recalls Hank. "So I sold him Skip A Barb as a yearling.

"Skip A Barb was out of one of the few outside mares I introduced into my program. Her name was Barbara Star, and she was by Star Duster and out of Gold Hen by Ding Bob.

"I gave Von Davidson, of Albuquerque, $5,000 for her after she had been the Honor Roll Halter Horse of 1956. I didn't buy her because she had that long show record, though. I bought her because of the Old Fred breeding that she had on the bottom side of her pedigree."

Jack Kyle showed Skip A Barb just long enough to earn his AQHA Championship, which he did in 1964. He then retired him to stud, crossing him on the good band of Wiescamp and Shoemaker-bred mares he owned in partnership with his brother-in-law Robert Johnson.

Skip A Barb sired six AQHA World Champions or Honor Roll horses. They were Pawnee Eagle, Skip Fancy Pants, Billiettas Jewel, Skip N' Stage, Barb A Leo, and Skip Dandy. He also sired 13 AQHA Champions, 10 Superior event horses, and the earners of 22 show Registers of Merit.

Skip N' Stage, a 1974 sorrel son of Skip

Skip Shi was a top-siring son of Skipper's King. Foaled in 1960 out of Shirley Nick by Nick W, he sired the earners of 3,721 AQHA show points. Skipper Chock, a 1971 gelding by Skip Shi out of Lady Chock, earned 1,689 open, amateur, and youth halter and performance points.

Photo by Dick Waltenberry, Courtesy of *The Quarter Horse Journal*

Skip A Barb was a 1960 stallion by Skipper's King out of Barbara Star by Star Duster. Sold to Jack Kyle as a yearling, Skip A Barb founded a family of halter and performance horses that is still winning today.

Photo by Darol Dickinson

Skipperette and Skipper's King were truly two of a kind, and they were Hank Wiescamp's kind.

A Barb, was out of Flying Stage by Stagehand. An AQHA Champion, Skip N' Stage was also a Superior steer roping horse, the 1978 AQHA Honor Roll Working Cowhorse, and the 1978 AQHA Honor Roll Steer Roping Stallion.

In keeping with the long-standing legacy of the Skipper's King family as superior breeding horses, Skip N' Stage also went on to become a top sire. Among others, he sired Sweet and Innocent, winner of the 1982 AQHA Superhorse competition.

Getting back to Skipperette and Skipper's King, it is important that they be put in the proper perspective as to where they fit in the overall Hank Wiescamp breeding program.

At the time that Hank bred these two horses, he had an excellent program of 25 years' duration already in place. He had, in his mind's eye, a goal for that program, and Skipperette and Skipper's King confirmed beyond a shadow of a doubt that he was on the right track.

More than any other two horses that he had bred up to that time, they represented what he was striving for. For their entire lives, and years afterwards, they were what he would try to duplicate.

Skipperette and Skipper's King were truly two of a kind, and they were Hank Wiescamp's kind.

Barbara Star, the dam of Skip A Barb, was one of the few mares Hank purchased to add to his breeding program. The 1956 AQHA Honor Roll Halter Horse, Barbara Star went on to become a top producer for Hank.

Photo by James Cathey

Although not as well known as his full brother Skip A Barb, Skip's Call was an excellent horse in his own right. Foaled in 1962, this sorrel stallion was sold by Hank to Robert Bruce, Walsh, Colorado. Shown here after standing grand at Hereford, Tex., in 1965, Skip's Call earned 36 open halter points.

Photo by Harvey Dolcater, Courtesy of *The Quarter Horse Journal*

12 The Sons Who Were Sold

. . . Hank sold a number of top Quarter Horse stallions during this time period who, under different circumstances, might have remained in Alamosa.

THE DECADE bounded by the late 1950s and the late 1960s was a period of rapid growth for Hank Wiescamp. His sale barn had prospered to the point that it was one of busiest in southern Colorado, he was in great demand as a auctioneer at registered Quarter Horse sales throughout the West, and his Old Fred-bred Quarter Horses were winning shows throughout the Rocky Mountain region at halter and in performance.

In addition, in the early 1960s he initiated Appaloosa and Paint Horse breeding programs patterned after, and utilizing some of the same blood as, his Quarter Horse program. He also developed a first-

Skipper Jr. was one of the first sons of Skipper W to be sold by Hank. Foaled in 1951, out of Mabel Question by Question Mark, Skipper Jr. was purchased by Glenn Ferrell, Windsor, Illinois.

Photo Courtesy of *The Quarter Horse Journal*

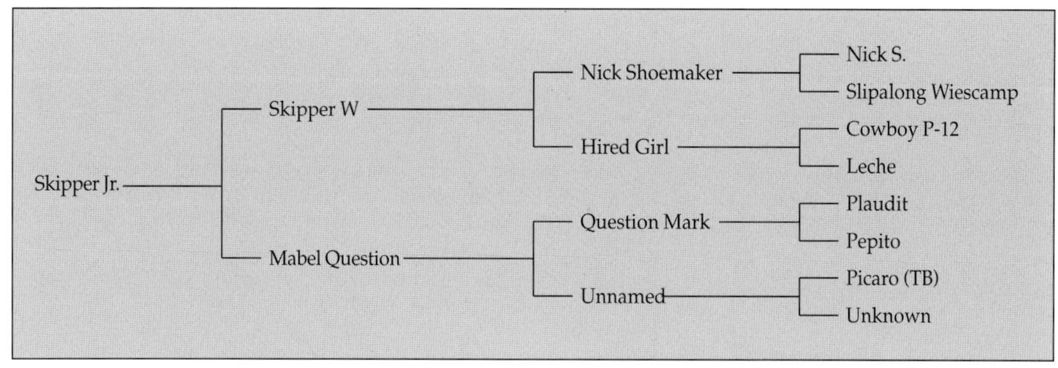

class herd of registered Hereford cattle of Prince Domino and Colorado Baldwin breeding.

With horse numbers that eventually reached over 800, and a purebred cattle operation that grew to 200 head, Hank was constantly in search of more land to support his ever expanding livestock operations.

In order to buy prime San Luis Valley farm land by the quarter-section (160 acres), and pay for it in cash as was his practice, Hank sold a number of top Quarter Horse stallions during this time period who, under different circumstances, might have remained in Alamosa.

The sales of these horses accomplished two things for Hank. First of all, they enabled him to buy the large amounts of land that he needed. Secondly, they put top Wiescamp-bred horses in virtually every corner of the country, where they were shown and bred with great success. As a result, the name-recognition and reputation of the Wiescamp Quarter Horses grew by leaps and bounds.

Although it would be impossible to list all the good stallions that Hank sold during these expansion years, several were especially noteworthy.

Skipper Jr., a 1951 sorrel stallion by Skipper W and out of Mabel Question by Question Mark, was one of the first top sons of Skipper W to leave Alamosa.

"I sold Skipper Jr. as a yearling to Glenn Ferrell of New Windsor, Illinois," remembers Hank. "Skipper Jr. looked a lot like ol' Skipper; that was why I named him the way I did. I also sold Glenn a yearling daughter of Nick W named Nicka Maria. She was out of Santa Maria, and she was a real Plaudit-looking filly. She was beautifully headed and necked, but kind of on the lightly muscled side as far as her conformation went.

"Skipper Jr. and Nicka Maria were top show and breeding prospects when I sold them to Glenn. I remember that he came here from Illinois and got 'em in a pickup truck with stock racks. I figured that those two would put him in the horse business, and they sure did."

Ferrell showed his new acquisitions throughout the Midwest in the mid- to late 1950s. Skipper Jr. became the first get of Skipper W to become an AQHA Champion when he was awarded that honor in 1958. Nicka Maria earned 14 halter points. Both horses were also shown extensively by the Ferrell boys, Arlie and Leo, in youth competition.

Although he sired only 80 registered

In addition to Skipper Jr., Ferrell also purchased Nicka Maria, by Nick W and out of Santa Maria, from Hank. Both horses were shown extensively throughout the Midwest in both open and youth classes. Here they are with their youth riders, Leo and Arlie Ferrell. Leo is on the buckskin Nicka Maria and Arlie is on Skipper Jr.

Photo Courtesy of Irene Ferrell

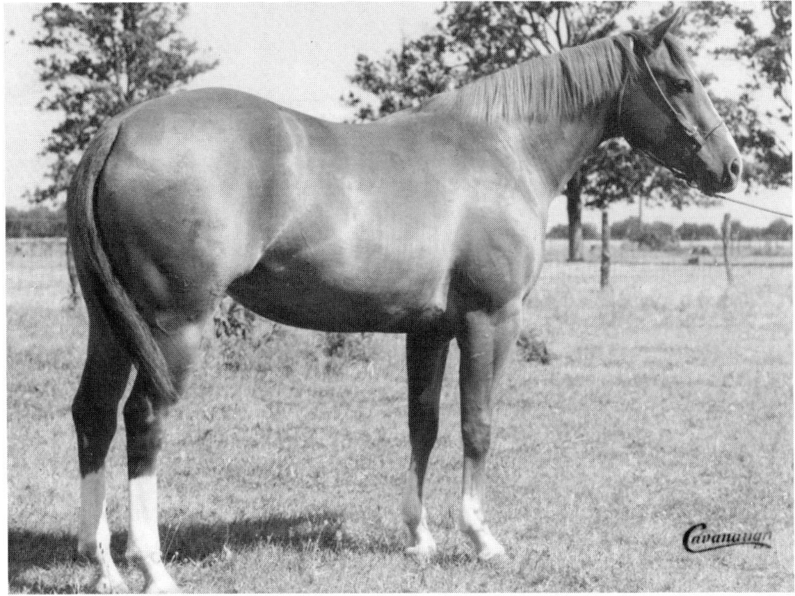

Nicka Maria was bred to Skipper Jr. in 1957, and the resulting foal was Skipa Maria, shown here. She went on to become an AQHA Champion and a Superior halter horse with 61 points. **Photo by Cavanaugh, Courtesy of Irene Ferrell**

offspring, Skipper Jr. made his mark as a sire. Thirty of his get were halter point-earners and twenty-one earned points in performance. Eight achieved their Registers of Merit, and five of these also secured their AQHA Championships.

In 1957, Glenn Ferrell bred Skipper Jr. to Nicka Maria. The resulting foal was Skipa Maria, who went on to become an AQHA Champion and a Superior halter horse. When the Ferrells bred Skipa Maria to Sir Teddy, whom they also purchased from Hank, they got Sir Teddy Too.

Sir Teddy Too was sold to Dr. Barry Wood of Carmel, Ind., and the horse developed into one of the top western pleasure sires of the 1970s and 1980s. Among others, he sired Teddys Soxy Lady, the 1983 AQHA World Champion Junior Western Pleasure Horse.

Skipper Jr. also sired Skipster. This chestnut stallion, foaled in 1963, was out of Pasamonte Easter by Golddust Shoemaker. A top show horse, Skipster earned

When Skipa Maria was crossed on the Wiescamp-bred Sir Teddy, she produced Sir Teddy Too. Sold by the Ferrells to Dr. Barry Wood, Carmel, Ind., Sir Teddy Too developed into a top halter horse and sire.

Photo Courtesy of ***The Quarter Horse Journal***

an AQHA Championship and a Superior at halter with 109 points.

Sold by the Ferrells to Clayton Benker, Lafayette, Ind., Skipster also developed into one of the Midwest's top show horse sires of the 1970s and 1980s. Included among his get, who earned in excess of 6,900 open, amateur, and youth points, was Skipster's Lad, the 1974 AQHA World Champion 3-Year-Old Stallion. In the late 1960s, Benker made a trip of his own to Alamosa in search of a Wiescamp-bred stallion. The horse he returned to Indiana with was Sheik's Command, a 1964 sorrel by Sheik's Image and out of Skip A Nurse by Skipper's King.

Sheik's Command earned 37 halter points during his show career and was a moderately successful sire, crossing especially well with the Skipper Jr.- and Skipster-bred mares.

Another one of the early sons of Skipper W Hank sold was Spot Cash, a 1950 sorrel out of Southern Queen by Brujo.

"We showed Spot Cash a little when he was young," relates Hank, "and he won a few shows at halter. As he matured, he did not retain that 'look' that I was striving for; he took after something on his maternal granddam's side that I never cared for, so I sold him to John Bauchman, of Seguin, Texas.

"Spot Cash did all right for John, and for several other people who owned him. That's the way it was with a lot of the studs I sold. Just because I couldn't find a spot for them in my program didn't mean that they couldn't go out and get the job done for other people."

Interestingly enough, Spot Cash was almost a total failure as a sire of show horses. He did sire one AQHA Champion, Skip Cash, a 1956 chestnut stallion out of H.J. Skippit.

Another son of Skipper W who enjoyed success after being sold by Hank was Skipper's Lad.

Skipster, a 1963 stallion by Skipper Jr. and out of Pasamonte Easter by Golddust Shoemaker, was an AQHA Champion and a Superior halter horse with 109 points. Owned for most of his life by Clayton Benker, Lafayette, Ind., he also developed into a top sire.
Photo Courtesy of *The Quarter Horse Journal*

Spot Cash was another of the early sons of Skipper W sold by Hank. Foaled in 1950, out of Southern Queen by Brujo, Spot Cash became most noted as a sire of breeding sons and daughters.
Photo Courtesy of *The Quarter Horse Journal*

Spot Cash made his most solid contribution as a sire of breeding horses. He sired the stallions School Cash, Sure Cash, Sir Barton, Super Chief, Silver Cash, Super Cash, and Cash Cole. Each of these horses was bred by Hank and each went on to become a successful sire.

Spot Cash also sired a number of top-producing daughters including Spanish Madam, Spanish Mama, Miss Walters, Spottette, Spotted Rose, and Kim Novak. Again, each of these mares was bred by Hank and each became a producer of either an AQHA Champion or a Superior title-earner.

Sure Cash was probably the top show son of Spot Cash. This 1954 palomino stallion was out of Stepaway by Nick Shoemaker.

"Sure Cash was a top halter horse," Hank relates. "He stood grand at the

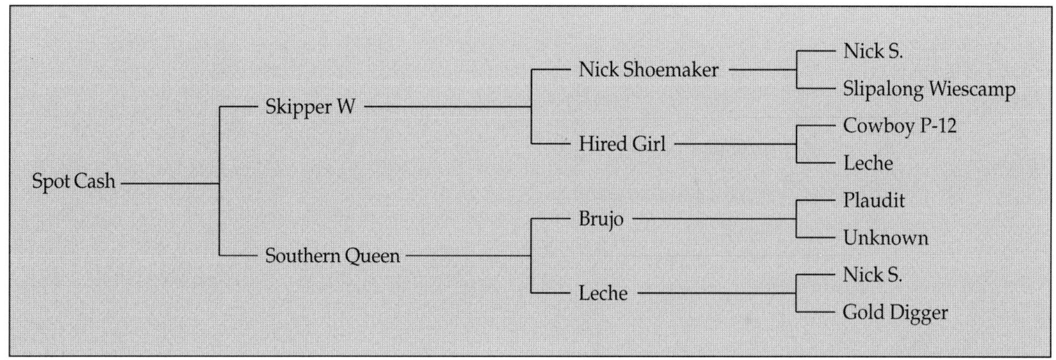

Denver National Western Stock Show as a coming 2-year-old, and he won the New Mexico State Fair and several other shows.

"I sold him to J.B. Ferguson of Wharton, Tex., when he was a 3-year-old. He didn't do too much as a sire down there, but I don't think it was all his fault. I never thought that they put him on the right kind of mares."

AQHA records show that Sure Cash sired two AQHA Champions and the earners of 406 halter and 180.5 performance points.

Another son of Skipper W who enjoyed success after being sold by Hank was Skipper's Lad.

"Like Spot Cash, we showed Skipper's Lad when he was young. He fared a little better than Spot Cash did. He earned 23 halter points. Like Spot Cash though, there were some things about Skipper's Lad that didn't compare well with the other sons of Skipper W that I was using in my program at that time, so I sold him.

"In the early 1960s, R.A. Furbush of Broomfield, Colo., was trying to put together a top Quarter Horse breeding program," continues Hank. "I sold him Skipper's Lad, along with some good mares, to head that program. Later on, I let him use Scottish. Those horses did a good job for him."

American Quarter Horse Association records reveal that Skipper's Lad sired the earners of 1,768.5 points. Four of his get were AQHA Champions, three earned Superiors in halter, and three were Superior performance horses.

Skipa Star and Lad's Imperial were two

Sure Cash was one of the sons of Spot Cash who excelled as a show horse. Foaled in 1954, out of Stepaway by Nick Shoemaker, Sure Cash was the grand champion stallion at the 1956 Denver National Western Stock Show. Hank sold him the following year to J.B. Ferguson of Wharton, Texas. **Photo by Darol Dickinson**

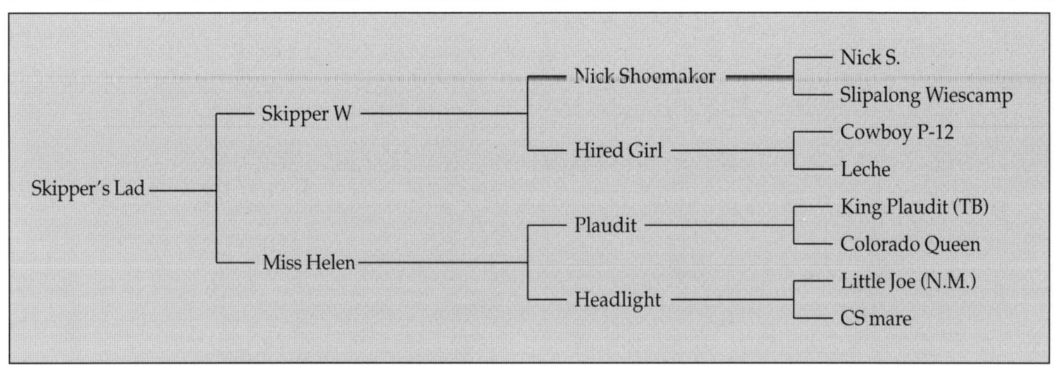

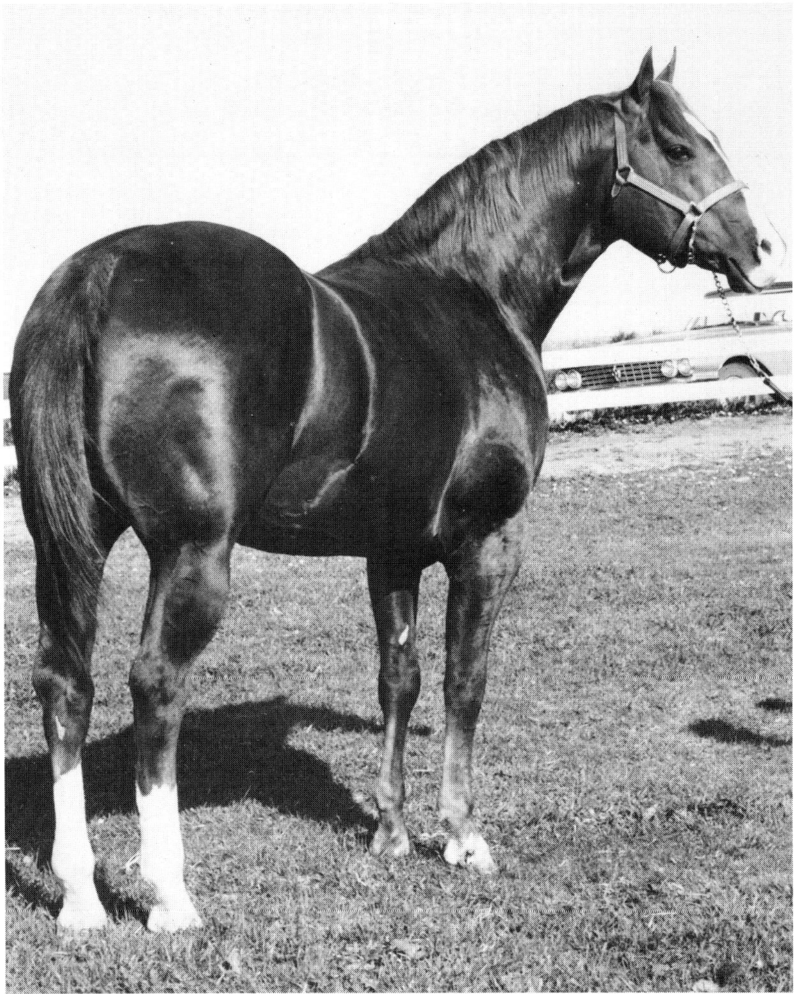

Here is Skipper's Lad, a 1952 stallion by Skipper W and out of Miss Helen by Plaudit. Sold by Hank to R.A. Furbush of Broomfield, Colo., as an 8-year-old, Skipper's Lad became a noted show horse and broodmare sire.

Photo by Darol Dickinson

of the best show horses sired by Skipper's Lad, and both went on to become successful sires in their own right.

Skipa Star, a 1973 chestnut stallion out of Pat's Dusty Star, earned his Superior at halter with 82 points, and was the 1975 AQHA World Champion 2-Year-Old Stallion. Retired to stud, he sired horses earning over 10,000 points. He sired 14 AQHA Champions, 35 Superior halter horses, and 26 Superior performance horses. Five of his get amassed seven AQHA World Championships.

Lad's Imperial, a 1974 sorrel stallion out of Miss Walters by Spot Cash, was bred by Duane Teten of Talmage, Neb., and sold to E.F. "Bud" Alderson, of Sharpsville, Ind., as a young horse.

Alderson showed him to his AQHA Championship and Superiors in halter and western pleasure. He won an all-around horse award at the 1978 Quarter Horse Congress in Columbus, Ohio, and placed at the 1978 AQHA World Show in halter and junior western pleasure.

As a breeding stallion, Lad's Imperial proved especially strong in siring performance horses. In all, his get earned over 4,400 AQHA performance points and 21 Superiors in riding events.

Yet another early son of Skipper W to leave Alamosa and make a name for himself as a sire was Sirlette, a 1952 sorrel out of Flamette.

Sirlette was the sire of five AQHA Champions including Leyba Chester, who was also the AQHA Honor Roll Steer

Lad's Imperial, a 1974 stallion by Skipper's Lad and out of Miss Walters by Spot Cash, greatly resembled his sire. Owned by E.F. "Bud" Alderson, of Sharpsville, Ind., Lad's Imperial was an AQHA Champion with Superiors in halter and western pleasure.

Photo by Harold Campton, Courtesy of *The Quarter Horse Journal*

Roping Horse of 1968, 1969, and 1970.

Sir Teddy, a 1955 palomino out of Silver Leche, was a son of Sirlette who proved himself both as a show horse and a sire. An AQHA Champion himself, he sired two AQHA Champions and three Superior western pleasure horses. Tee Crick, a 1966 sorrel daughter of Sir Teddy and out of June Cricket, earned 292.5 performance points and was the 1969 AQHA Honor Roll western pleasure mare.

Sir Teddy was also the sire of Sir Colonel, a 1968 Wiescamp-bred palomino stallion out of Skip's Aid by Skipper W. Sold to Bill and Sharlis Irwin of Aldergrove, B.C., Sir Colonel earned his AQHA Championship in 1983 and his get earned over 4,000 AQHA show points.

Sir Raleigh, a 1958 palomino stallion by Sirlette and out of Shirley Nick by Nick W, was another top sire who was not sold, but given away instead by Hank as a colt.

"Sir Raleigh contracted foal founder when he was born," says Hank. "I named him 'Sir' after Sirlette, and 'Raleigh' after the 'cure-all' medicine that was popular at the time he was born. I said it was going to take some powerful medicine to ever straighten him out.

"Harry Menicucii, from Elk Grove, Calif., was out here in 1959, looking at colts. I told him to just go ahead and load

Skipper Mingo, a 1964 stallion by Skipper's Lad and out of Spanish Bustle by Spanish Nick, was one of the top halter horses in the Rocky Mountain region in the late 1960s. He also developed into a successful sire.

Photo by Darol Dickinson

Here is Skipa Star, a 1973 stallion by Skipper's Lad and out of Pat's Dusty Star. A Superior halter horse and the 1975 AQHA World Champion 2-Year-Old Stallion, Skipa Star sired the earners of 14 AQHA Championships, 61 Superiors in halter and performance, and 7 world championships.

Photo by Darol Dickinson

Sir Teddy, a 1955 stallion by Sirlette and out of Silver Leche by Holy Smoke, was yet another of the Wiescamp-bred horses to leave Alamosa and make an impact. An AQHA Champion himself, Sir Teddy was the sire of two AQHA Champions and three Superior western pleasure horses. He was also the sire of the Wiescamp-bred Sir Colonel, an AQHA Champion and one of the top sires in the Pacific Northwest in the 1980s and 1990s.

Photo by Cavanaugh, Courtesy of Sharlis Irwin

Sir Raleigh, by Sirlette and out of Shirley Nick by Nick W, was given away by Hank as a yearling. Owned by E. Sonny Hannan of Petaluma, Calif., he went on to become one of California's top sires in the 1970s and 1980s.

Photo by Midge, Courtesy of Sonny Hannan

This good-looking palomino mare is Skippers Judy, by Sir Raleigh and out of Show Veil by Sirlette. An AQHA Champion with Superiors in halter and western pleasure, Skippers Judy was also the AQHA Honor Roll junior working cowhorse of 1972.

Photo by Ed Boland, Courtesy of Judy Frym

Yet another son of Skipper W Hank chose to sell was Skipador. Foaled in 1955 out of Cheri Mac, Skipador went on to sire six AQHA Champions, five Superior halter horses, and five Superior performance horses. Here is Skipador Joe, a 1969 sorrel gelding by Skipador and out of Kim Reed. Skipador Joe was an AQHA Champion with 442 open and youth halter points, and 236 open and youth performance points.

Photo Courtesy of *The Quarter Horse Journal*

Sir Raleigh up. I didn't care what he did with him, I just wanted him off the place.

"Well, he took him back to California and sold him to some folks who straightened his legs out and made him into a top sire. Who would've guessed it?"

Under the ownership of E. Sonny Hannan of Petaluma, Calif., Sir Raleigh was indeed one of California's top sires of the 1970s and 1980s. He sired two AQHA Champions, four Superior halter horses, and nine Superior performance horses. Skippers Judy, a 1968 palomino mare out of Show Veil by Sirlette, was an AQHA Champion with Superiors in halter and western pleasure. She was also the 1972 AQHA Honor Roll junior working cow horse.

Skip's Sierra Nick, a 1972 gray gelding by Sir Raleigh and out of Sierra Tammy, amassed 540 open performance points. He also won the 1981 AQHA World Show superhorse competition.

Skipador, a 1955 sorrel stallion by Skipper W and out of Cheri Mac, was another horse Hank showed and used as a breeding horse on a limited basis before selling him.

"Skipador was a fair halter horse and a fair sire," notes Hank. "He sired Skip Tres Bar and Skip's Pride for us, both of whom earned their AQHA Championships. Skip Tres Bar was also the high-point all-around horse for the Rocky Mountain Quarter Horse Association one year.

"But, by and large, Skipador did not get it done for us. He threw back to something that was behind Cheri Mac that was not what I was trying to perpetuate, so he had to go."

Like Spot Cash and Skipper's Lad, Skipador might not have been quite good enough for Hank to keep and use, but he did go on to become a moderately successful sire.

During the 1970s and 1980s, several of

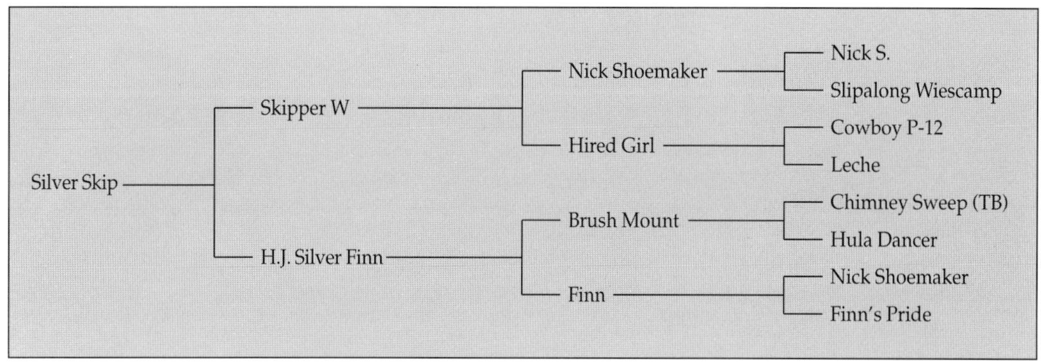

Silver Skip was the first stallion the well-known New Mexico rancher and horse trainer Jack Kyle purchased from Hank. By Skipper W and out of H.J. Silver Finn by Brush Mount, Silver Skip earned his AQHA Championship in 1958 and went on to sire five AQHA Champions. His daughters also crossed exceptionally well with Skip A Barb, the second stallion Jack got from Hank.

Photo Courtesy of *The Quarter Horse Journal*

the top show geldings in the nation were sons of Skipador. Skip Thrush, Skip Veto, Skipador Joe, and Skipajoy were all either open or youth AQHA Champions and, among them, they amassed 10 Superiors and 1,578 AQHA show points.

In all, Skipador sired six open and five youth AQHA Champions, five open and three youth Superior halter horses, and five open and one youth Superior performance horses.

Silver Skip was yet another son of Skipper W who did his part in spreading the reputation of the Wiescamp line.

"In the mid-1950s, Jack Kyle was one of the up-and-coming young hands in the Quarter Horse business," observes Hank. "I say 'hand,' and that's exactly what I mean. Back then, the boys who were in on the ground floor of the Quarter Horse shows were hands first and trainers second. For the most part, like Jack, they made their livings working on ranches, and the showing was just something extra.

"Anyway, Jack came to me, looking for a stud prospect. I sold him Silver Skip, a 1954 palomino son of Skipper, out of H.J.

Jack Kyle's namesake, the golden palomino gelding Jack Kyle, was by Silver Skip and out of Goldie Mount by Cripple Mount. He was shown to his AQHA Championship by both Kyle and owner Peggy Jo Dietmeir of Albuquerque, New Mexico. The versatile gelding competed in halter, western pleasure, reining, calf roping, heeling, barrel racing, and pole bending. He was also featured in a July 1966 article in Western Horseman *entitled "The Golden Gelding."*

Photo by Darol Dickinson

The athletic-looking Sir Skip was by Skipper W and out of Sis Nick by Nick W. Sold to Jerry Boomhower of Russell, Kan., in 1963, Sir Skip was the sire of a number of top show horses including Miss Sue Skip, winner of the 1969 NRHA Futurity.

Photo Courtesy of *The Quarter Horse Journal*

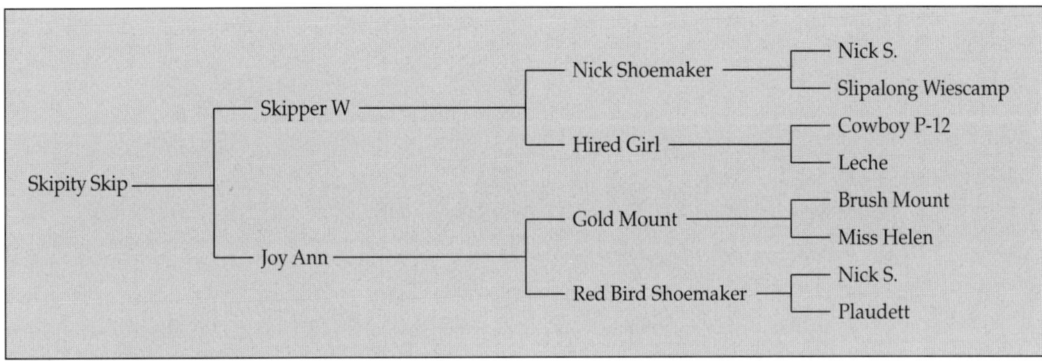

Silver Finn by Brushmount. Silver Skip did all right for Jack."

Under Kyle's tutelage, Silver Skip earned his AQHA Championship in 1958 with 13 halter and 41 performance points.

He was also the sire of five AQHA Champions, and the maternal grandsire of six.

For a short time during the early 1960s, Jack Kyle worked for Hank as a resident trainer. Spurred on by his modest success with Silver Skip, Kyle purchased a second stallion from Hank in 1962.

The stallion he chose was Skip A Barb, a 1960 sorrel by Skipper's King and out of Barbara Star. As chronicled in Chapter 11, the Jack Kyle-Skip A Barb combination proved to be a good one and has had a significant positive impact on the Quarter Horse breed.

And the list goes on.

Sir Skip, a 1958 bay son of Skipper W out of Sis Nick by Nick W, was sold to Jerry Boomhower of Russell, Kansas. He sired two AQHA Champions and five Superior event horses. Among his most noted offspring were Miss Sue Skip, the winner of the 1969 NRHA open futurity; El Skip, an AQHA Champion and the earner of 958 points; and Darin's Skip, an AQHA Champion and Superior western pleasure horse with 181 performance points.

Skipity Skip, a 1953 sorrel stallion by Skipper W and out of Joy Ann, sold to Joe Kirk Fulton, Lubbock, Texas. He sired three AQHA Champions and five Superior event horses.

Skip School, a 1957 palomino by Skipper W and out of School Madam by Nick W, went to Pat Dunning, Carrizozo, New Mexico. He was the sire of three AQHA Champions and five Superior event horses. One of his daughters, Skip's Schoolgirl,

Skipity Skip was a 1953 stallion by Skipper W and out of Joy Ann by Gold Mount. Sold to Joe Kirk Fulton, Lubbock, Tex., Skipity Skip was an AQHA Champion and the sire of three AQHA Champions. He also sired the Superior halter mares Skip's Robin, Skipity Oma, Skipity Miss, and Skipity Queen.

Photo by Orr's Studio, Courtesy of *The Quarter Horse Journal*

Skip Beau was a 1963 son of Skipper W out of Skip's Flame by Skipper's Lad. He was sold in the mid-1960s to Ron Riley of Alpine, California. He was an AQHA Champion and sired Skip Scamp, a 1968 gelding out of Cutie Bud. Skip Scamp was the 1976 AQHA world champion gelding and an AQHA Champion, and the earner of 579 show points.

Photo Courtesy of ***The Quarter Horse Journal***

earned 105 open and 572 youth performance points.

Skip Me, Stagehand, Skipper's Image, Skipper's Prince, Skip Beau, and Skipper's Smoke were yet other sons of Skipper W Hank sold during the 1950s and 1960s. They all went on to become AQHA Champion sires.

Of these latter stallions, Skipper's Smoke remains something of a mystery to his breeder to this day.

"Skipper's Smoke was without a doubt one of Skipper W's best sons," he exclaims. "He was a model to look at, and a top working horse. He was the RMQHA high-point all-around horse in 1962, and he earned 100 halter and 65 performance points. They could hardly beat him at halter.

"And he was out of Silver Leche, a great mare who was the dam of three AQHA Champions. He had the blood on both sides of his pedigree, but he just could not pass it on.

"It cost me over $100,000 to find out that he wouldn't work on my mares. I can't explain why; maybe it was that weedy ol' Thoroughbred mare, Sannatuga, he traced to.

"In any event, he couldn't get the job done, so I sold him."

Skipper's Smoke did eventually achieve a moderate sire record, but nowhere near what he should have, based on the quality of mares who were bred to him. AQHA records reveal that he was the sire of one open and one youth AQHA Champion,

Skip Me (top) and Skip's Image (bottom) were two halter champion sons of Skipper W who were only moderately successful as sires. Skip's Image, shown with owner Gordon Brown, Lake Village, Ark., after standing reserve at the 1962 San Antonio Livestock Exposition, earned 188 points at halter. Skip Me accumulated 13 halter and 12 performance points.

one Superior halter horse, and one Superior performance horse.

As extensive as this list of stallions sold by Hank during his expansion years is, the horses by and large represent only the first generation of the Skipper Ws.

Hank had sold show and breeding prospects to the general public before the 1950s and 1960s, and continued to do so in the years that followed.

It was during this time period, however, that he was the most aggressive about it. He was breeding some of the top Quarter Horse prospects in the country at a time when the breed was experiencing rapid growth and expansion.

As he has done throughout his life, Hank was quick to recognize the opportunities that were available, and acted on them to accomplish a little growth and expansion of his own.

"For the most part, the Quarter Horse stallions I sold during '50s and '60s paved the way for what I was able to put together land-wise.

"It's like I've always said. My horses own the ground they're standing on. They bought and paid for it. They don't owe me or anybody else a thing."

13 The Show Horses

"There I was, at my first show, with my first registered Quarter Horse, and she was the grand champion."

HANK WIESCAMP was in the horse business long before there were Quarter Horse shows.

There were rodeos, race meets, polo matches, and livestock expositions at the time that he began breeding and raising horses to sell, but Quarter Horse shows did not come into being until the early 1940s. By this time, Hank had been in the horse business for a decade and a half.

Being a promoter by nature, however, he saw the advent of the halter and performance horse show as a viable way to expose the general public to the type of horses he was raising, so he jumped into the horse show game with both feet.

"I entered my first Quarter Horse show by accident," he recalls. "It was in January of 1944, and I was taking a truckload of cattle up to Denver to sell.

"It was during the National Western Stock Show, and they were inspecting horses there for registration with the American Quarter Horse Association. I had never registered anything with the AQHA up to that time, but I took Flamette, a mare I had raised, up there to see if she was the

Skipper W was only shown three times: at the Denver National Western Stock Show and the Colorado and New Mexico state fairs. He championed all three. Here he is with George Mueller after his win in Albuquerque.

Photo by Cecil Hellbusch, Courtesy of *The Quarter Horse Journal*

Spanish Nick was the first Wiescamp-bred horse to earn an AQHA Championship, which he did in 1954. Campaigned in both Quarter Horse and Palomino shows, he is shown here standing grand at the 1954 New Mexico State Fair Palomino show. Pictured with him from the left: C.E. Botkin, judge; Barbara Hendricks, State Fair queen; Howard Babcock, president of the New Mexico Palomino Exhibitors Assn.; and George Mueller.

Photo Courtesy of Palomino Horse Breeders of America Inc.

kind they would approve.

"I just loaded her in with the cattle and hauled her up there. Helen Michaelis was doing the inspecting, and after she looked Flamette over and passed her, she said, 'Hank, this is a pretty good mare. Why don't you make a post-entry of her in the show?'

"They were holding their first Quarter Horse show at Denver that year, but I didn't know anything about it. Flamette sure wasn't ready to be shown. She was long-haired and unclipped, and she hadn't been conditioned at all.

"But I entered her anyway. Kenneth Gann got her cleaned up a little bit and led her into the ring. I can remember sitting way up high in the old coliseum, watching the class.

"They started leading in some of those aged mares from Oklahoma and Texas, and they were all pretty fat and slick. I said to myself, 'What have you got yourself into?' Then Kenneth came in with Flamette and I thought, 'Well, she doesn't look so bad out there after all.'

"Albert Mitchell was the judge, and he just pulled Flamette out and made her the grand champion mare. There I was, at my

Flamette, bred and owned by Hank, was the grand champion mare at the first Quarter Horse show held in conjunction with the Denver National Western Stock Show in 1944. Here she is after her victory. Flamette, by Booger and out of Aflame, was also the first horse Hank registered with the AQHA.

By the mid-1950s, the Wiescamp-bred horses were dominating the exhibitors' groups at the Rocky Mountain Quarter Horse shows. At the 1953 Pikes Peak or Bust show in Colorado Springs, Skipper W won the get-of-sire, and Southern Queen, the produce-of-dam. In the get-of-sire winner's photo (top), Leroy Webb holds Skip's Reward, Jack Kyle holds General Skip, and Bill Hendricks holds Skipper's Lad. In the produce-of-dam photo, Larry Walker (left) is at the head of Nye's Barney Google, while Kenneth Gann holds Spot Cash.

***Western Horseman* Photos**

first show, with my first registered Quarter Horse, and she was the grand champion.

"I don't think I'll ever forget that day."

At first, there were not a lot of shows to go to in the Rocky Mountain region. The Denver Stock Show, Colorado and New Mexico state fairs, Colorado Springs, and Santa Fe were the only shows that Hank chose to go to in the beginning.

The main accomplishments of the early Wiescamp show horses have been chronicled in preceding chapters. As recorded in them, Holy Smoke, Show Boat, and the

Hank even managed to get in a winner's photo every now and then. Here he is with the yearling filly Skip Nurse, by Skipper W and out of Night Nurse, after she had won her class at the 1955 Colorado State Fair.

***Western Horseman* Photo**

At the 1949 Denver National Western Stock Show, the Wiescamp horses swept the Quarter Horse and Palomino halter championships. Hank holds Skipper W, the grand champion Quarter Horse stallion, and Show Boat, the grand champion Palomino stallion, while Ray Moore, Briggsdale, Colo., hangs on to Spanish Rose, the grand champion Quarter Horse mare, and She Flew, the grand champion Palomino mare.

sons and daughters of Nick Shoemaker all piled up their share of show ring achievements during the mid- to late 1940s.

In 1949 at the Denver National Western Stock Show, the achievements of the Wiescamp show horse string hit an all-time high.

"In 1946, Guy Corpe came out here and bought all of my yearlings except for three," remembers Hank. "He shipped 'em back to California in a box car and hired a fella to ride along and take care of 'em. I set aside three horses who I wouldn't sell. They were Skipper W, Show Boat, and Spanish Rose.

The 1960s were the "Golden Age" for the Wiescamp show horses. They dominated the Rocky Mountain region in both halter and performance, and put Hank at or near the top in almost all of the breeders' lists maintained by the AQHA show department. Here are two of the top horses from that era. Skipper's Smoke (top), a 1956 stallion by Skipper W and out of Silver Leche, was the RMQHA high-point all-around horse in 1962. He was an AQHA Champion and Superior halter horse with 100 halter and 64.5 performance points. In this photo Leroy Webb holds Smoke after he was named the grand champion stallion at the 1963 Houston Livestock Show.

Silver Son, a 1960 stallion by Senator and out of Silver Leche, was also an AQHA Champion who earned Superiors in halter, reining, and calf roping. He amassed a total of 176 halter and 201 performance points and was the 1966 and 1967 AQHA Honor Roll calf roping stallion, and the 1969 AQHA Honor Roll steer roping horse.

Top Photo by Agri Photo Service, Bottom Photo by Darol Dickinson

Skip's Barred, a 1962 mare by Skip's Reward and out of Skipity Bar, was a Superior halter mare with 118 points. Shown here with Leroy Webb, she once stood grand at halter 33 times in a row.

Photo by Darol Dickinson

"Three years later, I took those three horses and She Flew to the Denver Stock Show. Skipper W was the Grand Champion Quarter Horse Stallion, Spanish Rose was the Grand Champion Quarter Horse Mare, Show Boat was the Grand Champion Palomino Stallion, and She Flew was the Grand Champion Palomino Mare.

"George Mueller hauled those horses up to Denver in an open cattle truck. I came back to Alamosa a day ahead of him, and a blizzard hit before he could get home with the horses. He called me from Walsenburg, and told me he didn't think he could make it over La Veta pass. That was before the new highway was built.

"I told him to put the horses up at the Walsenburg fairgrounds and get a room for the night. He said that he'd already tried that and couldn't get near the fairgrounds because of the snowdrifts.

"This was in the evening. I told him to come on, and if he wasn't home by 2 a.m., I'd come lookin' for him. About 1 a.m. I heard him coming down the road. He'd thrown a rod in the truck and it was 50 below zero, so the sound of that ol' motor knockin' really carried.

"We unloaded those horses from the truck and put 'em in the barn. The bed of the truck was covered with snow and ice,

Sailalong, a 1956 stallion by Skipper W and out of Brushalong, was another of the top Wiescamp show horses of the 1960s. An AQHA Champion, he was also one of the most consistent reining horses of his day. Leroy Webb is up on the athletic-looking stallion in this photo taken at Colorado Springs in 1961.

Photo by Darol Dickinson, Courtesy of *The Quarter Horse Journal*

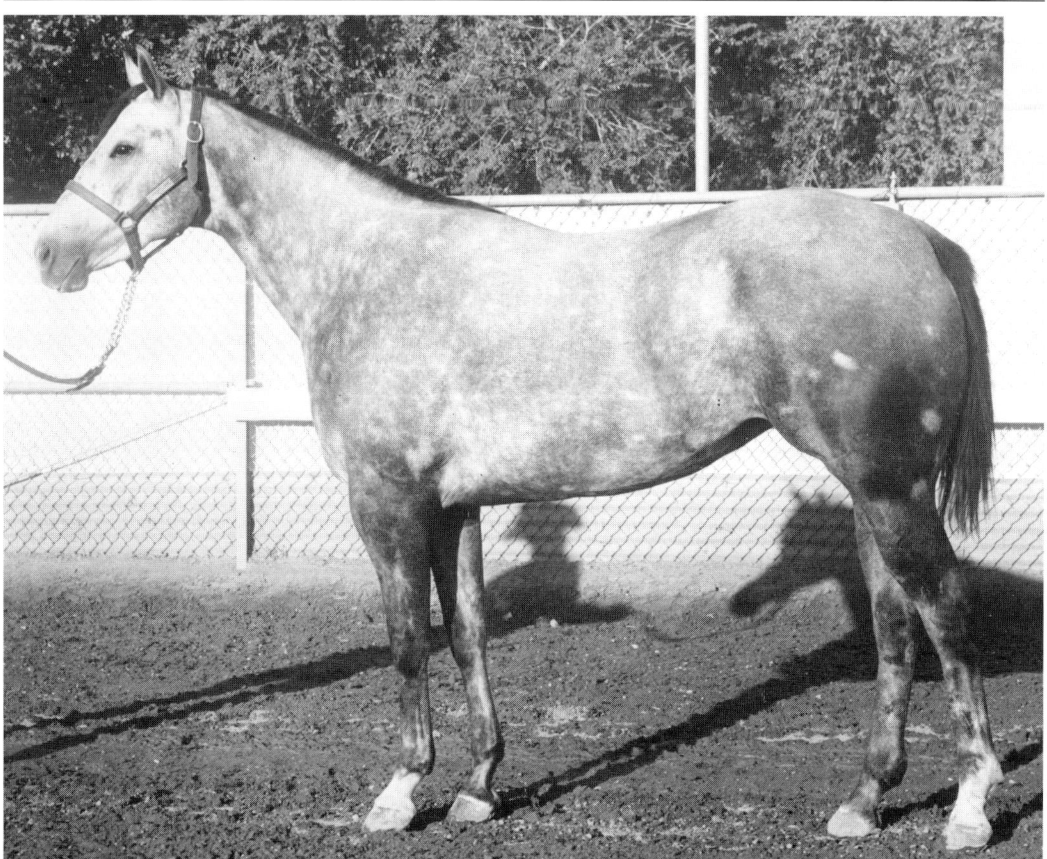

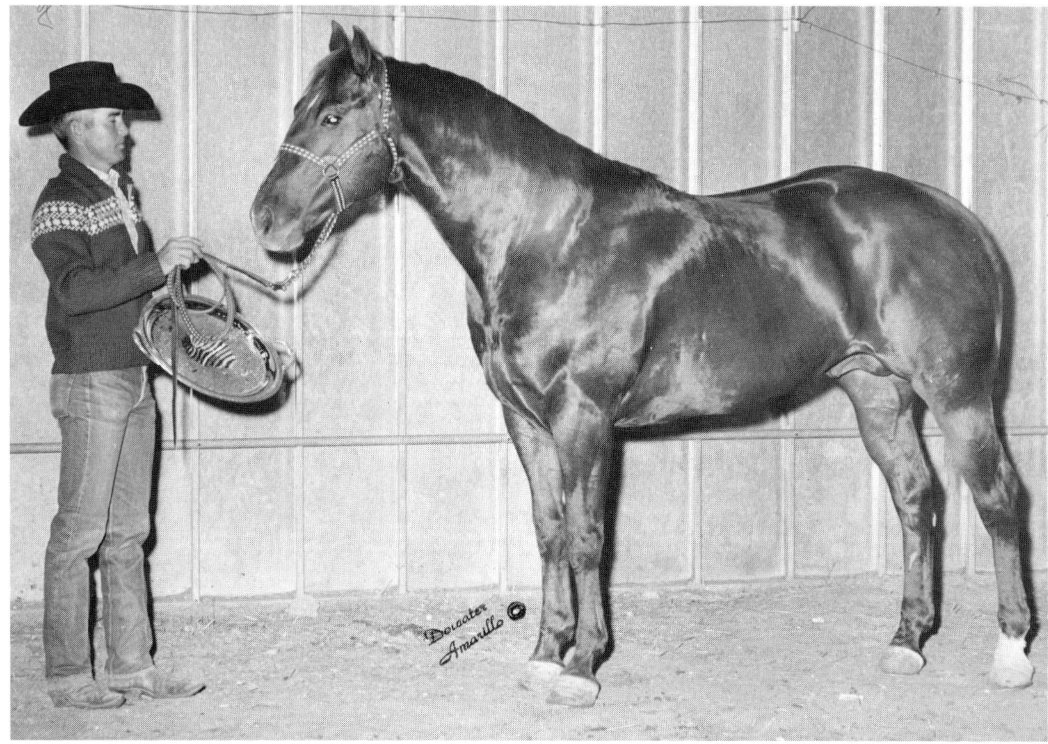

Skip's Ink (top), by Skipper W and out of Tetrama, and Skip Sir Bar by Skipper W and out of Twin Bar (TB), were two more of the Wiescamp horses who excelled in the show ring in the 1960s. Both were AQHA Champions, and both earned their Superiors in halter. In 1968, Skip Sir Bar was also the RMQHA high-point all-around horse and the AQHA Honor Roll steer roping stallion.

Top Photo by Darol Dickinson, Bottom Photo by H.D. Dolcater, Courtesy of *The Quarter Horse Journal*

Although he was not shown as heavily as some of the other Wiescamp horses, Skip Fare, a 1963 stallion by Skipper W and out of School Mama, did earn several championships at halter. Here, Larry Wilcox holds him after a win at a Grand Junction, Colo., show.

Photo by Lula Hayes

with indentations where the horses' hoofs had been.

"The next morning when I got up, it was 52 below zero! And do you know, not a one of those horses even got a runny nose out of the deal. Show horses had to be a bit tougher in those days."

By the mid- to late 1950s, the sons and daughters of Skipper W and Nick W had begun to make a firm impact on the regional show scene. Horses like Skipper's King, Skipperette, Skipadoo, Skipper's Lad, Spot Cash, General Skip, School Mama, Shirley Nick, and Scotch Maid proved to be the ones to beat wherever they appeared.

By this time, Hank was also winning almost all the get-of-sire and produce-of-dam classes that he entered. As a breeding group, the get of Skipper W, out of the Philmont and Ghost Ranch mares, were tough to beat when it came to quality and consistency of type.

Prior to the 1960s, the handling of the Wiescamp show horses had been entrusted to George Mueller, Kenneth Gann, and Clyde Swift.

"George, Kenneth, and Clyde were all top hands," notes Hank.

"George could make the best roping horse, Kenneth was the best with the race horses, and Clyde could make the best reining horse. But they could all break colts; they could all handle breeding stallions, broodmares, and young stock; and they could all doctor and shoe horses. They could all just do whatever was needed to run a large livestock operation.

"George Mueller was with me for over 30 years. In fact, he lived with me and my family in the sale barn for years. He was just like a part of the family and he always had time for my kids.

"Kenneth Gann worked for me almost as long as George did. He worked for me right up until he got sick from cancer and passed away. Although he didn't work for me as long as George and Kenneth did, Clyde put in his time here too. He would work awhile and then leave, and then come back and work some more.

"All three of those guys were a big part of this operation for a handful of years. I never thought they got as much recognition as they deserved."

By the 1960s, the Quarter Horse show scene had gotten so big that Hank felt the need to hire a full-time trainer to fit and show his horses. He chose first Jack Kyle, then Leroy Webb to fill the job.

Hank's name appeared on virtually every leading breeders list that the AQHA show department published in the 1960s.

The Wiescamp show horses of the 1960s not only looked good, they were top performance horses as well. Skipette (top), a 1959 mare by Skipper W and out of Sis Nick, was an AQHA Champion, earned a Superior in halter with 113 points, and was the 1964 AQHA Honor Roll calf roping mare. In this photo taken in Pueblo, Colo., she sets the brakes for Leroy Webb in a roping contest. Skip Tres Bar, a 1962 stallion by Skipador and out of Skipabar, was also an AQHA Champion and in 1966 was the RMQHA high-point all-around horse. Here, Leroy Webb heads on Skip Tres Bar at a show in Colorado Springs in 1966. That's Hugh Bennett on the heels.

Photos by Darol Dickinson

If there is a single era that can be designated the Golden Age of the Wiescamp show horse, it would have to be the decade of the 1960s.

Beginning with Skipper's Smoke and Sailalong, and ending with Skip Sir Bar, the Wiescamp halter and performance horses dominated the Rocky Mountain show scene in the '60s.

Skipper's Smoke, Skip's Princess, Skip Sir Bar, and Skip Tres Bar were all RMQHA high-point all-around horses during that time frame.

Skipper's Smoke, Sailalong, Skip's Princess, Skip On, Skip Barba, Sheik's Image, Skipette, Skip 3 Bar, Silver Son, Skip's Admiral, Skip's Ink, Skip Sir Bar, Skip's Barred, Skip Tres Bar, and Skip's Trama were all high-point halter and/or performance horses in the RMQHA during the decade, and the majority of them also earned their AQHA Championships and Superiors during that time period.

In addition, Skipette, Silver Son, and Skip Sir Bar were AQHA honor roll winners in performance. And there were scores of additional Wiescamp horses who were shown during the 1960s to a lesser degree, but who were still consistent winners whenever and wherever they were entered. Their numbers included horses like Skip Fare, Skip Twin Bar, Spanish Bar Girl, String's Nick, and Skip A Turn.

Hank's name appeared on virtually every leading breeders list that the AQHA show department published in the 1960s. In 1966, for example, he was the leading breeder of halter class winners (most winners), halter class winners (most wins), performance point-earners (most points), and performance class winners (most wins).

He was the third leading breeder of performance point-earners (most point-earners) and performance class winners (most winners). He was also listed as the second all-time breeder of AQHA Champions with 27, and the third all-time breeder of Register of Merit horses with 54.

By the end of the decade, the list of Wiescamp-bred AQHA Champions had grown to 37, and the Register of Merit earners to 66. In addition, Skipper W was listed as a leading sire of AQHA Champions, and both Spanish Joy and Silver Leche were among the leading dams of AQHA Champions. Simply put, the Wiescamp horses were at the top.

Unmistakably Wiescamp in looks and coloring, String's Nick was a 1964 stallion by Skippa String and out of Spanish Miss. The earner of 23 halter and 14 performance points, String's Nick is shown here winning his class at the 1966 Wyoming State Fair in Douglas.

Photo by Darol Dickinson

As the 1970s rolled around, Hank made the decision to cut back on the showing. By this time, Leroy Webb had moved on, and Hank did not hire a full-time trainer to replace him. He decided instead to place a few top prospects in the hands of outside trainers to condition and show.

At the top of the list of the horses Hank had campaigned during this era is Skip N Go, a 1969 sorrel stallion by Skipa Skipa and out of Skip V Bar by Bar Mount.

Skip N Go was given to Margaret Hammond to show. He qualified for his AQHA Championship in 1972 and also earned Superiors in halter with 75 points and in western pleasure with 123 points that same year. In 1976 he was the Grand Champion Quarter Horse Stallion at the Denver National Western Stock Show.

Silent Sheila, a 1973 sorrel mare by Sailalong and out of Skip Sassy by Skipper's King, was another of the top Wiescamp stars of the 1970s. Also shown by Margaret, Silent Sheila was an AQHA

Spanish Bar Girl, a 1964 mare by Scoot's Bar and out of Spanish Sister, also won her class at the 1966 Wyoming State Fair. The earner of 12 halter points, she was just one of the many young halter mares that Hank had lightly shown in the 1960s.

Photo by Darol Dickinson

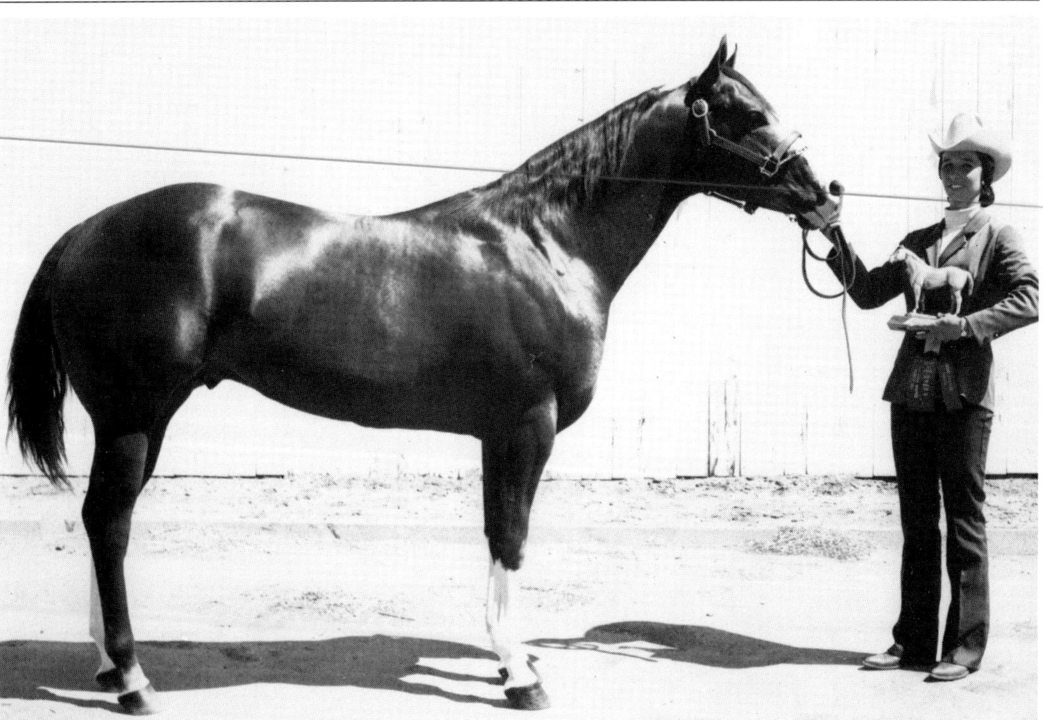

Skip N Go, a 1969 stallion by Skipa Skip and out of Skip V Bar, was the acknowledged superstar of Wiescamp's show string in the 1970s. Hank was reported to have turned down $100,000 for the big sorrel stallion, who earned Superiors in halter and western pleasure en route to his AQHA Championship. Margaret Hammond holds him here, after his win at the 1972 Block and Bridle show in Lincoln, Nebraska.

Western Horseman **Photo**

Silent Sheila, a 1973 mare by Sailalong and out of Skip Sassy, represented the ultimate in femininity during her show career. Like several of her contemporaries, she was an AQHA Champion with Superiors in halter and western pleasure. Margaret Hammond holds her in this photo taken in 1975.

Photo by Potter, Courtesy of Margaret Hammond

Champion with Superiors in halter and western pleasure.

Skip's Chita and Skip's Style were also shown during this era with great success. Skip's Chita, a 1970 mare by Skippa String and out of Skip's Delighted by Skip's Bar Boy, was an AQHA Champion and a Superior halter horse. Skip's Style, a 1971 mare by Skip Fare and out of Skip Drama by Skip's Reward, earned the same honors.

Skip's Barber, a 1971 stallion by Skippa Lark and out of Skip Barba by Skip's Reward, was yet another successful 1970s-vintage Wiescamp show horse. Shown by Sunny Jim Orr, he earned 34 halter points. He also went on to become the sire of several of the greatest Wiescamp show horses of the 1980s.

Spanish Array, a 1980 stallion, was by Skip's Barber and out of Spanish Galla by Skip's Bid. While still owned by Hank, Spanish Array stood grand at the Denver National Western Stock Show and the Colorado State Fair.

Sold to Marsha Miller and Glen Hudleston, of Carrier, Okla., Spanish Array went on to earn a Superior at halter and be named the 1985 AQHA World Champion Aged Stallion.

Skip So Smooth, a 1982 stallion by Skip's Barber and out of Smooth Maiden by Skip's Bid, earned 28 halter points. He also stood grand at the 1986 and 1987 Colorado State Fair, 43 years after the

Skip's Style, a 1971 mare by Skip Fare and out of Skip Drama, was a good-looking palomino mare from a long line of good-looking palomino mares. She earned her AQHA Championship and Superior halter award in 1975 with 56 halter, 15 hunter under saddle, 4 heading, and 4 heeling points.

Photo Courtesy of Margaret Hammond

Wiescamp-owned Holy Smoke had accomplished the same feat.

Skip So Smooth was the last show horse Hank campaigned to any degree.

"After Skip So Smooth, I just decided it was time to quit showing horses," he relates. "Sometimes I don't figure out things as quick as I should. It took me years to figure out that too few of my big-time show horses ever went on to become big-time breeding horses.

"I don't know what there is about it. Maybe it's all the time they spend in box stalls. Or maybe it's all the time they spend on the road. But I can tell you one thing for sure. It takes something out of them. They don't ever get it back.

"I can go down the list of all the top horses I had hauled extensively over the years, and I can't point to a single one who lived to old age, or who set the world on fire as a breeding stallion or a producing mare.

"The early ones, like Skipper W, Skipper's King, and Skipperette were different. They made breeding horses. But then, they hardly ever saw a barn, and they weren't hauled to death.

"The show horse business can be hard on horses. It got to the point where I had to decide whether I wanted to win awards or breed horses.

"It wasn't too hard a decision to make."

The beautifully headed Skip's Chita, by Skippa String and out of Skip's Delighted, also earned her AQHA Championship and a Superior in halter. **Photo by LeRoy Weathers**

14 THE QUEST FOR SPEED

"... I always believed that speed was necessary in the type of working horse that I set out to raise."

JUST AS HE sought from the very beginning to put looks and athletic ability into the horses that he raised, so too did Hank strive to inject speed into them.

"Speed was never the most important trait to me," he states. "Conformation and working ability were. But I always believed that speed was necessary in the type of working horse that I set out to raise.

"Speed was necessary to cut a cow, and catch a calf or steer. And I always did like straight race horses. So, from the days of the Remount studs on, I always made speed a part of my formula."

From the beginning, Hank always had a race horse or two on the track. For 3 years in a row, he had the winner of the Colorado Futurity. O'Possum won the 1945 edition of that race, followed by Joker W. in 1946, and Spanish Rose in 1947. In 1948, Scooter W. was the American Quarter Racing Association's Champion Running Stallion.

In the mid-1950s, Scottish acquitted himself quite well as a race horse. Of almost pure Old Fred breeding, Scottish was a solid AAA runner, a AAA sire, and a AAA maternal grandsire.

It was only natural, then, that the first

Skippa String, a sorrel stallion foaled in 1958, by Rukin String and out of H.J. Skippa by Skipper W, was the first in a long line of top horses bred by Hank through the use of speed-bred outcross stallions. Shown in this 1962 race win photo, from the left, are Charlotte and Hank Wiescamp, trainer J.J. Phillips, and jockey Bobby Harmon.

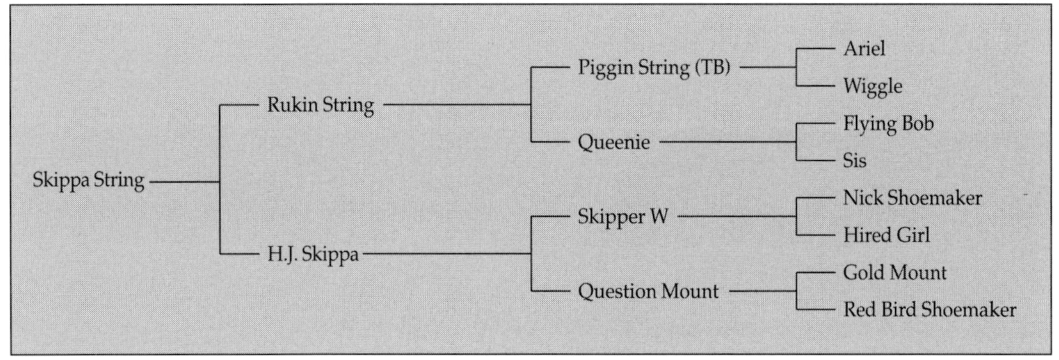

outcross stallion that Hank chose to use in his program would be a well-known running horse of fashionable breeding.

"I leased Rukin String in 1956 and 1957 to use on my Old Fred-bred mares," he states. "He was sired by Piggin String (TB), the World Champion Quarter Running Stallion in 1945-46, and the co-champion in 1943-44. And Piggin String was a Ben Brush-bred horse, just like Maple Prince and Chimney Sweep. This was the Thoroughbred family that has just always seemed to cross the best with my horses.

"Rukin String's mama was Queenie, the World Champion Quarter Running Horse in 1945-46, and the Champion Quarter Running Mare in 1945-46. And Rukin String was, himself, the Champion Running Stallion of 1953. So I figured that he had the speed and he had the blood.

"People second-guessed me when I leased him," continues Hank. "They didn't think that he was good-looking enough to use on mares like Skipperette, School Mama, and Spanish Rose.

"But I knew I could make it work. I needed him as an outcross, and then I planned to breed whichever of his sons and daughters that I kept back to horses from my Old Fred line. It worked out all right."

During the 2 years that Hank used Rukin String, he got several breeding-caliber stallions and a number of solid-producing broodmares.

School Meister, a 1957 bay stallion out of School Mama; and Silver String, a 1957 palomino stallion out of Silver Leche, were two of the better Wiescamp-bred sons of Rukin String.

Dunny String, a 1958 dun stallion by Rukin String and out of Sagey, earned his AAA rating on the racetrack and was also used as a breeding stallion.

Skipperita, a 1957 bay mare by Rukin String and out of Skipperette, earned her Register of Merit in racing. She was also the dam of 16 foals, including several race starters and a number of daughters who found their way into the Wiescamp broodmare band.

Skipakin, a 1958 daughter of Rukin String and out of Skiparado, was the dam of 10 AQHA performers, including Sailalong Skip, a Superior halter horse with 98 points, and Mill Iron Ruk, a Superior reining horse with 68 performance points.

Spanish String, String Again, and String Madam were additional Rukin String daughters who proved to be good producers for Hank.

But the most important legacy that

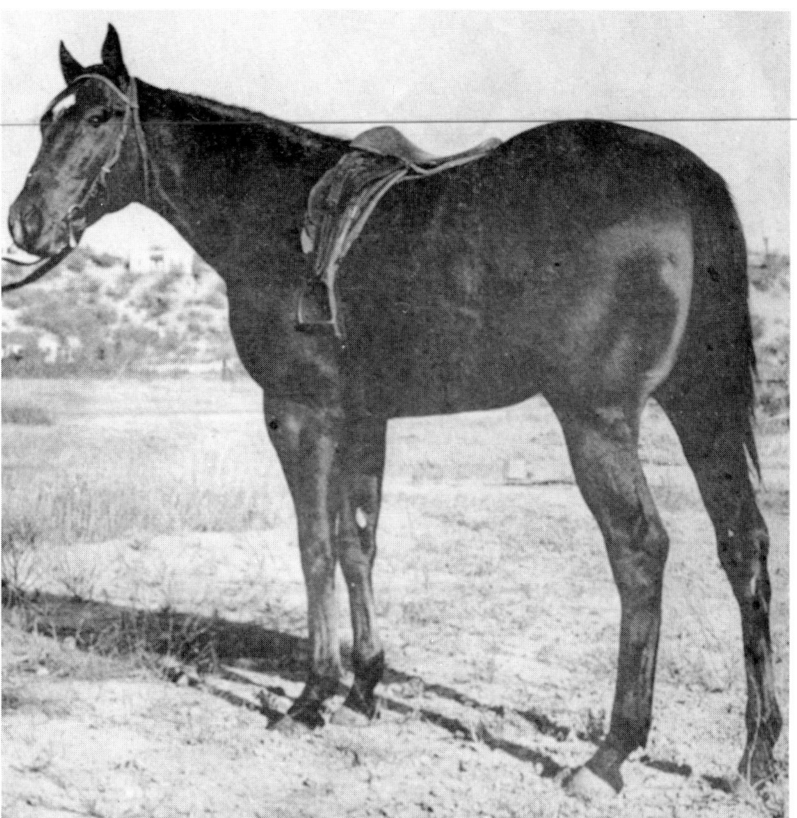

Rukin String, a 1950 stallion by Piggin String (TB) and out of Queenie by Flying Bob, was the Champion Quarter Running Stallion of 1953. He was leased by Hank in 1956 and 1957 to use on his Old Fred-bred mares.

Rukin String left the Wiescamp breeding program was as the sire of Skippa String.

This sorrel stallion, who was foaled in 1958, was out of H.J. Skippa by Skipper W. H.J. Skippa's dam was Question Mount by Gold Mount.

As mentioned in Chapter 9, Question Mount was a little spooky as far as her temperament went. Her grandson took after her in that respect.

"Skippa String was not a bad-dispositioned horse," says Hank, "but he was high-strung. We broke him right here and put him in his first starting chute here. The first time we put him in one, he jumped right out of it.

"We put him back in, and he crawled out again. My brother Shorty was helpin' us with him. He asked me, 'By gosh Hank, do you expect to race him?'

"I said, 'You bet. He's the kind who'll get it done. Don't you worry about him. He'll settle down.' And he did. He broke out real nice, and all of his colts did too. The first two or three times they were handled, they were spooky. But, once they found out what you wanted, they would try to please you.

"When it was time to run Skippa String, we took him down to La Mesa Park at Raton. They didn't have any maiden races scheduled, and I wasn't going to put him in a claiming race, so I just entered him in an allowance race. He won it going away.

"Walter Merrick once told me that Skippa String was one of the most honest race horses he'd ever seen. And he did it all on hay and oats."

Skippa String achieved a solid AAA rating on the tracks. In 1960 he won the Nursery Handicap at La Mesa Park, and in 1962 he won the C.L. Maddon's Bright Eyes Handicap at Albuquerque.

Retired to stud, Skippa String was the sire of two AAA race horses, three AQHA Champions, and four Superior halter horses. His get earned a total of 1,008 halter points and 269.5 performance points in AQHA-sanctioned competition.

String Of Gold, a 1964 palomino gelding by Skippa String and out of Skip's Gold Bar by Bar Mount, was an AQHA Champion who amassed 601 open and 101 youth halter points. Skippa Cord, a 1966 black stallion by Skippa String and out of Skip Doll by Skipper's Lad, was also an AQHA Champion and Superior halter horse.

And, as documented in the previous

String Of Gold, a 1964 palomino gelding by Skippa String and out of Skip's Gold Bar by Bar Mount, was an AQHA Champion with 601 open and 101 youth halter points.

Photo by Tom Esler, Courtesy of *The Quarter Horse Journal*

St Skippa, shown here as a 2-year-old in 1984, is an excellent example of the results Hank got when he incorporated speed bloodlines into his breeding program. The good-looking buckskin traces to Skippa String on both sides of her pedigree and also to Double Dancer, ST Bar D (TB), Scottish, and Bright Bar. Despite all of her outcrossed blood, St Skippa retains the classic Wiescamp look.

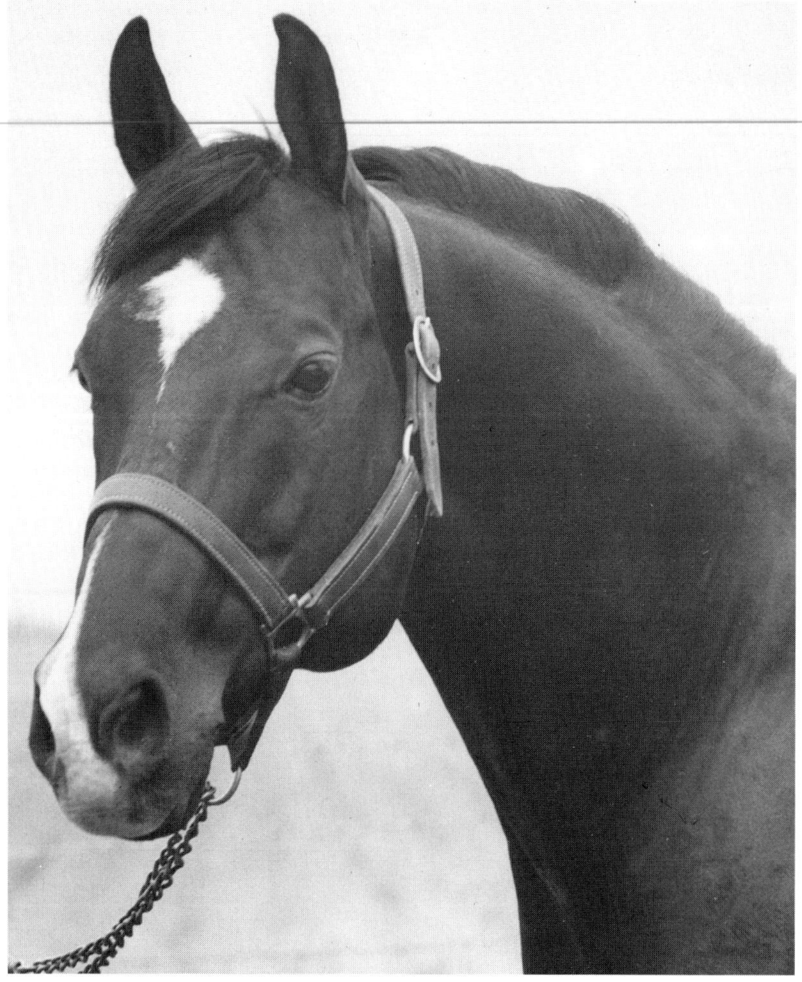

After Rukin String, Hank leased this Three Bars (TB) son, De Witt Bar, to use on his Old Fred-bred mares. Foaled in 1951, this AAA race-rated black stallion was out of Dialie Mc by Chicaro Bill.

Photo by Western Livestock Journal, Courtesy of *The Quarter Horse Journal*

chapter, the Skippa String daughter Skip's Chita also earned her AQHA Championship and Superior halter award.

Finally, Bart String, a 1964 sorrel stallion by Skippa String and out of Cherry Barta by Bart B.S., and Skippa Sure, a 1967 black stallion by Skippa String and out of Sure Bar by De Witt Bar, both achieved AAA ratings on the track.

Like a number of other Wiescamp stallions, however, Skippa String made his greatest impact on the program as a sire of breeding animals.

Skip's Chant and Skip's Cadet, full brothers by Skippa String and out of Skipperette, were both used by Hank for a number of years as herd sires. And the daughters of Skippa String proved to be consistently outstanding producers.

Shasta String, a 1966 palomino mare by Skippa String and out of Spanish Shasta by Spanish Nick, was the dam of three performers who earned a total of 1,321.5 AQHA points. Old Lady Irwin, a 1974 palomino mare by the Wiescamp-bred Sir Colonel and out of Shasta String, was an AQHA Champion who earned seven Superiors and 879 points.

Skippa Twin, by Skippa String and out of Skip Twin Bar by Skipper W, was the dam of the point-earners Skippa Twin and Skip To Array, and she was also the dam of the top Wiescamp sire St Limit.

Still other top-producing daughters of Skippa String were String Relic, Skip Anna, Skippa Kay, Skippa's Hope, Stringette, Silent Skippa, Skippa Bid, Skippa Lick, Skippa Show, Skippa Scot, and Skip Sister.

"I believe that Skippa String was one of the nicest horses we ever raised," concludes Hank. "He had the gas, he had the looks, and he was one of the most athletic horses I've ever owned. He paid his way every day of his life."

The second speed-bred horse Hank leased was De Witt Bar, a AAA-rated son of Three Bars (TB), out of Dialie Mc by Chicaro Bill. Foaled in 1951, this black stallion was used by Hank in 1955 and 1956.

By this time, Hank had decided that the

Few photographs exist of Bar Mount, who played a very definitive role as a sire on the Wiescamp ranch during the 1960s. The sire of seven AQHA Champions, and the maternal grandsire of nine more, Bar Mount is shown here at the Wiescamp ranch as a 4-year-old.

Photo by Carolyn Bignall, Courtesy of Carolyn Bignall

Skipper Bar, a 1959 sorrel stallion out of Skipper's Maid by Skipper W, was one of the first AQHA Champions sired by Bar Mount. He achieved the honor in 1964.

Photo by Darol Dickinson

Skip O Bar, a 1961 sorrel stallion by Bar Mount and out of Skip Queen by Skipper W, qualified for his AQHA Championship in 1966.

Skippit Bar was another son of Bar Mount who earned his AQHA Championship. The sorrel stallion was foaled in 1961, out of Sea Skipper by Skipper W.

Photo by Darol Dickinson, Courtesy of *The Quarter Horse Journal*

Three Bars-bred horses and his Old Fred-bred horses were born to be crossed on each other.

"There were several good lines of Thoroughbreds out there when I started using the Three Bars horses," notes Hank. "Horses like Piggin String, Depth Charge, and Spotted Bull could all add some speed to your program, but Three Bars could add that conformation as well.

"In size, type, and coloring, he reminded me of the Coke Roberds horses I had seen in the 1920s and 1930s. That's why I used his blood. Over the years, I bought or leased four of his sons and grandsons, and, at one time, I owned four of his daughters.

"In 1960, I made a deal with Art Pollard to lease Lightning Bar for several years. Art was going to use him up to June 1, and I was going to get him for the rest of the year. He died of colitis X before I could ever use him.

"Lightning Bar was far and away the best son of Three Bars I ever saw. I can't help but think that he would have really

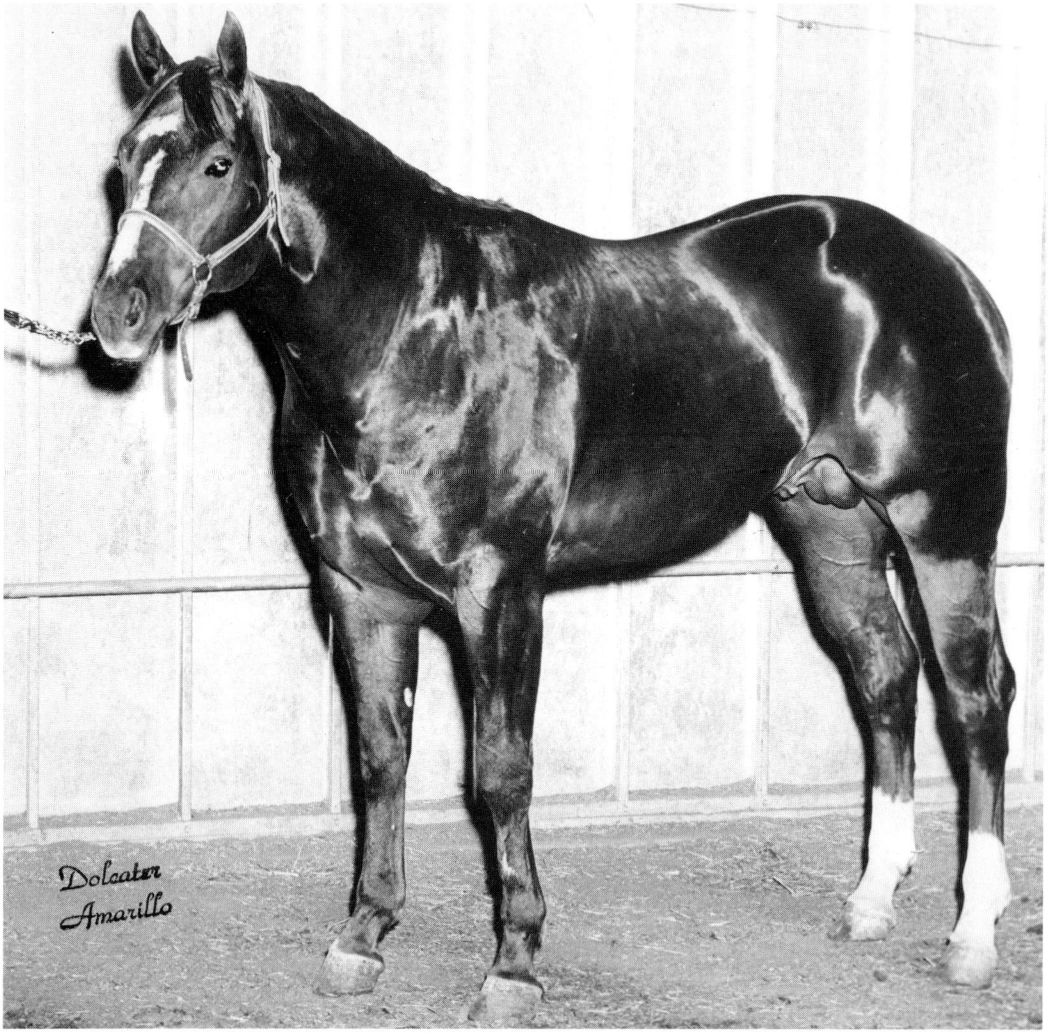

Scoot Baron, a 1962 sorrel stallion by Bar Mount and out of Scooter's Charm by Scooter Lad, earned his AQHA Championship in 1962.

Photo by H.D. Dolcater, Courtesy of *The Quarter Horse Journal*

crossed well with my mares."

As an individual, De Witt Bar did not quite measure up to Lightning Bar. During the 2 years that Hank leased him, however, he did do a creditable job as a sire.

The top Wiescamp-bred stallion De Witt Bar is credited with siring would have to be Bar Mount, a 1956 sorrel stallion out of Question Mount.

AQHA records reveal that Bar Mount was the sire of seven AQHA Champions and three Superior halter horses. Six of the AQHA Champions were bred by Hank, with three of them out of daughters of Skipper W, two out of Spanish Nick mares, and one out of a daughter of Scooter W.

Bar Mount was also an excellent broodmare sire. His daughters produced nine AQHA Champions, nine Superior halter horses, seven Superior performance horses, and the earners of over 4,000 AQHA show points.

Here is Splash Bar, a 1963 sorrel stallion by Bar Mount and out of Skip Irish by Skipper's King, who earned 40 halter and 12 performance points. He was also the sire of several top show horses, including Splash Bar Maid, who earned 250 halter points.

Photo by Darol Dickinson

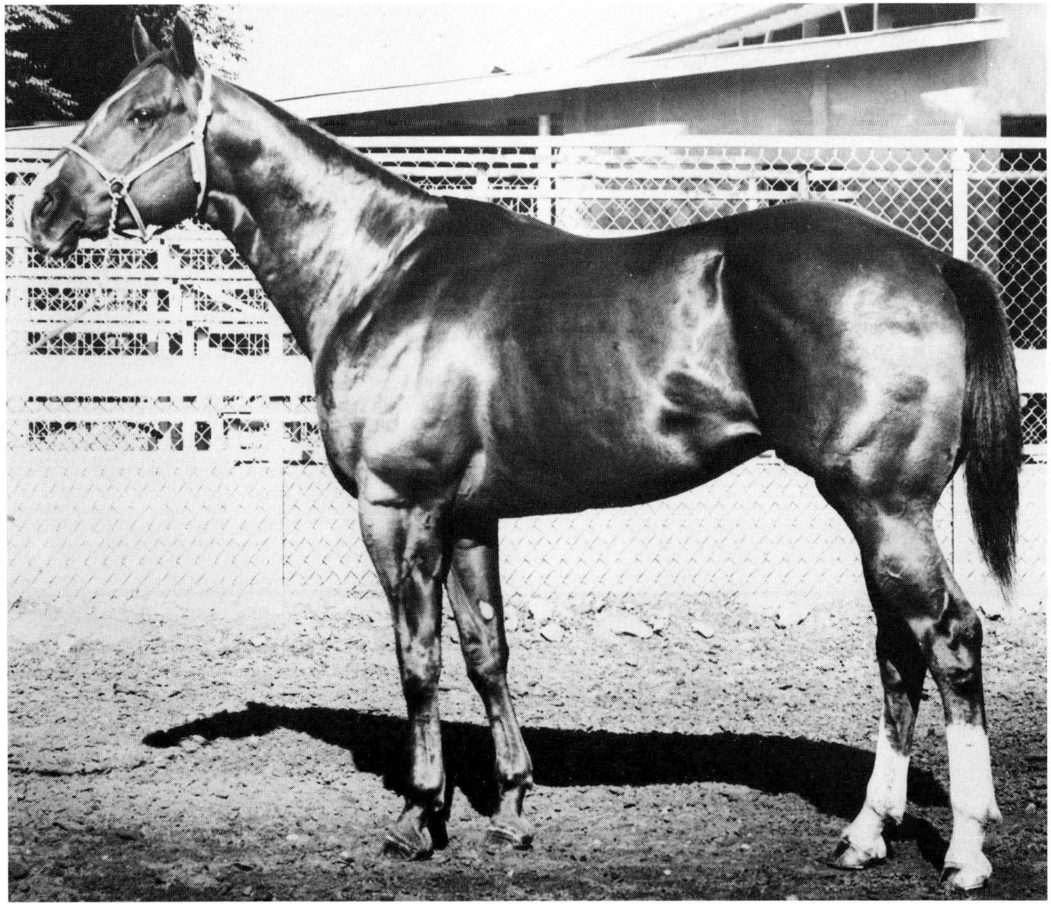

South Bar, a 1961 sorrel stallion by Bar Mount and out of Southern Babe by Skipper W, displays the classic Wiescamp look of the 1960s. Slim-necked, with an excellent shoulder and top-line, South Bar earned 11 halter points.

Photo by Darol Dickinson

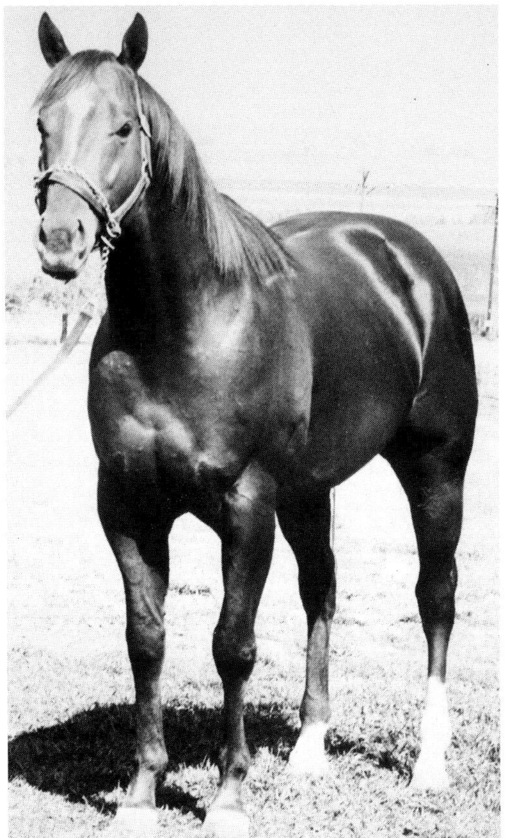

Sir Bar, a 1955 stallion by Parker's Trouble and out of Twin Bar (TB) by Three Bars (TB), was used on a limited basis by Hank in the early to mid-1960s. He sired several good broodmares during that time.

Photo by Darol Dickinson, Courtesy of *The Quarter Horse Journal*

Shasta Bar, Southern Bar, Skip's Gold Bar, Silent Bar, Skipover Bar, Skip All Bars, Skip's Gift, Bar Lassie, Social Bar, Skip's Gift, Skipover Bar, Skip's Bar Maid, Skip V Bar, Skip By Self, Skip's Design, Skip's Trick, Scotch Mount, String Mama, and School Mother were all top-producing Bar Mount mares.

In addition, the Bar Mount sons Skip 3 Bar, Skip Barette, Scoot's Bar, South Bar, Skippit Bar, Skip O Bar, Scoot Baron, and Skip Bardoo were all good to top sires.

"Bar Mount was not a big horse," observes Hank, "and, thanks to Question Mount, his foals had a little buck in 'em. But he was one of the better early outcross stallions I used. He helped my program more than he hurt it."

Another son of Three Bars (TB) Hank used was ST Bar D (TB), who was out of Little Victory (TB).

"I bought ST Bar D (TB) from Paul and Carolyn Crabb, of Arlington, Kan., in 1960," notes Hank. "I used him here, on a limited basis, for a couple of years. I also let R.A. Furbush use him some during that same time. He sired several good horses for each of us."

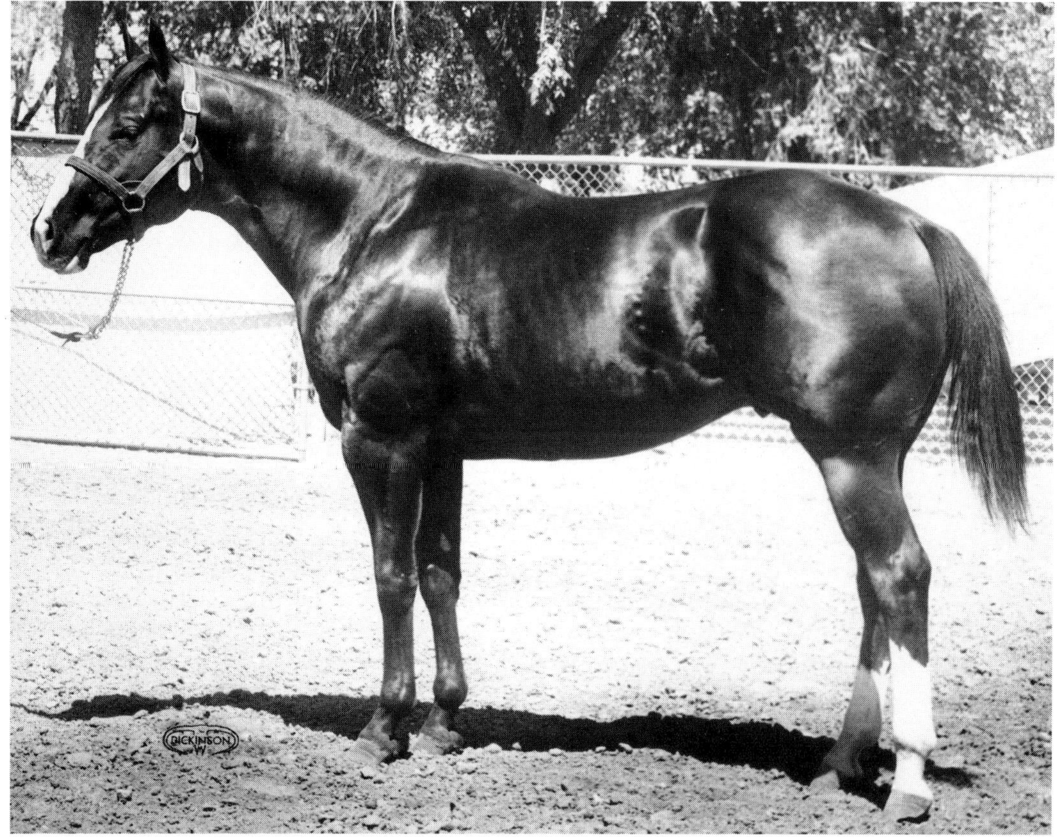

St Three Bar, a 1961 black stallion by ST Bar D (TB) and out of Skip Mama by Skipper's Lad, earned his AQHA Championship in 1976. He accumulated 41 halter and 18 performance points.

Photo by Darol Dickinson

Among the top show and race horses sired by ST Bar D (TB) was Elm's Bar Maid, St Three Bar, and Skip The Bar. Elm's Bar Maid, a 1961 buckskin mare out of School Marm by Monte Carl, was a Superior halter horse with 77 points. St Three Bar, a 1961 black stallion out of Skip Mama by Skipper's Lad, was an AQHA Champion, and Skip The Bar, a 1962 bay stallion out of H.J. Skippa, earned a AAA rating on the track.

Hank also used Sir Bar, a grandson of Three Bars (TB), in his breeding program.

"I bought Sir Bar's dam, Twin Bar (TB), who was by Three Bars (TB), in the fall of 1954," says Hank. "She was bred to Parker's Trouble, a AAA running horse who was by Ed Echols and out of Little Nellie Bars, who was also by Three Bars (TB). Sir Bar was the resulting foal.

"I used Sir Bar very limitedly when he was a young horse, and then I let R.A. Furbush use him when he was a 6-year-old. I got him back the following year, and used him a little heavier. He got us some good mares who crossed back on our Old Fred-bred stallions very well."

The beautiful-headed Elm's Bar Maid was a 1961 buckskin daughter of ST Bar D (TB), out of School Marm by Monte Carlo. A Superior halter horse with 77 points, Elm's Bar Maid is shown here as a 2-year-old.

Photo by Darol Dickinson, Courtesy of *The Quarter Horse Journal*

The outcross stallion Hank used during the early 1970s was Double Dancer, a 1963 stallion by Double Bid and out of Lena's Bar (TB) by Three Bars (TB). In addition to Double Dancer, Lena's Bar was also the dam of Jet Smooth and Easy Jet.
Photo by Darol Dickinson, Courtesy of *The Quarter Horse Journal*

Among the good broodmares Sir Bar sired were Summer Madness, Spanish Dress, String of Slippers, Scotch Rocketina, Skips Maiden, and Skippits Wand.

One of the running stallions Hank used who did not work out was Pasamonte Paul.

"We leased Pasamonte Paul for the 1963 breeding season," recalls Hank. "He was a good-looking horse; a little long in the back, but still a nice horse. He had the blood. He was by Suggested, a sprinting Thoroughbred from the same family as Plaudit, and he was out of Pasamonte Baybright by Golddust Shoemaker.

"And he was a race horse. He was a AAA runner when we leased him, and he returned to the track the following year and was the 1964 Champion Quarter Running Stallion.

"But he just couldn't get it done here as a breeding horse. I think we only kept a couple of studs and two or three mares by him. Sometimes it works, and sometimes it don't. Pasamonte Paul was one of the times it didn't."

The two stallions by Pasamonte Paul Hank did use for several years were Skip Monte, a 1964 palomino out of Sassy Skip by Skipper W, and Skipper's Pasa, a 1964 palomino out of Skipper's Model by Skipper's King. Pasa Cherry, Pasa Mama, and Show Pasa all made it into the Wiescamp broodmare band.

Returning to the blood of Three Bars (TB) for his next outcross stallion, Hank used Double Dancer for three breeding seasons in the early 1970s.

"I have always been a fan of Walter Merrick and his horses," says Hank. "Walter worked for Howard Linger here in the San Luis Valley at about the same time I was working for Clyde Helms. We share some of the same roots.

"One of the best mares Walter ever raised was Lena's Bar (TB). She was a daughter of Three Bars (TB), out of Lena Valenti (TB) by Grey Dream (TB).

"Walter raced Lena's Bar on the Quarter tracks and got her AAA rating. Then, in 1962, he bred her to Double Bid, the 1959 Champion Quarter Running Stallion, and got Double Dancer. Double Dancer was a good-looking chestnut stallion who earned a AAA rating on the tracks. We leased him from Walter in 1969, 1970, and 1971."

The first top horse Double Dancer sired for Hank was St Dancer, a 1970 sorrel stallion out of String Madam by Rukin String.

"St Dancer was a top conformation horse," says Hank. "I've raised thousands of horses over the past 60-plus years, and I

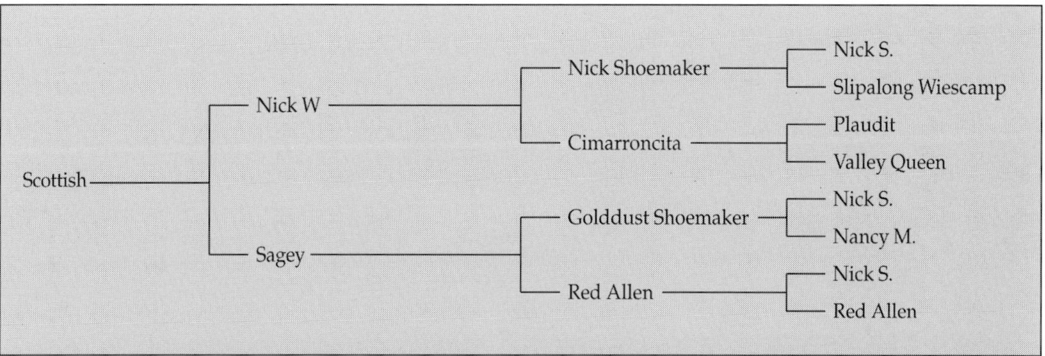

Scottish, a 1953 buckskin stallion by Nick W and out of Sagey by Golddust Shoemaker, was AAA-rated on the tracks. Retired to stud, he became the founder of an important female line within the Wiescamp family of horses. In this mid-1950s photo, Kenneth Gann holds Scottish after a race win at Centennial Race Track in Denver. Hank and Larry Wiescamp are at the buckskin's shoulder. The jockey is unidentified.

Photo Courtesy of Charlotte Wilcox

can't recall a single one of 'em who had a better shoulder than St Dancer. And he had the gas too. He achieved a speed index of 90, which is equivalent to AAA time under the old rating system.

"And he was a breeding horse. He established the 'Saint' line of horses who have done so well for us in recent years. They are good-looking horses who can run and also perform in the show and rodeo arena.

"In a lot of ways, St Dancer represents what I have always tried to get when I went to a speed outcross. He was a Three Bars (TB) on the top, and Rukin String on the bottom. He had the blood, and he had the speed, and yet he looked like an Old Fred horse. And he crossed exceptionally well with my mares. He was a success story."

In addition to St Dancer, Double Dancer sired the good runners Scotch Double and Scotch Dance. Scotch Double, a 1971 sorrel

Scotch Coin, a 1965 sorrel mare by Scottish and out of Super Miss by Super Cash, was one of the Old Fred bred mares who crossed exceptionally well with the Three Bars (TB) line of running horses. Scotch Coin had a speed index of 100 and was a multiple stakes winner. She was bred and owned by Larry and Charlotte (Wiescamp) Wilcox of Alamosa, Colo., and that's Charlotte at the left in this win photo taken at Centennial Race Track in Denver in 1968.

Photo by Ralph Morgan, Courtesy of Charlotte Wilcox

Scotch Double was a 1971 mare by Double Dancer and out of Scotch Coin. She was the earner of over $11,000 and was a futurity winner.

Photo by Gloria Loose, Courtesy of Charlotte Wilcox

Here is Smooth Coin, a 1970 mare by Jet Smooth and out of Scotch Coin. She earned over $77,000 on the tracks and was the 1973 Champion Quarter Running 3-Year-Old Filly.

Photo by Gloria Loose, Courtesy of Charlotte Wilcox

mare out of Scotch Coin by Scottish, had a speed index of 97 and was a futurity winner. Scotch Dance, a 1972 bay gelding out of Scotch Barta by Scottish, had a speed index of 92.

Double Dancer also sired a number of good broodmares during the time he was in Alamosa, including Scotch Double, Shesadoll, Social Stylist, Senorita Dancer, Spanish Rhapsody, and Skippity Dance.

The final horse to whom Hank has turned as an speed outcross, and who he is currently using as a sire, is Fly Duino, a 1983 gray stallion by *Beduino (TB) and out of Little Dandy Mae, a granddaughter of Three Bars (TB).

"I really like the *Beduino (TB) line," observes Hank. "The sons and daughter of *Beduino (TB) made a big splash on the Quarter tracks a few years ago, and now they're doing the same thing in the breeding barns.

"Fly Duino has excellent stock horse conformation, which he gets from both *Beduino (TB) and Three Bars (TB), and he is crossing real well with my line-bred mares.

"When I started outcrossing to speed horses in the 1950s," concludes Hank, "I looked to it to put some speed and hybrid vigor into my line of horses, without losing the type. I was experimenting with the mix then, trying to get that perfect horse, and I'm still experimenting today. The day I quit will be the day they bury me."

15 The Appaloosas

"... Loretta spent some time at Cecil's in the late 1950s and developed a liking for Appaloosas. So we got into the Appaloosa business."

IN THE LATE 1950s, Hank made the decision to start an Appaloosa breeding program. The decision was based, in part, on his daughter Loretta's interest in the spotted breed.

"Cecil Dobbin of Colorado Springs was a friend of mine," recalls Hank. "In the late 1950s he brought an Old Fred-bred

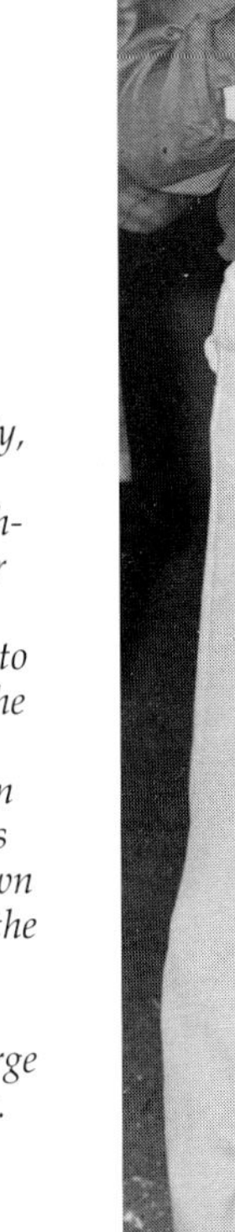

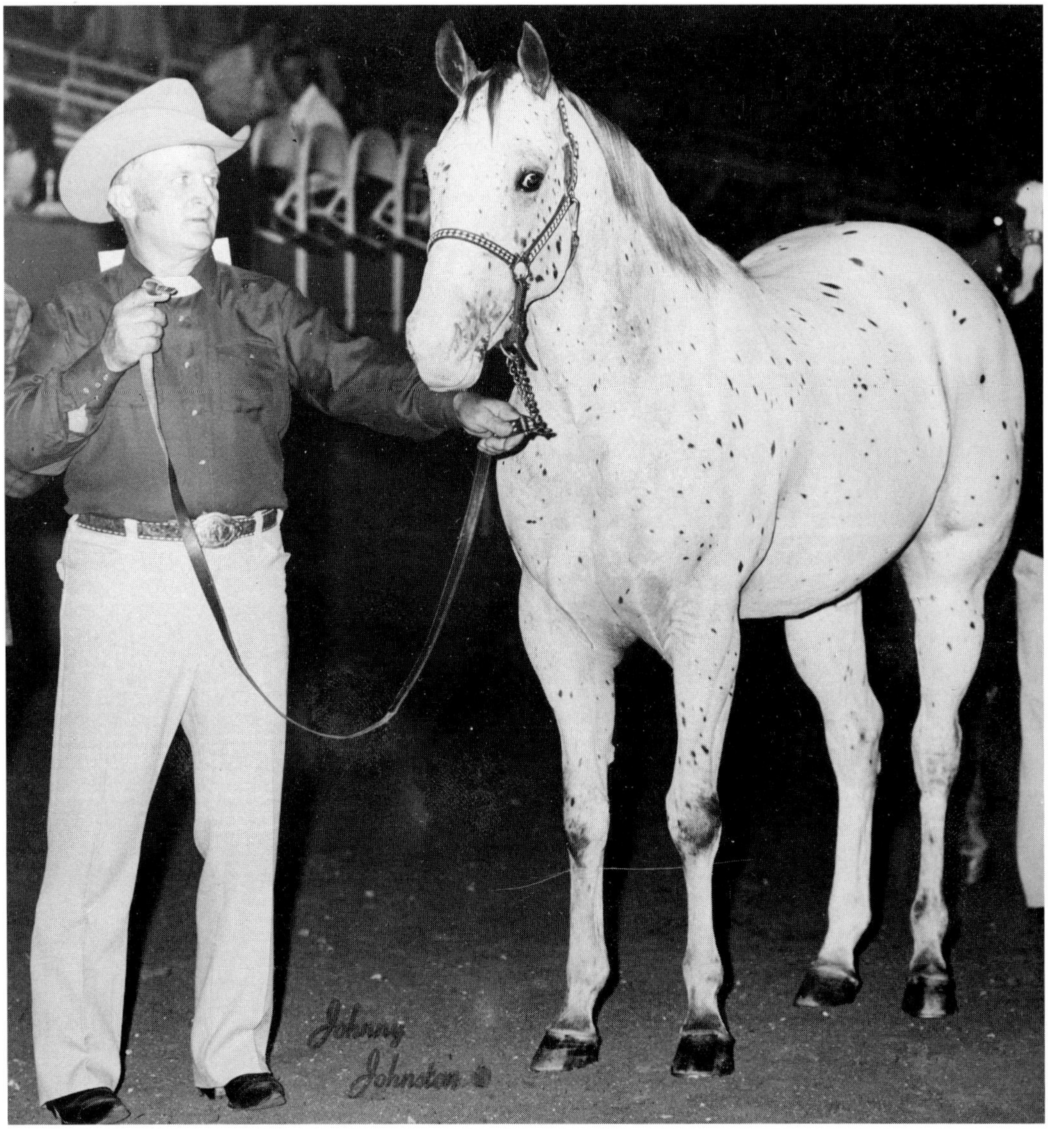

Plaudit's Southern Lady, a 1970 mare by Sir Red Plaudit and out of Southern Bar (AQHA) by Bar Mount, was the type of horse that Hank set out to breed when he entered the Appaloosa business. Southern Lady once won 25 halter championships in a row, and she is shown here standing grand at the 1972 Texas State Fair. Long-time Wiescamp Appaloosa handler George Brunelli is the exhibitor.

Photo by Johnny Johnston, Courtesy of George Brunelli

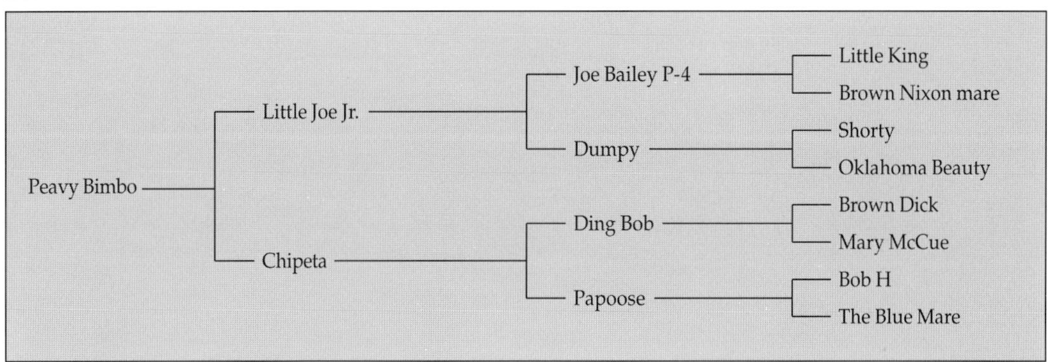

Peavy Bimbo was the first Appaloosa stallion used by Hank. By Little Joe Jr. (AQHA) and out of Chipeta (AQHA), Peavy Bimbo sired a number of daughters who went on to become top broodmares. This photo of the colorful buckskin was taken at Hank's in the early 1960s.

Photo by Darol Dickinson

Appaloosa stallion by the name of Bright Eyes Brother into this country. He was named that because he was a brother to the famous AQHA race mare, Maddon's Bright Eyes. Both were out of Plaudette.

"I was familiar with this blood because Joy Ann and Question Mount, two of my better mares, were out of Red Bird Shoemaker, who was by Nick S. and out of Plaudette.

"Anyway, Loretta spent some time at Cecil's in the late 1950s and developed a liking for Appaloosas. So we got into the Appaloosa business."

Hank began his Appaloosa program with the purchase of two mares, Robert's Frosty Ruth and Miss Lovely, at the September 1960 Carey Appaloosa Ranch sale in Denver. Laramie Lassie, a good roan mare of Coke Roberds breeding, and

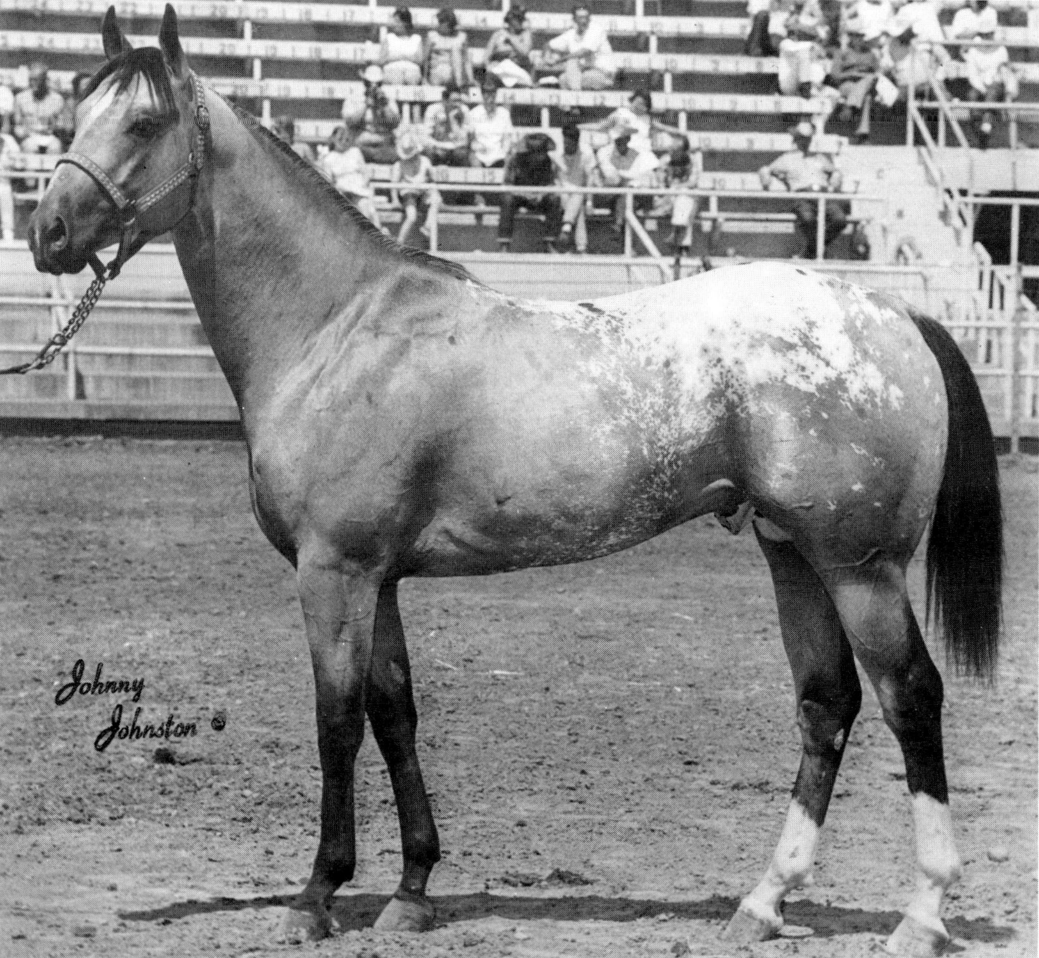

The best Wiescamp-bred son of Peavy Bimbo was Peavy's Fireball, a 1964 stallion out of Little Cowgirl (AQHA). Here he is after winning the 3-year-old stallion class at the 1967 National Appaloosa Show in Walla Walla, Washington.

Photo by Johnny Johnston

Cheyenne Maid, a Wyoming-bred mare, were added shortly thereafter.

In the late fall of 1960, Hank located a weanling stallion he thought would cross well on his small band of Appaloosa mares. This was Red Plaudit, a red leopard-patterned horse by Juaquin and out of Wavy by *Wave Of Eire (TB). Also appearing in the colorful youngster's pedigree were Booger Red and Plaudit, two horses Hank was very familiar with.

"Red Plaudit was bred by Clara Wilkins, a neighbor of mine," says Hank. "She had been raising this line of Juaquin leopard Appaloosa horses for a number of years. They were generally pretty good-headed, with small spots over their bodies except where their face and leg markings were. Often times, their rear ends were solid-white, almost like there was a white blanket laid on top of the leopard color. They were attractive.

"I liked some things about Red Plaudit and figured I could make him work, so I bought him."

To fill in as a herd sire until Red Plaudit was old enough to handle the chore, Hank purchased a half-interest in Peavy Bimbo, one of the better-known Appaloosa stallions of that era.

"I knew all about Peavy Bimbo and his kinfolks," Hank relates. "He was a good-headed buckskin horse with a white blanket over his hips that was full of dark gold spots. Both of his parents were registered Quarter Horses.

"His sire, Little Joe Jr., was a top show

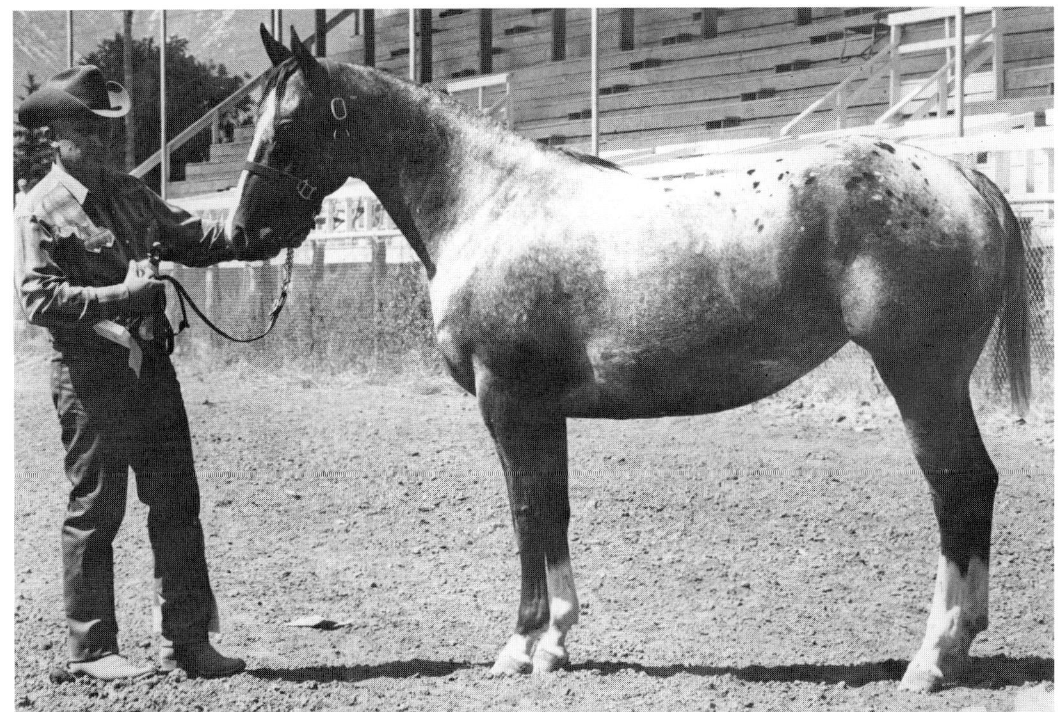

Bimbo's Lassie, a 1964 mare by Peavy Bimbo and out of Laramie Lassie by TK Roany, had the blood of the well-known Coke Roberds horses on both sides of her pedigree. The black roan mare was shown for several years before being placed in the Wiescamp broodmare band. She is pictured here with George Brunelli after standing grand at a Colorado Appaloosa show in the late 1960s.

Photo by Camera San Juan, Courtesy of George Brunelli

horse who once held the world's record for 440 yards around a turn. Bimbo's dam was a mare named Chipeta. She was listed as a roan Quarter Horse mare, but she was really a roan Appaloosa.

"Chipeta was a straight-bred Coke Roberds/Marshall Peavy-bred mare," continues Hank. "She was by Ding Bob, who was a great-grandson of Old Fred, and she was out of Papoose, a double-bred Old Fred mare.

"Chipeta's full sister, Margie, was one of the top show and race mares in the country in the early 1940s. And when Marshall Peavy gave Papoose to Jack Casement after she was an old mare, she produced Cherokee Maiden, another one of the early Quarter Horse greats.

"So I knew what was behind Peavy Bimbo when I bought half-interest in him. I had to give $10,000 for that half-interest, but I figured I could make it work."

Appaloosa Horse Club records reveal that Hank used Peavy Bimbo for three breeding seasons—from 1961 through 1963. Peavy's Fireball, a 1964 buckskin stallion out of Little Cowgirl (AQHA), was probably the top Wiescamp-bred son of Peavy Bimbo. He was the national champion 3-year-old stallion in 1967, and showed great promise as a sire before his untimely death of colic in 1968.

Chipeta Bimbo, a 1962 palomino mare out of Spanish Lady, and Bimbo's Lassie, a 1964 black mare out of Laramie Lassie, were the two top show mares sired by Peavy Bimbo during his stay at Wiescamp's.

Sold to Laura Brest of Rapid City, S.D., Chipeta Bimbo went on to become a top halter, performance, and race mare. Bimbo's Lassie, who was retained by Hank, was one of the top Appaloosa halter mares in the Rocky Mountain region in the mid- to late 1960s.

The main contribution that Peavy Bimbo made to the Wiescamp Appaloosa program was not as a sire of show horses, however, but as the sire of broodmares. Peavy's Dunn, Bimbo's Princess, Brite Peavy, Scotch Lady, Skips Peavy, Peavy's Blackbird, Bimbo's Lassie, and Bimbo's

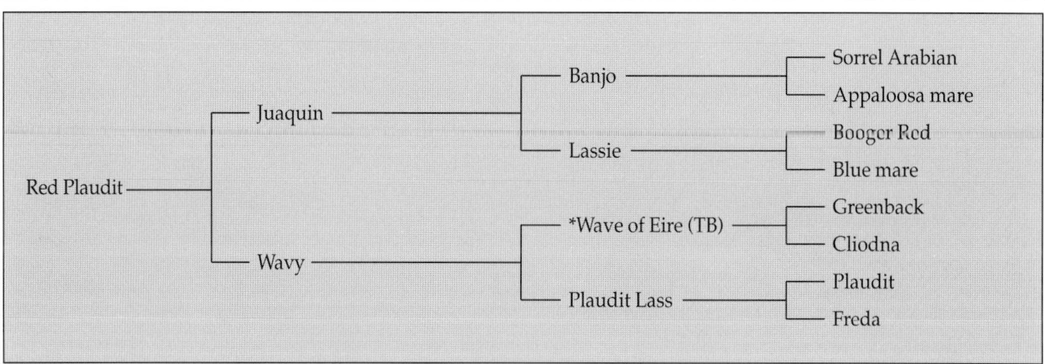

Here is one of the few existing photos of Red Plaudit, the colorful stallion who founded Hank's well-known line of Plaudit Appaloosas. It was taken of the then-yearling stallion after he had won his class at the 1961 Colorado State Fair. That's Leroy Webb at the halter.

Photo by Darol Dickinson

Lady were all retained by Hank as broodmares. Bred to Red Plaudit and his sons, they excelled as producers.

In 1962 Red Plaudit was test-bred to two solid-colored mares. The results from these breedings were the loud-colored leopard stallions Signal Fire and Prince Plaudit. Signal Fire was sold and wound up becoming a moderately successful sire in the Pacific Northwest. Prince Plaudit became a legend.

"Prince Plaudit's dam, Princess Rita, was a nice mare with some good breeding," says Hank. "She traced to Red Dog P-55, Ding Bob, and King Plaudit (TB). The year before I bred her to Red Plaudit, I bred her to Peavy Bimbo and got a nice filly I kept.

"Prince Plaudit was a nice colt. He was kind of gangly as a yearling, but he grew out of that. We showed him as a 2-year-old at the Colorado State Fair, and he was the grand champion there.

"Then in December of 1965, we sold him and a bunch of good Quarter Horse mares to Carl Miles."

Carl Miles was the energetic oilman from Abilene, Tex., who had made Joker B. into

Plaudit-Roulette, a 1974 stallion by Red Plaudit and out of Skip Rullah by Skip's Reward, was shown as a yearling and a 2-year-old in the Rocky Mountain region and then sold. Here he is with George Brunelli after one of his yearling wins.

Photo by Scott Trees, Courtesy of George Brunelli

one of the best-known Appaloosas in the country in the early 1960s. Joker B. was by Red Dog P-55, and was out of Blue Vitrol, a Roberds-bred Appaloosa mare.

Miles had done a lot of research into the Roberds bloodlines and was very high on them, so it was only natural that when he began looking around for a young Appaloosa stallion to replace Joker B., his search would take him to Alamosa.

"I'll never forget when Carl came here to look at horses," says Hank. "He was already pretty interested in Prince Plaudit, and he told me that he was also interested in looking at some mares.

"When he got here, I had the mares whom I had decided I would sell all up in pens. I had them arranged in groups of about six or so, and each pen had a little different price.

"Well, we spent all day looking at mares. We discussed their breeding, we discussed their show records, and we discussed their production records. During all that time, Carl never said much. I was beginning to wonder, 'What's the deal with this guy? Is he here to buy horses, or is he just a tire-kicker?'

"At the end of the day, Carl wanted to review everything we'd looked at, and everything we'd said. He had been jotting things down in a little notebook as we went along, and he started reviewing all of those notes.

"By this time, I was beginning to get a little impatient. I wasn't sure where the guy was coming from. Finally, he looked up at me and said, 'Mr. Wiescamp, I've decided to buy Prince Plaudit, and I want to buy some mares to go with him. You've sure shown me some good mares today. The trouble is that I'm not sure I'm a good enough horseman to figure out

Plaudit's-Scarlet, foaled in 1975 out of Sassy Scarlet by Skip 3 Bar, was one of the last sons of Red Plaudit. He was shown successfuly as a young horse and then used by Hank as a breeding stallion until the Wiescamp Appaloosas were dispersed.

Photo Courtesy of George Brunelli

"I thought to myself, 'Man, if he can't make a go of it in the Appaloosa business with this set of horses, nobody can.'"

which of these mares will cross the best on Prince. I'm afraid that the only way I'll ever be sure of making the right choices is to take them all.'

"And that's what he did. He bought 'em all. I sold Prince Plaudit and over 30 head of mares to Carl. And he got some good ones. Stepaway was one of 'em, Cheri Mac was another, Skip Mama was another, and Sis Nick was another.

"I sold to Carl daughters of Nick Shoemaker, Plaudit, Show Boat, Music Mount, Skipper W, Nick W, Spanish Nick, Shawnee Sheik, Sheik's Image, Skipper's Lad, Spot Cash, Skippa String, and Bar Mount. I sold him the mothers of Sure Cash, Skipador, and Skipette.

"I thought to myself, 'Man, if he can't make a go of it in the Appaloosa business with this set of horses, nobody can.'"

Miles did make a go of it. Using the same energy and promotional skills that had made Joker B. a household name, he set about building a program based on the greatest concentration of Wiescamp breeding ever assembled outside of Alamosa.

Prince Plaudit had been shown three times prior to being purchased by Miles, standing grand each time. Shown as an aged stallion by Miles, he stood grand at such events as the Denver, Fort Worth, and San Antonio livestock shows.

Retired to stud and bred to the Wiescamp mares, he became the best known and most successful Appaloosa sire of his era.

Appaloosa Horse Club records show that Prince Plaudit sired the earners of over 40 national or world titles and 30 reserves. His get placed in the top 10 at the national and world level more than 175 times. In get-of-sire competition, Prince Plaudit won the nationals in 1969, 1975, and 1976, and the world in 1975.

The majority of his early show and breeding stars were out of the Wiescamp mares. Prince's Bird, a five-time national and world champion, was out of Skip Bird by Skipper W. Prince's Mac, a three-time world champion, was out of Cheri Mac.

Prince's Lauri, a three-time world champion driving horse, was out of Skip In Scotch by Skipper's King. Prince's Sheik, a two-time world champion reining horse, was out of School Dress by School Meister. Prince's Nancy, a two-time national champion, was out of Sheik's Reign by Sheik's Image.

Prince's Question, Prince's Show Lady, Prince Charlie Boy, Princess Copper, and Prince Skiphustle were all national or world champions, and all were out of Wiescamp mares.

And, as would be expected, the sons and daughters of Prince Plaudit out of the Wiescamp mares went on to become great breeding horses in their own right. Howdy Prince Plaudit, Prince's Nick, Prince Hank, Prince PL Bar, Prince's Mac, Prince Plaudit Jr., Prince's Fury, Prince's Image, Prince Edward, and Prince Spot Cash were all sons of Prince Plaudit out of Wiescamp mares. All were highly successful sires. And the daughters of Prince Plaudit out of the Wiescamp mares did just as well.

The impact that Prince Plaudit and his descendants have had on the Appaloosa breed was far-reaching and continues to this day. In whatever way you choose to measure it, the Prince Plaudit tale is one of the greatest success stories in the history of the Appaloosa breed.

Back at the Wiescamp ranch in the early 1960s, Hank's Appaloosa program was beginning to take on a successful air of its own. The year after Prince Plaudit was foaled, another son of Red Plaudit hit the ground who would wind up having a great impact on the Appaloosa breed. This was King Plaudit.

"King Plaudit was out of Cheyenne Maid," relates Hank. "She was bred by Everett Coy, of Torrington, Wyoming. We never were able to pinpoint her breeding, but the way that she produced, there had to have been some good horses behind her.

"King Plaudit was a highly colored colt. He was a sorrel with a big solid white blanket from his shoulders back. He was good-headed and had a world of conformation. I sold him to Wallace Barbee of Houston, Tex., and he went on to make a top show horse and sire."

Like Prince Plaudit, King Plaudit was shown by his new owner and fared well, standing grand at some of the bigger shows on the southern plains. Retired to

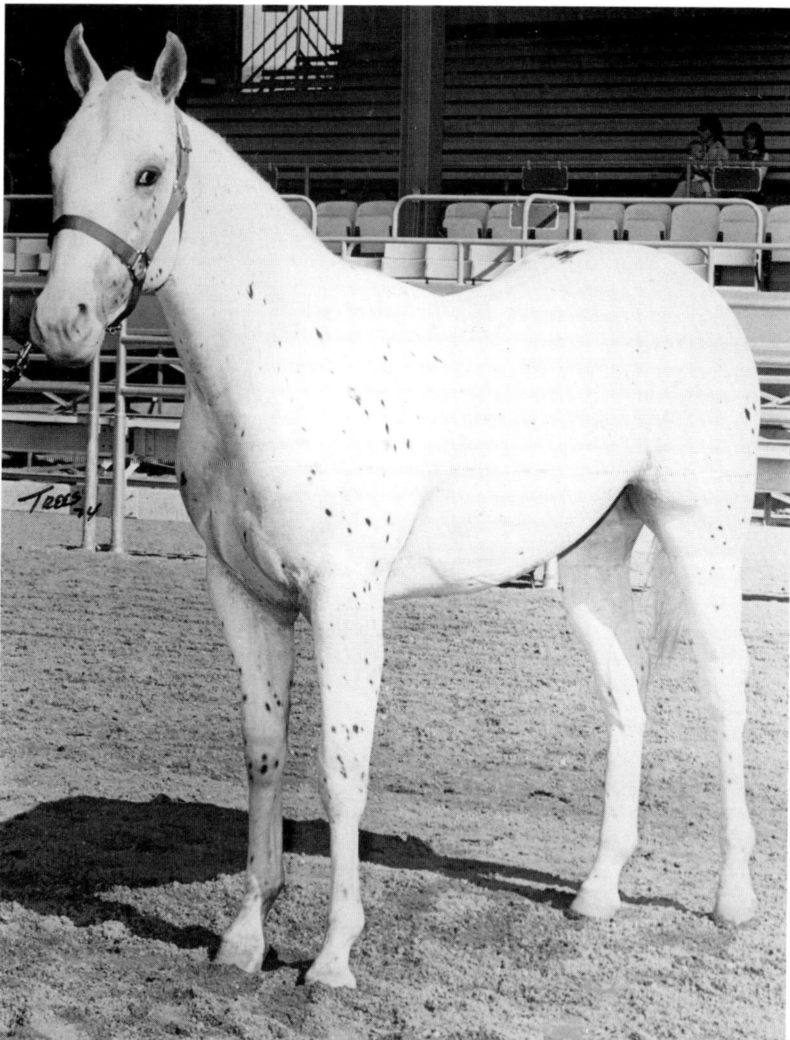

Skip It Sure, a 1973 mare by Skippa String (AQHA) and out of Sure Plaudit by Red Plaudit, seemed destined for great things as a show horse and broodmare. Shown here as a yearling, she was killed by lightning before she had a chance to live up to her promising potential. **Photo by Scott Trees, Courtesy of George Brunelli**

Plaudits Double-Me, a 1974 mare by Sir Red Plaudit and out of Plaudita's Rita by Red Plaudit, was shown seven times as a 2-year-old and won her class every time. Here she is with George Brunelli after her win at the prestigious Estes Park, Colo., show.

Photo by Michelle, Courtesy of George Brunelli

stud, he also became one of the leading sires of his day.

Spring Plaudit, a 1970 mare out of Sassy Breeze, and Bar Plaudit, a 1971 stallion out of Sugar Bee Bars, were two of his greatest show get. Among his other champions were Skip Plaudit, Plaudit Doll, Russo's Candy Spots, Plaudit's Skipperette, Splash Plaudit, Streak Plaudit, and Schoolgirl Plaudit.

Also like his famous half-brother, King Plaudit was a national champion in get-of-sire competition. His victory came at the 1971 Appaloosa Nationals in Las Vegas.

Prince Plaudit and King Plaudit were without a doubt the two sons of Red Plaudit who had the greatest impact on the Appaloosa breed. There were, however, several other sons of his who acquitted themselves well as show and/or breeding horses.

"When I bred Sir Plaudit, I felt I had taken the Appaloosa program to the next level."

Plaudit Rebound, a 1968 stallion out of Scotch Lady (the Appaloosa, not the Quarter Horse), Skipper-J-Plaudit, a 1974 stallion out of Skipper's Joy, and Plaudit's-Scarlet, a 1975 stallion out of Sassy Scarlet, were sons who were retained by Hank.

Others, such as Plaudit's Gold, Plaudit's Red, Major Plaudit, Bim Plaudit, Royal Plaudit, Brite Plaudit, Plaudit's Roulette, and Supreme Plaudit, went on to achieve success after being sold.

Sir Plaudit, a 1966 black leopard stallion by Red Plaudit and out of Laramie Lassie, is rated by Hank as being one of the very best sons of Red Plaudit.

"When I bred Sir Plaudit," comments Hank, "I felt I had taken the Appaloosa program to the next level. He was just as good-headed as his daddy, and he was way better in every other way. He had the

Prince Plaudit, a 1963 stallion by Red Plaudit and out of Princess Rita, was one of the most successful products of the Wiescamp Appaloosa program. An all-time leading sire of the Appaloosa breed, Prince is shown here with George Brunelli after standing grand at the 1965 Colorado State Fair.

Photo by Darol Dickinson

muscle; he had the looks. He was my choice to go on with, but I never really got the chance to. He died young."

Among the few foals that Hank did get by Sir Plaudit were two that he considers to be among the best Appaloosas he ever bred.

Sir Red Plaudit, a 1968 red roan stallion, was out of Skylark by Shawnee Sheik. Plaudit's Southern Lady, a 1970 leopard mare, was out of Southern Bar by Bar Mount.

"Sir Red Plaudit did not have the charisma that Sir Plaudit had," comments Hank. "But he had a lot good points and I kept him as a breeding stallion until I got out of the Appaloosa business. One of the good colts I raised by Sir Red Plaudit was Big Bluffer, a 1973 model out of Bimbo's Princess by Peavy Bimbo. Bimbo's Princess was out of Princess Rita, the dam of Prince Plaudit. I sold Big Bluffer to Bob and Shirley Allen of Albion, New York. They gelded him and won the world with him as a 2-year-old.

"Two other good show horses I got from Sir Red Plaudit were Plaudits Double Me and Plaudits Red Rose. They were full

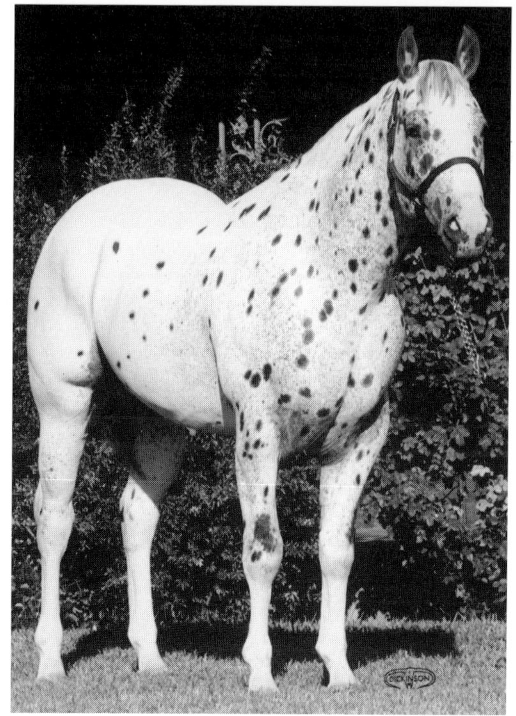

Here is Prince Plaudit as a mature horse at Carl Miles' ranch outside Abilene, Texas. The colorful leopard sired over 40 national and world champions and won the get-of-sire at either the national or world show 4 times.

Photo by Darol Dickinson

Prince's Shiek was another member of Prince Plaudit's first foal crop who achieved success as a show horse. Foaled in 1967 out of School Dress by School Meister, he was a two-time world champion Appaloosa reining horse. He is shown here with John Brown up after winning the senior reining at the 1972 Houston Livestock Show.
Photo by Jim Keeland, Courtesy of *The Appaloosa Journal*

sisters out of Plaudit's Rita by Red Plaudit. I showed Double Me seven times as a 2-year-old and she placed first every time. Red Rose was grand and reserve champion many times.

"Plaudit's Southern Lady was a beautiful mare. She was a feminine version of her daddy. I showed her and she won a lot of the big shows for us. She was the grand champion mare at the 1972 Texas State Fair. She beat at least six national or world champions in that show alone."

Red Plaudit was also the sire of several other top daughters, such as Plaudit's Lady and Sure Plaudit, whom Hank first showed and then placed in his Appaloosa broodmare band.

At first Hank just bred Red Plaudit to the Appaloosa and Quarter Horse mares he had purchased expressly for that purpose. Eventually, however, he bred him to some of his top Old Fred-bred Quarter Horse mares.

"When I decided to breed some of my own mares to Red Plaudit," he says, "I didn't deal from the bottom of the deck. I bred him to mares like Skipper's Joy, who stood grand at Denver. I bred him to some of my best Bar Mount mares, like Skip's Gift and Skip's Design. I bred him to daughters of Skipper W, Skip's Reward, and Skip 3 Bar.

"Red Plaudit was a good horse. He had an exceptional head. And he did some good for me. But, just like Skipper W, the main reason he was successful was because of the mares I put him on. I had that good set of Peavy Bimbo mares, and I added some of my better Quarter Horse mares to the mix. What stud couldn't have gotten it done with that set of mares?"

In 1969, pleased with the way that the Peavy Bimbo mares were crossing on his Red Plaudit stallions, Hank arranged for the lease of several top Appaloosas of similar bloodlines from Lane Hudson of Denver.

Among the horses he leased were Genevieve Peavy, a daughter of Peavy Bimbo, and Bright Delight, a daughter of Bright Eyes Brother. These two mares were both national grand champions at halter.

Mighty Marshall, a young stallion by Mighty Bright (by Bright Eyes Brother) and out of Overdue Peavy, a maternal half-sister to Peavy Bimbo, was also leased for a year to be bred to the Red Plaudit mares.

By the mid- to late 1970s, Hank's

The early get of Prince Plaudit, out of the Wiescamp mares, literally rewrote Appaloosa show and breeding history. Here is Prince's Helen, a 1967 mare by Prince Plaudit and out of Skip Mama by Skipper's Lad. She is pictured with ApHC Hall-of-Fame trainer Harry Reed after winning the 2-year-old filly class at the 1969 Houston Livestock Show & Rodeo.

Photo by Jim Keeland

Prince's Nick, a 1967 stallion by Prince Plaudit and out of Stepaway by Nick Shoemaker, is another example of the type of Appaloosa that was produced when Prince Plaudit was bred to the great set of Wiescamp mares that Hank sold to Carl Miles in 1965. Prince's Nick is shown here as a 3-year-old with Harry Reed. He went on to become a top show horse and sire.

King Plaudit, a 1964 stallion by Red Plaudit and out of Cheyenne Maid, was another Wiescamp-bred Appaloosa who went on to achieve fame as a show horse and sire.
Photo by Darol Dickinson

Appaloosa program was at its peak. The sons and daughters of Red Plaudit had been crossed on Hank's good Quarter Horse mares, and the results of those crosses were now in production. The better daughters and granddaughters of Red Plaudit had been bred to stallions like Skippa String and Skip N Go.

Second- and third-generation Red Plaudit stallions such as Go South, by Skip N Go and out of Plaudit's Southern Lady, and Plaudit Jet, by Plaudit Rebound and out of Laramie Lassie, were heading the breeding program. Top young mares such as Plaudit's-Step-Way, Plaudit's-Stepagain, Plaudit's Orchid, and Plaudit's So-So were being added to the broodmare band.

Then, simply put, the clock ran out on the Wiescamp Appaloosas.

In 1983 Hank made the decision to end his Appaloosa breeding program. By this time, Loretta had suffered the stoke that severely curtailed her involvement with the horses. Grant Wiescamp, into whose name the bulk of the Appaloosas had been transferred, was too engrossed in the daily management of the overall operation to devote the time that was necessary to ensure the program's continuation.

For one of the few times in his life, Hank decided to have a sale. In May of 1983, at the Alamosa sale barn, he dispersed his Appaloosa breeding operation.

In reflecting back on the years during which he was involved with the Appaloosas, Hank's observations are short and to the point.

"I tackled the Appaloosa business the same way that I tackled everything else," he states. "If I was going to be in it, I was going to give it everything I had. I was going to try to make it a success.

"When I look back on the impact that Red Plaudit, Prince Plaudit, King Plaudit, and some of the other Appaloosas I bred have had on the breed, I would have to say that I did just that."

Another great show daughter of Prince Plaudit was Prince's Show Lady. Foaled in 1970 out of Skip Mama, Show Lady won the senior western pleasure class at the 28th National Appaloosa Show in Sacramento, California. Owner A.F. Jackson of Kerrville, Tex., rode the blanket-hipped mare to her big win.

Photo by Johnny Johnston, Courtesy of *The Appaloosa Journal*

The impact that the blood of the Wiescamp horses had on the Appaloosa breed was far-reaching. Skip Bright, a 1975 stallion by Skipper's Lad and out of Bright Starlette by Bright Eyes Brother, was one of the breed's leading show horses and sires in the late 1970s and early 1980s. He's shown here with A.F. Jackson after standing grand at the 1977 Southwestern Exposition and Fat Stock Show at Fort Worth.

Photo by Don Shugart

16 The Paints

". . . as far back as I can remember, I've always had some good Paints around."

AROUND THE same time that he got into the Appaloosa business, Hank got into the registered Paint business. He had, however, owned Paint Horses for many years before that.

"When I was buying the Philmont and Ghost Ranch mares in the early 1940s, there were some good Paint mares in with them," he recalls. "Several other big ranches around Cimarron, like the WS, also had some top Paints.

"Remember now, that this was 20 years before the Paint registry came into being. But then, like now, colorful horses were easy for me to sell. So, as far back as I can remember, I've always had some good Paints around. I'd pick 'em up through farm sales and trades, and I never had any trouble reselling 'em."

One of the Paint Horses acquired by

Skip Again, a 1966 sorrel tobiano mare by Skip Hi and out of Skip Lady by Skip Hi, was one of the best of the first-generation Paint Horses bred by Hank. She was an American Paint Horse Association Champion, a Superior halter horse with 119 points, and tallied 79 points in open performance. In 1969, she was also the reserve national champion 3-year-old mare.

Photo by Marge Spence

*Here are the first two Paint mares Hank registered with the American Paint Stock Horse Association. School Girl #792, left, was a 1950 brown tobiano mare sired by Cowboy P-12 and out of Spot Time. Sky Hi #793, the sorrel tobiano mare, was a 1954 mare by Advantage (TB) and out of Wavy by *Wave of Eire (TB).*

Hank in the late 1950s was a sorrel and white tobiano mare by the name of Sky Hi.

"Sky Hi was bred by Howard Linger, the long-time executive secretary of the AQHA," notes Hank. "She was sired by Advantage (TB), a Remount Thoroughbred, and she was out of a mare by *Wave of Eire (TB), an imported Thoroughbred. *Wave of Eire (TB) was well-known in this part of the country as a sire of top ranch horses and polo ponies.

"Sky Hi didn't have much white. I bred her to Skipper's Lad in 1958, and she foaled Skip Hi the following spring. His loud color came as kind of a surprise to me."

In 1962, the American Paint Stock Horse Association was formed with Rebecca Tyler of Gainesville, Tex., as one of its chief architects. Rebecca had known Hank for years prior to this and convinced him to register Skip Hi with the fledgling organization.

"Rebecca came to visit me in the summer of 1962," says Hank. "She was laying the foundation of the American Paint Horse Association at that time. I registered Skip Hi in 1963 because of Rebecca. They gave him number 8."

From the onset, all of the Paint Horses were registered in Larry Wiescamp's name, and they were branded on the left jaw with his Lazy T brand.

"I wanted to keep the Paints separate from the Quarter Horses, and I wanted to get Larry more involved. That's why we did it the way we did."

After registering Skip Hi, Hank went ahead and registered the Paint mares he had accumulated over the years and began a Paint breeding program in earnest.

"I had bought and sold a lot of Paints by the time the registry for them was formed," says Hank. "Over the years, I kept a few of the better mares. These were the ones that we wound up registering.

"Those first mares were good ones. They had to have been, or I wouldn't have kept 'em. And they had some good 'hot' blood behind 'em. There were daughters of Remount Thoroughbred horses such as

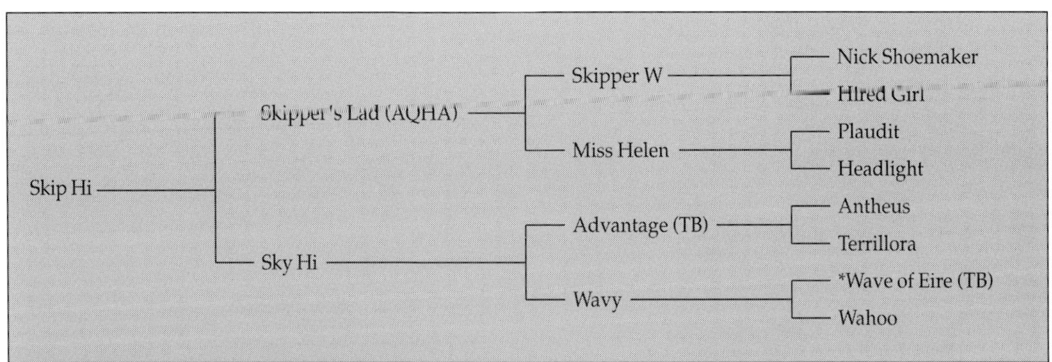

Skip Hi, a 1959 sorrel and white stallion by Skipper's Lad (AQHA) and out of Sky Hi, founded the well-known family of tobiano Paints that Hank raises to this day.

Photo by MaryAnn Czermak, Courtesy of *The Paint Horse Journal*

"When I got into the Paint business, I didn't start at the bottom. I was several rungs up on the ladder. . . ."

Advantage (TB), After Dark (TB), and Isolater (TB) among 'em. And there were daughters of Gold Heels, Tadpole, and Moon, who all had a shot or more of Coke Roberds breeding.

"When I got into the Paint business, I didn't start at the bottom. I was several rungs up the ladder, I'll grant you that."

Although American Paint Horse Association records do reveal that he earned 1 reining point, Skip Hi's most profound influence on the Paint Horse breed was not as a show horse, but as a sire.

From a total of 120 registered get, he was the sire of 37 performers who earned 466 open halter and 995 open performance points. They also accumulated 275 points in youth and amateur competition. Five were APHA Champions.

Skippa Streak, a 1964 tobiano stallion by Skip Hi and out of Cheyenne Lil, was his sire's first show superstar. Sold by Hank as a yearling, he was a two-time national champion in western pleasure, a three-time reserve national champion at halter, and an APHA Champion with 100 halter and 178 performance points.

Skippa Streak also went on to become a highly successful sire in his own right. APHA records reveal that he was the sire of 46 performers who earned 687 open halter and 2,747 open performance points. Of his get, 11 were APHA Champions, 9 were national champions, and 22 earned Superiors in halter and/or performance.

Skippetta, a 1967 tobiano mare by Skippa Streak and out of Jackie Van (AQHA), was a Supreme Champion, a national champion halter and calf roping horse, and an APHA Champion with 101 open halter and 161 open performance points.

In 1974, Hank leased Skippa Streak back and bred him to a dozen of his top mares. Skip's Artist, a 1975 tobiano stallion out of Skip's Aid by Skip's Lad, was one of the foals that he got.

Sold to Marsha McGovney of Penalosa, Kan., Skip's Artist went on to become one of the Paint Horse breed's all-time leading performance sires. Through 1995, his get had earned 343 Registers of Merit and over 13,000 performance points.

By the time the late 1960s rolled around, Hank had decided not only to breed Paints, but to show a few as well.

"I would guess that Skip Again was about the first top Paint we showed," he recalls. "She was a 1966 mare, by Skip Hi and out of Skip Lady by Skip Hi. I usually do not breed father to daughter, but I did in this case and it turned out all right.

"Skip Again was a nice mare. She would have been nice no matter what color or breed she was. We showed her quite a bit in the late 1960s and early 1970s and she won her share. She earned her APHA Championship and had over 100 halter points. In 1969, she was the reserve national champion 3-year-old mare."

Skip Hi sired a number of other Paints for Hank who went on to become successful show horses. Skipolator, a 1967 tobiano mare out of Risolator, and Skippa Rope, a 1968 tobiano stallion out of Baby Doll McCue, earned their APHA Championships.

Skipover, a 1964 tobiano stallion out of Silver Sash (AQHA) earned 7 halter and 76 performance points. Skip-A-Dollar,

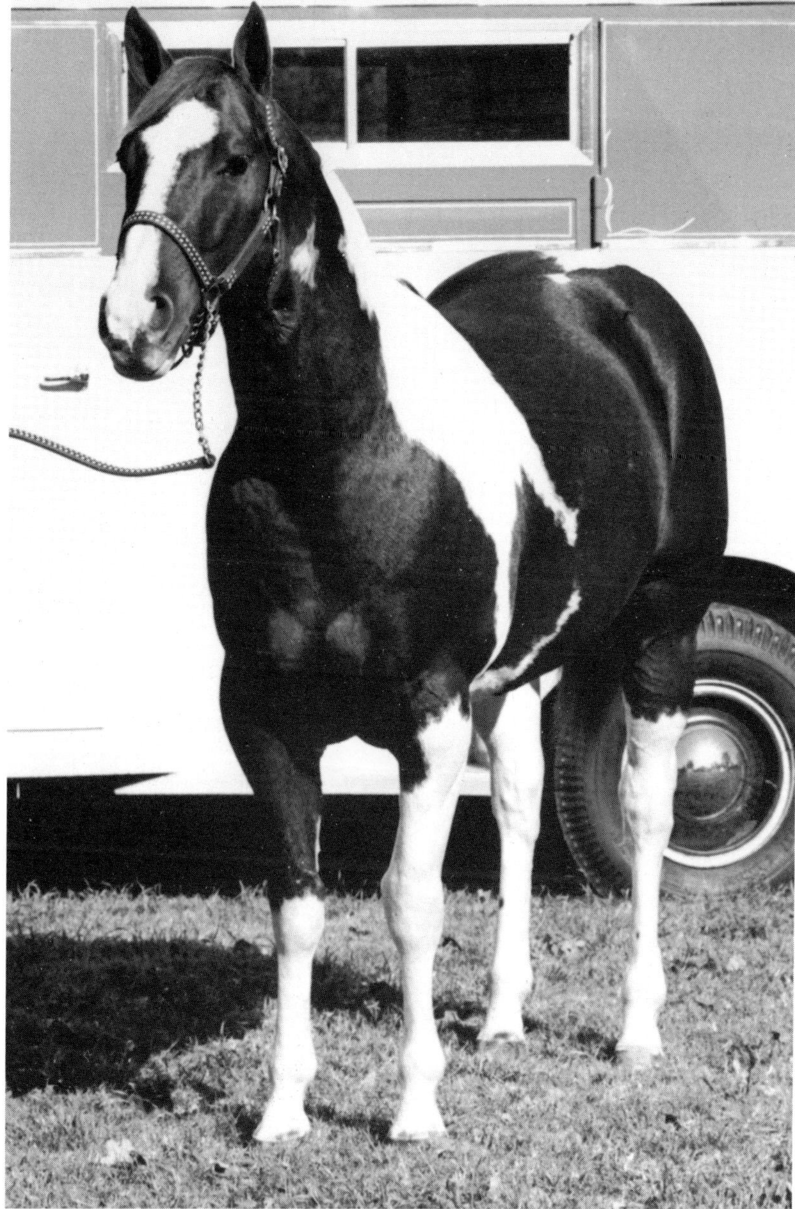

Skippa Streak, a 1964 sorrel tobiano stallion by Skip Hi and out of Cheyenne Lil, was his sire's first show superstar. He was a two-time national champion in western pleasure and a three-time reserve national champion at halter. He also went on to become a leading Paint Horse sire. **Photo by Marge Spence**

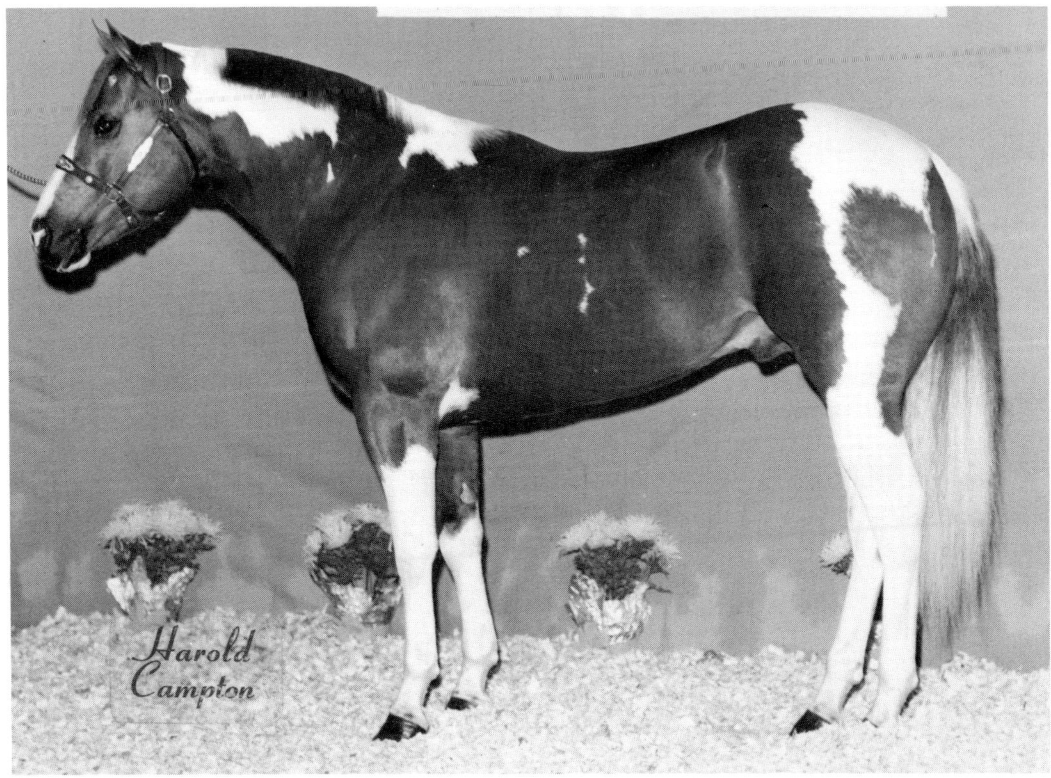

Skip's Artist, a 1975 sorrel tobiano stallion by Skippa Streak and out of Skip's Aid by Skip's Lad, was bred by Hank and sold as a young horse to Marsha McGovney of Penalosa, Kansas. He went on to become a leading sire of Paint performance horses.

Photo by Harold Campton, Courtesy of Marsha McGovney

HF Skip Supreme, a 1982 sorrel tobiano mare by Skip's Artist and out of Skip Supreme, won the 2-year-old western pleasure futurity at the 1984 APHA World Show in Fort Worth.

Photo by Don Shugart, Courtesy of Marsha McGovney

Skipolator, a 1967 sorrel tobiano mare by Skip Hi and out of Risolator by Isolater (TB), was an early Wiescamp-bred APHA Champion. She earned 28 halter and 50 performance points in seven events.

Photo by Marge Spence

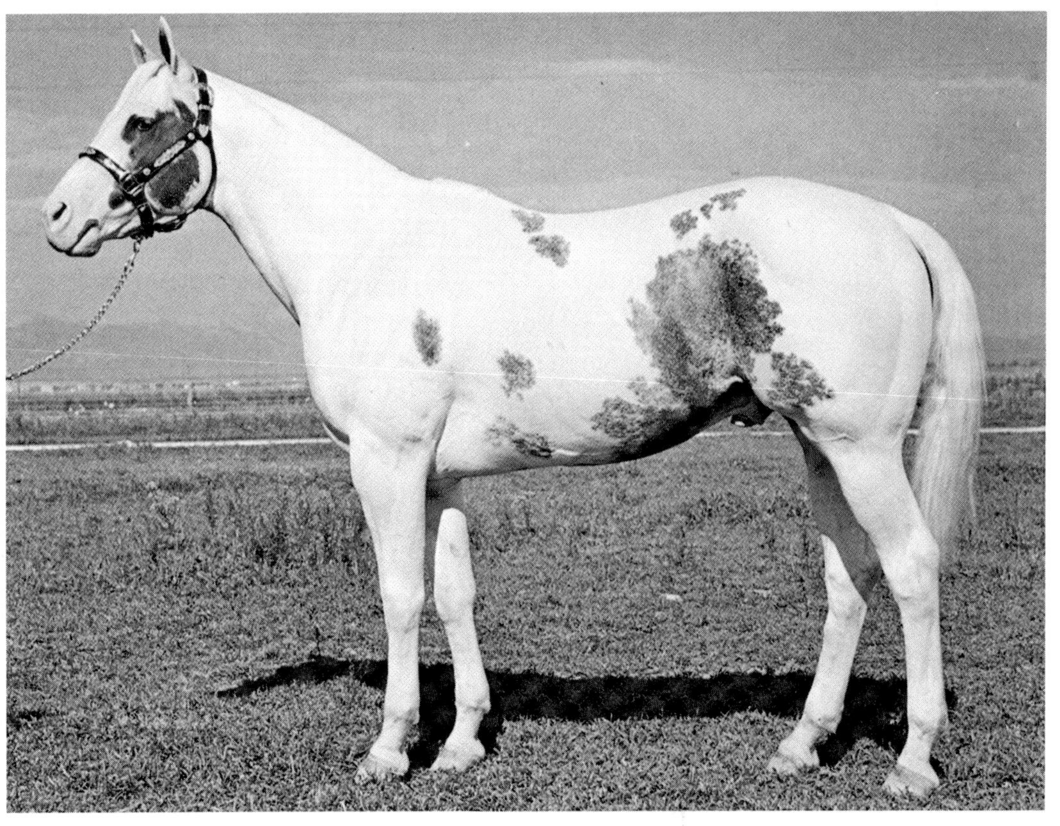

Skippa Rope, a 1968 tobiano stallion by Skip Hi and out of Baby Doll McCue by Cotton McCue, was another early APHA Champion produced by the Wiescamp Paint program. He earned 30 halter and 65 performance points en route to his championship, and went on to sire five open and youth national champions and seven open and youth APHA Champions.

Photo by Darol Dickinson

Skip Mount, a 1969 sorrel overo gelding by Skipper's Lad and out of Sassy Sheila (AQHA) by Skip 3 Bar, was one of the most durable show horses of his era. He was an open APHA Champion and also earned four youth APHA Championships with four riders. He is shown here with Kip Boomhower of Russell, Kan., aboard.
Photo by Harold Campton, Courtesy of Jerry Boomhower

Skip Sue, Skipper's Dude, and Skip's Nick were all point-earners at halter and/or in performance.

In the late 1960s, Hank sold Skip Hi to Robert and Jo-An Soso of Live Oak, California. He continued to do the same good job for them as a sire that he had done for Hank.

Skip's Bandit, a 1972 tobiano gelding out of Sunglow Senorita (AQHA), earned his APHA Championship. Skip's Shine, a 1973 tobiano mare out of My Shiny Flash (AQHA), earned 45 open halter points, and Skip And Scamp, a 1979 tobiano stallion out of Scamp's Easter (AQHA), earned 75 open performance points.

Skip Hi changed hands twice more during his lifetime and was owned by Lynn Henry of Crows Landing, Calif., at the time of his death in 1983.

The Paint stallion that Hank chose to replace Skip Hi was Skip's Lad, a 1964 sorrel tobiano out of Skip Joy.

"Skip Hi had done me some good," relates Hank. "He left me with a nice set of young mares. But it was time to take the Paint program to the next rung on the ladder, and Skip's Lad was the horse I chose to do that.

"Skip's Lad was colored a lot like his daddy. He had a little more white. He looked more like my Quarter Horses though. And why shouldn't he have? He was a grandson of Skipper's Lad on the top, and he was out of Skip Joy, one of my good Skipper W-bred Quarter Horse mares.

"Skip Joy was by Sir Teddy, an AQHA Champion son of Sirlette, and she was out of Skipper's Joy, one of the better daughters of Skipper W. With mares like Miss Helen, Silver Leche, and Joy Ann close up in his pedigree, I figured Skip's Lad would get it done as a sire. He didn't disappoint me."

Skip's Lad sired only 43 registered foals. Twenty-two of them were APHA perform-

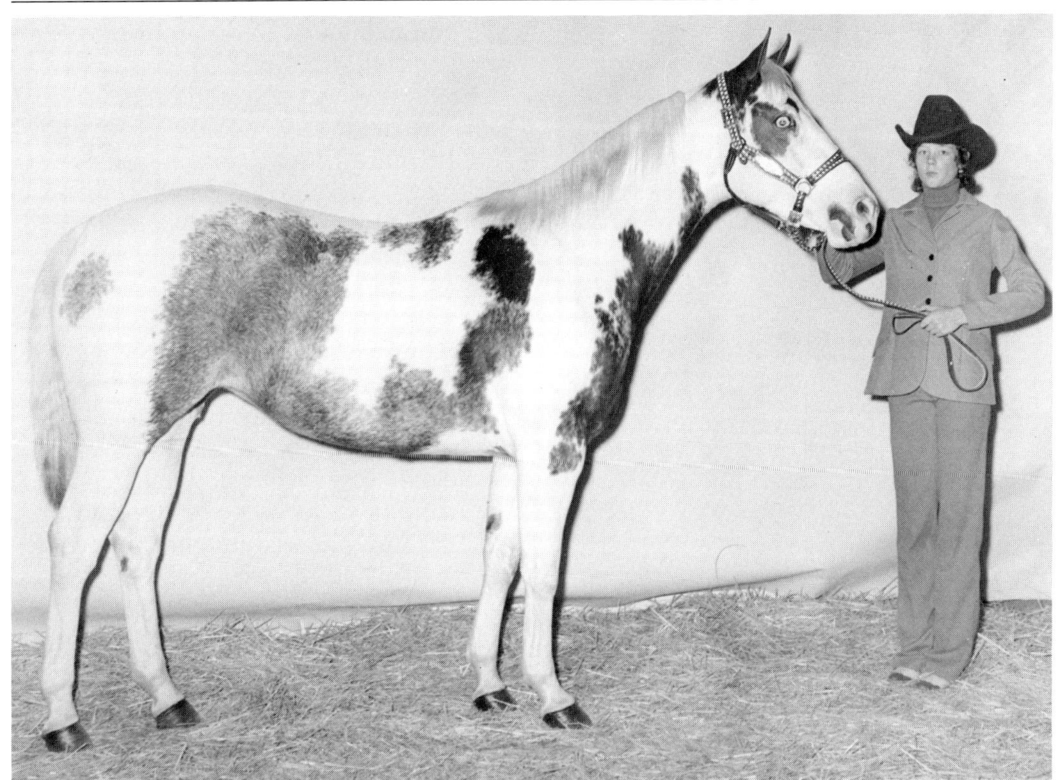

Skiparette, a 1971 sorrel tobiano mare by Skip's Scholar (AQHA) and out of Slip Hi by Skip Hi, was another top Paint youth horse bred by Hank. Shown here with Skiparette is Denise Boomhower of Russell, Kan., one of several youths who showed the colorful mare.

Photo Courtesy of Jerry Boomhower

Here is a pair of young broodmares who are part of Hank's current Paint breeding program. They are shown in a mountain meadow west of Alamosa that Hank bought years ago and that his wife, Freda, resowed by hand. Says Hank of the meadow, "It's as close to Heaven as I've found on this earth."

Photo by Darrell Dodds

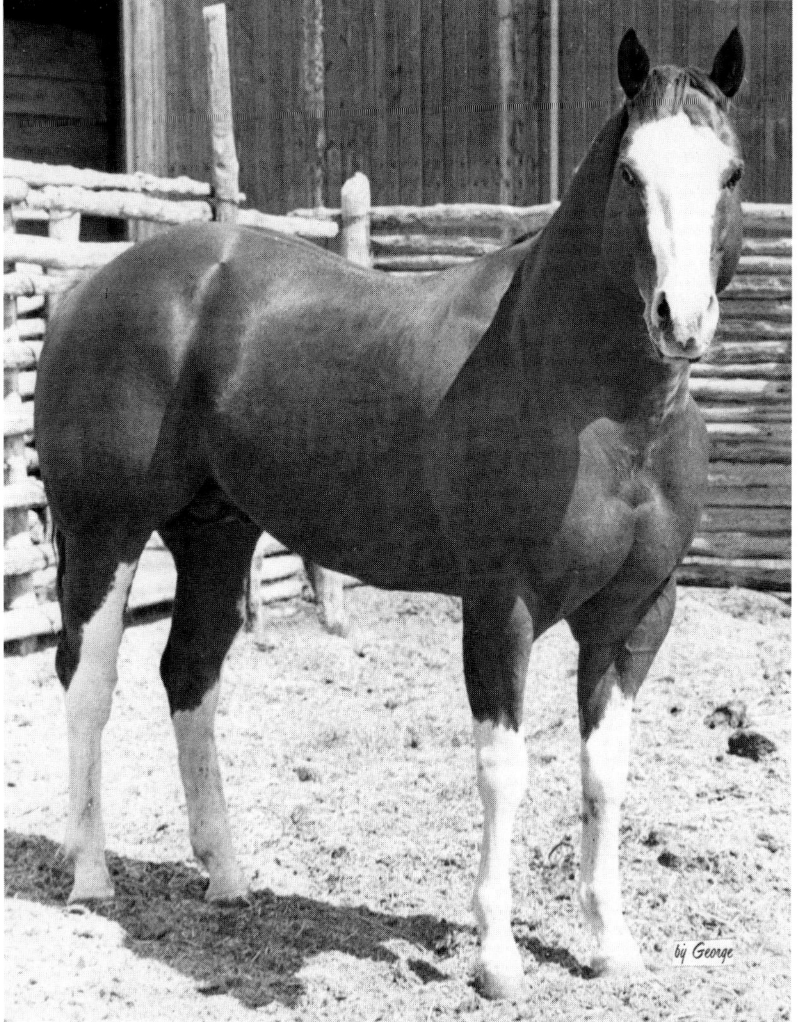

ers, and they earned a total of 337 open halter and 366 open performance points. Five were APHA Champions, and three earned Superiors in halter or performance.

Skip Mount, a 1969 overo gelding out of Sassy Sheila (AQHA) by Skip 3 Bar, was one of the most durable Paint show horses of his day. In open competition he was an APHA Champion and a Superior halter horse with 110 points. As a youth mount, he earned APHA Youth Championships with four riders.

Cream 'N Sugar, a 1969 dun tobiano mare by Skip's Lad and out of Bally Bars by Boulder Bars, was another top open and youth show horse.

"Bally Bars was one of the good early mares we registered with the association," recalls Hank. "She was one of the few legitimate cropouts that we put into our original Paint broodmare band. She came by her excess white markings honestly because she went back to Old Fred on both sides of her pedigree."

Cream 'N Sugar lived up to all of the potential that the good breeding behind her sire and dam bequeathed her. In open competition she was an APHA Champion with Superiors in halter and trail. Shown in youth, she tallied three APHA Youth Championships and five youth Superior awards. All told she accumulated 724 points in APHA-sanctioned competition.

Still another top all-around show horse by Skip's Lad was Skip's Kitty, a 1970 mare out of Kitty's Pride by Crazyweather.

"I let my neighbor Walt Alsbaugh breed some mares to Skip's Lad," says Hank. "One of the mares he bred to him was Kitty's Pride, an overo mare who traced to Cowboy P-12 and Plaudit. So she had the blood to nick on Skip's Lad, and she did."

Like Skip Mount and Cream 'N Sugar, Skip's Kitty did well in both open and youth competition. She was an APHA Youth Champion with three youth Superior awards, and earned 384 open and youth points.

Among the other good show horses sired by Skip's Lad while Hank owned him were the APHA Champions Skipadoo, a 1968 tobiano mare out of Skip Shi, and Skip's Champ, a 1969 tobiano stallion out of Skip's Flash.

Skip's Lad was also the sire of Hank-A-Chief, one of the leading sires of the Paint Horse breed.

"I let Rebecca Tyler breed Cherokee Maiden, her Paint show mare, to Skip's Lad," says Hank. "She got a loud-colored stud colt she named Hank-A-Chief, and he went on to become a top sire."

Hank-A-Chief sired a total of 473 registered foals. In open competition they earned a pair of national championships, 14 APHA Championships,

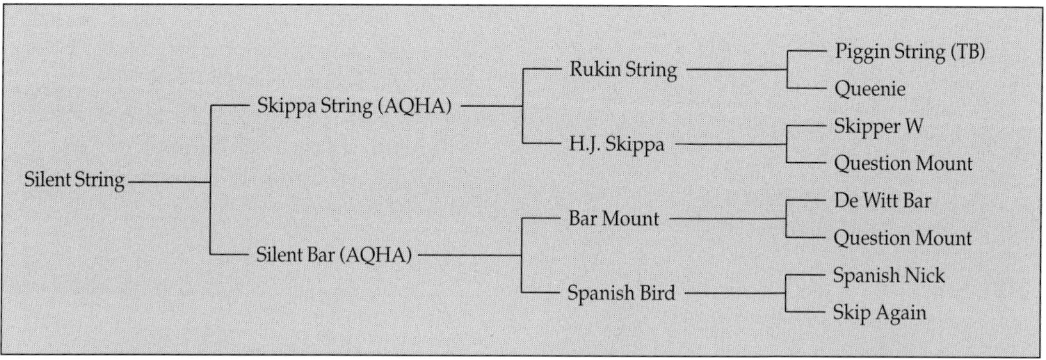

Shown on the opposite page and here are two shots of Silent String, a 1965 stallion by Skippa String (AQHA) and out of Silent Bar (AQHA) by Bar Mount. Although his high stockings and one white spot made him ineligible for registration with the AQHA, Hank rates the classy sorrel stallion as one of the greatest individuals to ever come out of his Quarter Horse breeding program. Silent String was eventually registered with the APHA, and exerted a positive influence on the Paint breed.

Photos by George

and 13 Superior awards. In the youth and amateur divisions, they earned 12 APHA Championships and 13 Superior awards. Altogether, they earned over 7,000 open, youth, and amateur show points.

In the late 1960s, Hank decided to sell all of his Paints. As was noted earlier, he sold Skip Hi to Robert and Jo-An Soso of Live Oak, California. The original deal that Hank made with the Sosos was to sell them Skip Hi, Skip's Lad, and all of the Paint broodmares.

Shortly after this, however, and before the bulk of the horses were physically transferred, Robert Soso was killed in a farm accident. Hank and Jo-An decided that she would be better off with fewer horses, so in the end, she got Skip Hi, Skip's Lad, and half of the mares.

Skip's Lad died shortly after this, and

Because of the intensified Old Fred blood that was behind the Wiescamp Quarter Horses, they sometimes produced excess-white foals or cropouts. Here is Skip Barta, a 1969 overo mare by Skip 3 Bar (AQHA) and out of Skipper's Barta (AQHA) by Skipper's King. The powerfully built mare was an early APHA Champion and a multiple producer of the same. **Photo by George**

Hank (center) with his friends Bette Zane Smith and Ed Roberts discussing broodmares and foals in one of Hank's mountain pastures. Ed is the executive secretary of the American Paint Horse Association. This picture was taken by Darrell Dodds, editor of the Paint Horse Journal, *in June 1993.*

the Paint Horse breed was robbed of one of its most promising young sires.

It should be noted that, from day one, Hank bred for the tobiano pattern in his Paints, even though he did get some overos.

"I've always bred for tobianos in my Paints for two reasons," he notes. "First of all, they breed stronger, colorwise. Secondly, tobianos almost always have normal-colored eyes with dark linings around them.

"We are at 7,500 feet above sea level in this valley, and horses with blue eyes and pink pigment around those eyes don't do well here. They develop a lot of cancer."

Breeding the family of Quarter Horses that he does, however, it was inevitable that Hank would get some with excessive white markings. These horses, of course, were not eligible for registration with AQHA and many wound up being registered as Paints.

Skip Barta, a 1969 overo mare by Skip 3 Bar and out of Skipper's Barta by Skipper's King, was one of the first Quarter Horses with excess white Hank registered with the APHA. She was put on the show circuit and earned her APHA Championship. Retired to the broodmare band, she also excelled as a producer.

Silent String, a 1965 sorrel stallion by Skippa String and out of Silent Bar by Bar Mount, was another early excess-white Quarter Horse; Hank had no choice but to register him as a Paint.

"Silent String was one of the greatest horses I ever raised," states Hank. "He was turned down by the AQHA because his stockings were too high and he had a white spot on his belly. I got a personal letter from Howard Linger, who was the executive secretary of the AQHA at the time. He said turning Silent String down was one of the hardest things he had ever had to do as an employee of the association.

"But turn him down he did, so I registered him as a Paint."

Silent String lived out his entire life on the Wiescamp Ranch. He was only shown one time, at Pueblo, Colo., and stood grand. Used lightly by Hank in his Paint program, he sired 72 registered foals.

Nine of his foals earned 318 open halter and 72 open performance points. Silent Princess, a 1976 overo mare out of Skip Barta by Skip 3 Bar, was the reserve national champion 2-year-old mare in 1978 and the reserve national champion 3-year-old the following year. She was also a Superior halter horse with 156 open halter points.

Silent Barta, an overo full sister to Silent Princess foaled in 1977, was also a Superior halter horse, as was String Twice, a 1977 overo mare by Silent String and out of Skippa Challenge (AQHA) by Skippa String.

Skippa Twice, a 1975 overo stallion by Silent String and out of Skipaletta by Skippa String, earned 38 halter points. Silent Cord, a 1978 overo stallion by Silent String and out of Skip Fantacia by Skip Rama, earned 46 performance points in five events.

"As far as the Paint program goes," remarks Hank, "Silent String did sire a number of good show horses for us. But the main thing that he did was sire sons and daughters who went on to become great sires and producers in their own right.

"Silent String was one of the greatest sires I've ever raised."

Skippa Scotch, a 1969 overo stallion by Skippa String and out of Scotch Charm by Skipper's King, was another excess-white Quarter Horse who was registered with the APHA.

Sold as a young horse by Hank to Bob and Chris Jones of Smithfield, Tex., Skippa Scotch wound up in the hands of Ronnie

Silent Princess, a 1976 sorrel overo mare by Silent String and out of Skip Barta, was a two-time reserve national champion at halter. She was also a Superior halter horse with 156 open halter points.

Photo by Alfred Janssen III, Courtesy of *The Paint Horse Journal*

Silent Chant, a 1976 cropout Paint stallion by Skip's Chant and out of Spanish Bar Girl, was campaigned on the Paint Horse show circuit and earned 18 halter points.
Photo by Alfred Janssen III

Stallings of Aubrey, Texas. Stallings showed him to his APHA Championship and, in 1977, won the national championship in calf roping on him.

Skippa Scotch sired only 53 registered foals, but 27 of those were performers. They accumulated 12 open, youth, and amateur APHA Championships, 8 national and world titles, and close to 5,000 points in APHA competition.

In recent years, St Sheila, a 1979 excess-white Quarter Horse stallion by St Dancer and out of Silent Sheila by Sailalong, has made his presence felt in the Wiescamp Paint program.

"In a lot of ways, St Sheila was a greater individual than Silent String," observes Hank. "We tried to get him registered the way he should've been—as a Quarter Horse—but they turned him down, so we put him in the Paints.

"He had the size, he had the conformation, he had the class, and his mama was one of our great mares. The only way I would have changed things would be to have a field full of horses just like him."

The Wiescamp Paint Horse program continues in full swing today. Managed by Larry Wiescamp's son, Shane, with guidance from Hank, it continues to produce both tobiano and overo horses who are in demand as show and breeding prospects.

"I've always had Paints," concludes Hank. "I've tried to breed 'em up over the years. I've tried to make 'em look just like my Quarter Horses with a little extra color. The only thing that loud color on a horse does is make him more saleable. It always has, and it always will."

Skippa Scotch, a 1969 stallion by Skippa String (AQHA) and out of Scotch Charm (AQHA) by Skipper's King, was yet another cropout product of Hank's Quarter Horse program. Shown as a Paint, Skippa Scotch was an APHA Champion and the 1977 national champion calf roping horse.

Photo by George

St Sheila, a 1979 stallion by St Dancer (AQHA) and out of Silent Sheila (AQHA) by Sailalong, was also denied registration in the AQHA because of the high white on two of his legs. Registered with the APHA, he had a positive influence on Hank's Paint program.

Photo by Dr. Jerry Burkey, D.V.M.

17 The Modern Sires

"Because we didn't have the show horses on the road like we did in previous years, I guess they thought we'd gone out of business."

BY THE MID-1980s, the Wiescamp Quarter Horse program had taken on a new personality.

Hank had drastically cut back on his horse show involvement.

He placed most of his emphasis during the latter part of the 1980s on just keeping the ship afloat during the recession that hit the horse industry hard at that time.

Throughout most of this time period, Hank continued to breed his Quarter Horses with the same intensity and on the same scale as he ever did. By the late 1980s, his horse numbers ballooned to over 1,000 head. In 1988, and again in 1989, he held gelding sales in the Alamosa

St Dancer, a 1970 stallion by Double Dancer and out of St Madam by St Three Bar, had a positive impact on the Wiescamp breeding program in the late '70s and early '80s. He is shown here after winning a 350-yard race at La Mesa Park in Raton, N.M., in 1973. With him are trainer Lonnie Stokes and jockey Tim Wortman. The man on the far right is unidentified.

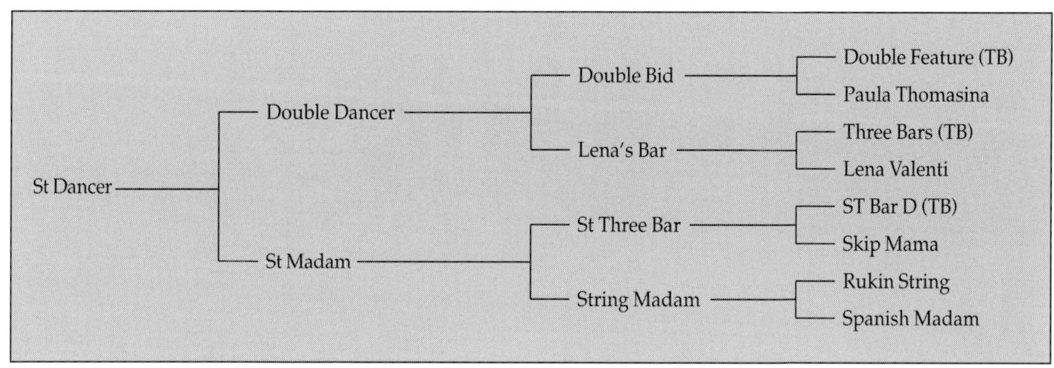

sale barn to market some of the good ranch and show type geldings he had accumulated.

Even as breeders throughout the country were scaling back or dispersing their breeding herds, however, Hank maintained his optimism that the market would return, and continued to work diligently with the breeding program that he had initiated almost 60 years prior.

This was a time of transition in that program. Skipper's King, Skip's Reward, and Skippa String, the cornerstone breeding stallions of the 1960s and 1970s, had been replaced by a younger set of sires. The influence of the three older stallions would be felt for years to come through the Wiescamp broodmare band, but the bulk of the herd sire duties now belonged to horses such as Skip's Bid, Skip's Supreme, Skippa Lark, St Dancer, and St Limit.

"Some people kind of forgot about us," observes Hank. "Because we didn't have the show horses on the road like we did in previous years, I guess they thought we'd gone out of business. But we were right here all the while, breeding the same kind of horses that we've always bred."

Skip's Bid, a 1967 palomino stallion by Skipper's King and out of Spanish Shasta by Spanish Nick, was one of the older stallions who heralded in the modern era.

"Skip's Bid was a big horse," says Hank. "He would stand 15.3 and weigh 1,400 pounds. He wasn't as classy as his dad, but he sure had the size and the substance. His mama was one of our better-producing Spanish Nick mares.

"Skip's Bid was a great sire of females. His daughters were better than his sons, and they went on to make great broodmares."

Very few of Skip's Bid's offspring were ever sold by Hank, and as a result, few were shown. Skipannette, a 1971 mare out of Skiporita by Skipper W, was shown and earned 28 halter and 18 performance points.

Skip's Supreme, a 1967 sorrel stallion by Skip's Reward and out of Scooter's Charm by Scooter Lad, was also used as a sire by Hank during this time frame.

"Skip's Supreme did not do quite as good a job for us as Skip's Bid did," he remarks. "He did sire Scotch Supreme, an AQHA Champion, and Skips Mist, who earned 94 halter points. And he sired one son, Shieks

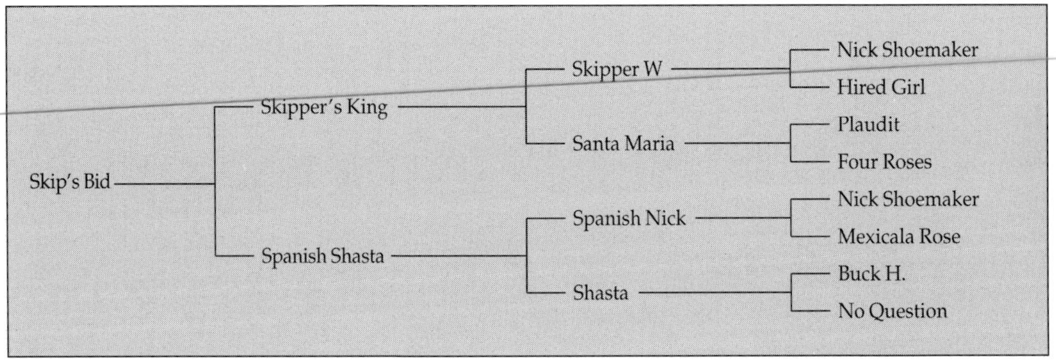

Here are two shots of Skip's Bid, a 1967 stallion by Skipper's King and out of Spanish Shasta by Spanish Nick. The 15.3-hand, 1,400-pound palomino became a noted broodmare sire for Hank. The handler is George Brunelli.

Photo by Louise Stewart, Courtesy of Benham and Louise Stewart

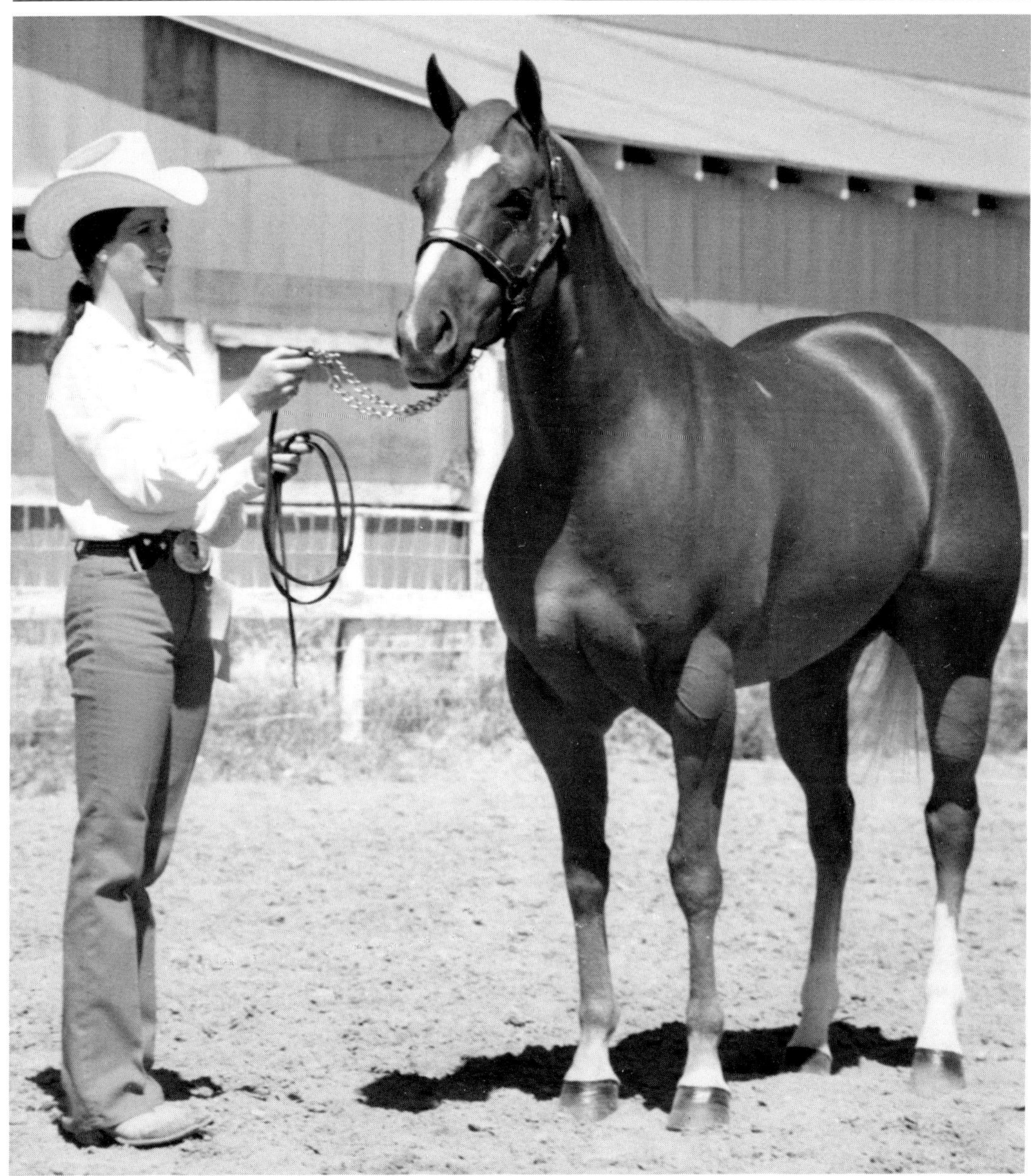

Skipannette, a 1971 mare by Skip's Bid and out of Skiporita by Skipper W, was taken out of the Wiescamp broodmare band in 1975 to be conditioned for the show ring. Campaigned by Margaret Hammond, she earned 28 halter and 18 performance points.

Photo Courtesy of Margaret Hammond

"Skip's Barber was an extremely breedy horse. He had that class that I'm always striving for. He had that look."

Lass, who went on to make a breeding horse. But, for the most part, Skip's Supreme didn't get the job done for us, so we sold him."

There was yet another stallion foaled in 1967 Hank used as a breeding stallion. This horse, Skippa Lark, proved to be a great sire and was a mainstay of the Wiescamp program for almost 20 years.

"Skippa Lark was by Skippa String and out of Skip Alone by Skipper's Lad," says Hank. "He lacked a little in the head and was a little long in the back, but he sure made up for those two shortcomings with a lot of other strengths. He had a super neck, a nice long hip, and great inside muscle in his hind legs. He also had a real nice front end.

"I had to work awfully hard to get the right kind of mares out of him. The problem was not in how he crossed with my mares; he crossed well with about every family of mares that we put him on. I just had to work at getting the kind of heads on his daughters that would let me put them into my broodmare band.

"I got it done though. By the time he died in 1986, Skippa Lark left me with a great set of mares. And I'll guarantee you that the best ones stayed right here."

Although Skippa Lark's main impact on the Wiescamp program was as the sire of

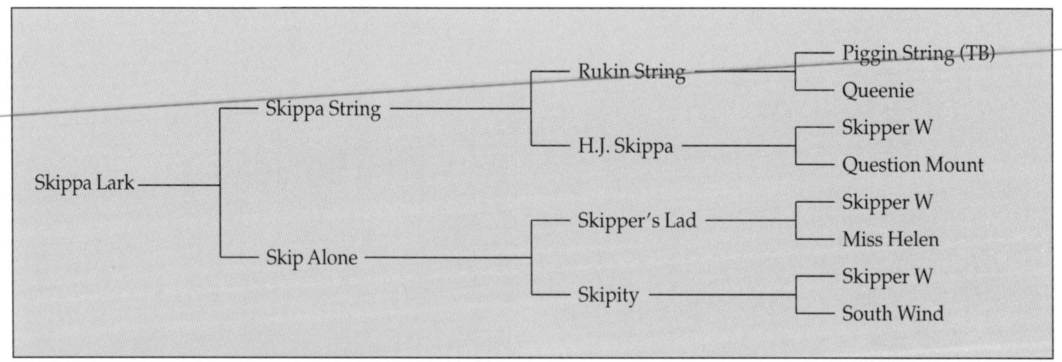

Skippa Lark, a 1967 stallion by Skippa String and out of Skip Alone by Skipper's Lad, also left his impression on the modern Wiescamp breeding program. He sired a number of top show horses and a set of daughters who are an integral part of Hank's current broodmare band. **Photo by Jeanne Luckey**

breeding horses, he also sired a number of top show horses.

Premium Skip, a 1977 palomino stallion out of Skippits Premium by Skip 3 Bar, earned 34.5 halter and 63 performance points en route to his AQHA Championship. Skips Angelical, a 1983 sorrel mare out of Skip Angel by Skip's Supreme, was both an open and amateur AQHA Champion, and garnered four Superior awards and 368 AQHA points during her 6-year show career.

Sierra Scheme, a 1987 sorrel stallion by Skippa Lark and out of Sierra Royal by St Royal, earned his AQHA Championship, and Sheiks Romance, a 1978 bay stallion by Skippa Lark and out of Sheiks Dream by Sheik's Image, was a Superior western pleasure horse.

Streak of Summer, a 1977 mare by Skippa Lark and out of Summer Streak by Skippa Streak, was a Superior halter horse with 87 points. Skiponaire, a 1977 mare by Skippa Lark and out of Skip's Debonair by Skipper's King, also earned a Superior in halter with 100 points.

At the 1979 AQHA World Championship Show, Streak of Summer was the reserve world champion 2-year-old mare, and Skiponaire placed third. These two mares were bred by Hank's son-in-law, Larry Wilcox, of Alamosa.

Still other point-earners by Skippa Lark were Skip's Barber, a 1971 stallion out of Skip Barba by Skip's Reward, who earned 34 halter points; and Surenuffskippa, a 1981 stallion out of Skips Tabu by Skipper's King, who earned 29 halter and 28 performance points.

Skip's Barber, who was retained by Hank as a breeding stallion after his show days were over, became a top sire.

"Skip's Barber was an extremely breedy horse," notes Hank. "He had that class that I'm always striving for. He had that look. We didn't get many foals by him, but the ones we did get were good, and very few of 'em ever left Alamosa."

Spanish Array, a 1980 stallion by Skip's Barber and out of Spanish Galla by Skip's Bid, was one of the few. While he was still owned by Hank, Array was shown at the Denver National Western Stock Show and the Colorado State Fair by Margaret Hammond. He championed both shows. Sold to Marsha Miller and Glenn Huddleston

Sierra Scheme, a 1991 stallion by Skippa Lark and out of Sierra Royal by St Royal, was sold to Volker Laves of Wenden, Germany. The sorrel stallion earned his AQHA Championship competing solely in Europe.

Skip Tama, a 1970 stallion by Skippa Lark and out of Skip Drama by Skip's Reward, was sold to Benham and Louise Stewart of Glenwood, Georgia. He went on to become one of the all-time leading sires of Palomino show horses.

Photo by Louise Stewart, Courtesy of Benham and Louise Stewart

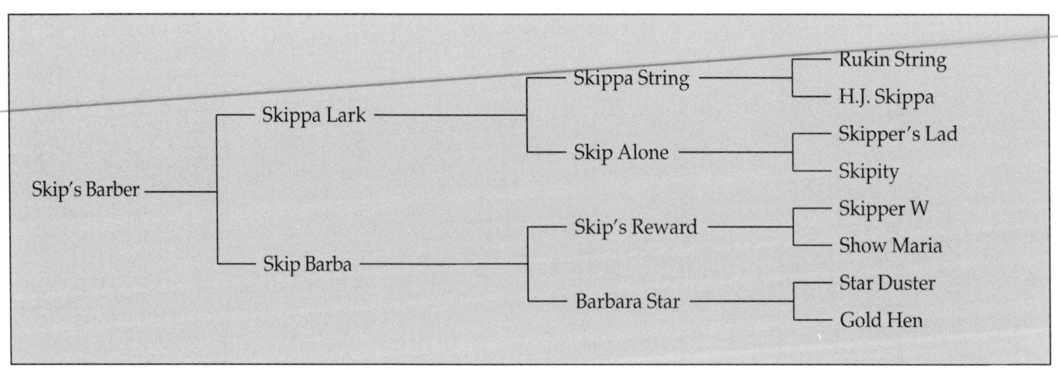

of Enid, Okla., he was the 1985 AQHA World Champion Aged Stallion.

Skip So Smooth, a seven-eighths brother to Spanish Array, out of Smooth Maiden, stood grand at the 1986 and 1987 Colorado State Fair and earned 28 halter points.

"Spanish Array and Skip So Smooth were both nice horses," comments Hank. "Array didn't have quite as good a head as Skip So Smooth did. He's made a name for himself, though, as a show horse and a sire.

"I had high expectations for Skip So Smooth as a breeding horse. But he never lived long enough to prove himself. He died young. It's like I've said about the show horses: They are rarely worth a damn after they're done showing. They either die young, or they never reproduce the way you think they should. That's just the way it is."

"St Dancer was a freak. He was so much better than either his sire or dam, that you just had to look at the three of 'em and shake your head."

In addition to Spanish Array and Skip So Smooth, Skip's Barber was also the sire of Spanish Will, a 1976 mare out Spanish Sister by Spanish Nick, who earned 39 halter points.

Like so many of his predecessors, though, Skip's Barber made his greatest impact on the Wiescamp program through his daughters.

"You know, Skipper's King was a great sire of mares," says Hank. "And so was his son, Skip's Bid. Although it's a little early to say for sure, I feel that Skip's Barber will be a great broodmare sire too. His daughters are crossing exceptionally well with whatever male line I put 'em on. Years from now, they might be talking about the Skip's Barber mares in the same way that they're talking about the Skipper's King mares today. If I had as many daughters of Barber as I once did of King, there would be no doubt about it."

Several years after Skippa Lark arrived on the scene, another stallion was born at Alamosa who would establish a dominant male line during the 1980s.

St Dancer, a 1970 son of Double Dancer out of St Madam by St Three Bars, was raced before he was placed at stud. From seven starts he placed in the money four times and achieved a speed index of 90.

As a race sire, he had seven starters, five of whom earned their Registers of Merit. St Agent, a 1979 stallion out of Scotch Rockette by Scottish, earned a speed index of 94. Scotch Sipper, a 1978 mare out of Scotch Coin 2 by Scottish, achieved a speed index of 93.

"St Dancer was a freak," says Hank. "He was so much better than either his sire or dam, that you just had to look at the three of 'em and shake your head. He had the best shoulder, *bar none,* of any horse I ever saw. He also had a super front end, with just the right kind of long muscle. As a result, he was one of the best movers I ever saw.

"And I'll tell you something about freaks. When they're that much better than either of their parents, it's very

Skip Barba (top) was a 1965 mare by Skip's Reward and out of Barbara Star. Shown here with Leroy Webb, she was one of the stars of the Wiescamp show string during the late 1960s. She also excelled as a broodmare, producing, among others, Skip's Barber (bottom), a 1971 stallion who earned 37 halter points. That's Sunny Jim Orr at the halter.

Top Photo by Louise Serpa

Skip So Smooth, a 1982 sorrel stallion by Skip's Barber and out of Smooth Maiden by Skip's Bid, was a seven-eighths brother to Spanish Array. He earned 28 halter points and stood grand at the 1987 Colorado State Fair.

Photo by K.C. Montgomery

Spanish Array, a 1980 sorrel stallion by Skip's Barber and out of Spanish Galla by Skip's Bid, was the 1985 World Champion Aged Stallion.

seldom that they can reproduce themselves.

"So that made St Dancer a double freak, because he could, and did, breed as good as he was.

"He was one of a kind."

From a limited number of registered foals, 66 to be exact, St Dancer sired several sons who were placed in service in the Wiescamp program.

St Limit, a 1975 stallion out of Skippa Twin by Skippa String, was used for nine seasons. Among others, he sired the Superior halter mare Skippa Jean and the top halter and roping mare St Skippa.

St Limit's full brother, St Twin, had four race starts, winning two and earning his racing Register of Merit. He was also used as a breeding stallion by Hank for a number of years.

And the St Dancer mares, few that there were, went on to make top producers for Hank, crossing exceptionally well with the Skippa Lark and Skip's Barber lines.

Skip N Go, Hank's great halter and performance horse, was also destined for a prominent place in the Wiescamp breeding program after his show career ended in 1972. Like Skip So Smooth, however, he died before his full potential was ever realized.

"Skip N Go only got the chance to sire two full foal crops for us before he passed away," relates Hank. "I sure would have liked to have had the chance to use him longer. We did put him on some of our best mares, and he did leave us with several good sons and a dozen or so top daughters."

In the 1990s, Hank's leading sire is Skippers Ring, a 1980 stallion by Skipper's Sport and out of Skip N Ring by Skip's Chant.

"'Ringer,' as we call him, is not much to look at," admits Hank. "When people go down stud row, and look at the stallions who are lined up on it, he's the last one they pick as an individual.

"But when I show them his sons, who we've kept as breeding prospects, and his daughters, who we've picked to put in the broodmare band, they change the way they look at him. Then they try to buy one of his foals.

"We have not sold a single one of his sons while they were still stallions. We have sold a few geldings and mares by him, but we're going to see how his sons do as sires before we ever let one go."

The horse that Hank has put in the No. 1 hole on stud row is Skippers Zane, a 1991 son of Skippers Ring, out of Skips Agree, one of the best daughters of Skip's Barber. "We are excited about this colt. He's one of the best. We're going to give him some of our best mares," notes Hank.

"If he doesn't work, we've got two of his full brothers, and one of them might.

"You know, I've been breeding this family of Old Fred horses since the 1930s. I started with those Philmont and Ghost Ranch mares.

"First I used Barney Owens on 'em, then Holy Smoke, then Nick Shoemaker, and

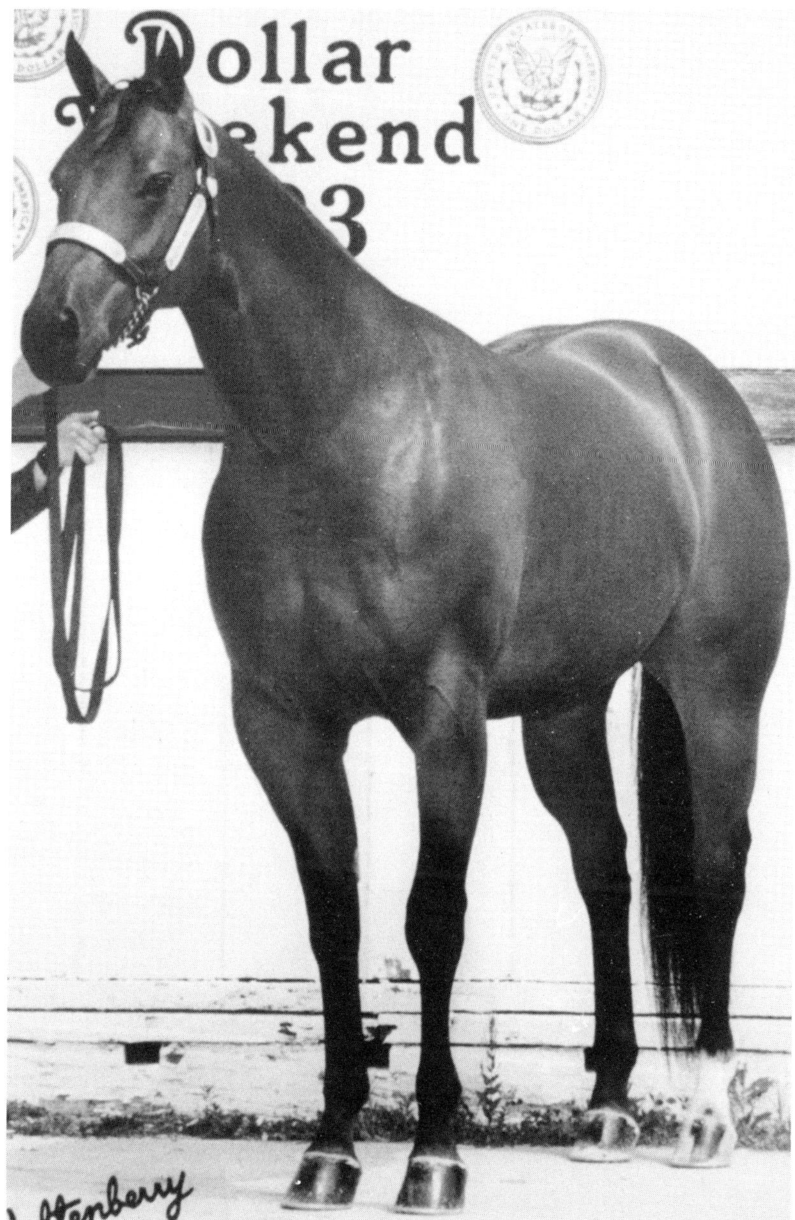

Spanish Trump, a 1989 bay gelding by Skippers Ring and out of Spanish Sent by Skippa Lark, had earned 59.5 open, amateur, and youth halter points through 1995.

Photo by Dick Waltenberry

Skips Mist, a 1974 mare by Skip's Supreme and out of Skip's Blonde by Skipper's King, was a top Wiescamp-bred show mare of the late 1970s. She was a Superior halter horse with 97 halter points. She is shown here with Charles Crawley.

Photo by Don Trout, Courtesy of *The Quarter Horse Journal*

then Skipper W. I've gone right down the line since then, crossing the descendants of those original horses on each other. I've worked in my outcrosses over the years, but I've always stayed with this one family of Old Fred horses.

"I've never changed the type of horse that I raise. I have no time for fads and fashions. Even if I wanted to keep up with them, which I don't, I'm not smart enough to figure them out. They change too often.

"When it comes to breeding and raising horses, I set my stake way out there a long time ago, and I'm still working toward it. I'm not there yet.

"I'm a little closer than I once was, that's a fact. But I still haven't got it plumb right yet. I still haven't raised that perfect horse.

"I guess I'll just keep trying until I do."

Hank has always taken great pride in the fact that he has bred for just one type of Quarter Horse: a middle-of-the-road, good-looking athlete. The horses shown on this page are two modern examples of the Wiescamp breeding program, and both horses are out of the same mare, proving the prepotency of this broodmare.

The top photo shows St Duino, a 1989 mare by Fly Duino and out of St Jewel by St Limit. She is shown after winning her first race, a 350-yarder, at La Mesa Park in 1991. That's Hank on the far left and Greg Howard, who works for Hank, on the right. The jockey is Anthony G. Archuleta. The mare is owned by Hank and his long-time friend, Bette Zane Smith. Hank is now using Fly Duino, and some of his sons and daughters, in his program. He related, "I had Bette, whose opinion I could rely upon, look at Fly Duino, who was at Los Alamitos in California at the time. I bought the horse based on her evaluation, and he is doing a real good job for me. St Duino was his first foal, and won the first time we started her."

The bottom photo is of St Topaz, by Skips Avant and out of St Jewel. Owned and shown by Margo Ball, St Topaz is a four-time world champion in Palomino competition. He's shown here with Margo and her brother, Wayne Ball, at the 1995 PHBA World Championship Show in Tulsa.

Photo of St Topaz by K.C. Montgomery

EPILOGUE

HANK WIESCAMP'S involvement in the horse industry has spanned over 7 decades. During that time, there have been tremendous changes in almost every aspect of the industry.

When Hank got into horses in the mid-1920s, they were still an important source of power and transportation in the city, on the farm and ranch, and in the Army. His original horse trading and breeding program was designed to produce animals in support of the cavalry and carriage horse segments of the still-active "horse power" industry.

As the age of mechanization transformed the role of the horse in America from utilitarian to show and recreational, Hank's horse breeding program was able to make the transition with remarkable ease. His horses were the type needed.

Hank participated in the exciting days of early growth and expansion of all four of the major stock horse registries. His involvement with those associations was of enough significance to get him inducted into the Palomino Horse Breeders of America's Hall of Fame in 1981, and the American Quarter Horse Association and Appaloosa Horse Club halls of fame in 1994. It seems a safe bet that, when the American Paint Horse Association initiates its hall of fame, Hank will be inducted into it as well.

The Wiescamp-bred horses have competed successfully in the show ring and on the racetrack for over a half-century. They were in on the advent of the modern horse show in the early 1940s, and they continue to make their presence felt in the show ring to this day.

Through all this, life on the Wiescamp ranch in Alamosa, Colo., remains remarkably unchanged.

Hank still breeds his horses with the same goals that he established in the 1920s. He has the same eye for a horse that has stood him in such good stead over the years. His breeding, handling, and feeding practices are virtually the same.

Literally hundreds of uniformly built Wiescamp mares still graze in irrigated pastures on the outskirts of Alamosa. They are, for the most part, managed just as their ancestors were 70 years ago.

People from throughout this country and from abroad continue to make the trip to southern Colorado to visit Hank and view his horses. The number of visitors has not declined. If anything, it has increased.

Those visitors view the Wiescamp horses just as thousands of other people have over the years: as they naturally are. They are not kept in show barns and they are not professionally groomed.

Despite the lack of show fitting, the Wiescamp horses continue to sell just as well as they ever have. In recent years, Hank's foreign sales have increased dramatically. Wiescamp-bred horses can now be found in Canada, Panama, Germany, Poland, Argentina, and Uruguay. One individual, Volker Laves, owner of the Circle L Ranch in Wenden, Germany, has imported over 50 of Hank's horses to Europe.

Much of the Wiescamp family continues to live in and around Alamosa. Hank, of course, still lives in the yellow house that Nick Shoemaker built in 1945.

Ron Wiescamp's widow, Jean, lives on the east edge of town. In partnership with her son, Ron Jr., she maintains a Saler beef cattle operation. Ron and Jean's three daughters, Tammy, Debby, and Laura, have all married and moved away from the valley.

As a result of a debilitating stroke, Loretta Wiescamp is institutionalized.

Larry and Charlotte Wilcox live on their ranch southwest of town. They continue to breed both running and show horses. They

Larry Wiescamp took this classic shot of Hank and a 7-year-old buckskin mare named St Skippa in 1989. It bears a striking resemblance to Dwayne Brech's cover painting of Hank and Skip's Napoleon. Dwayne did not have access to this photograph when he was working on his painting; his research photos of Hank and Napoleon were taken by Kathy Kadash in the fall of 1995. The object lesson to be taken from this is that Hank's horses look today just as they've looked for decades; the way that Hank has bred them to look. They are, in every sense of the word, a family of horses.

have a daughter, LaWanda, and a granddaughter, Lakayla, who live in Denver, and a son, Justin, who still lives at home.

Larry Wiescamp's widow, Kathy, lives on the south edge of Alamosa. Their two children, Brandi Lee and Shane, still live in the area.

Grant Wiescamp, wife Chelle, and son Cody live on their farm southwest of town.

As this book goes to press, Hank is nearing his 90th birthday. Due to his age, the question is often asked, "What does the future hold in store for the Wiescamp horse?"

"Everybody wants to know that," says the venerable horseman. "They all want to know what'll happen to the horses after I'm gone. All I can tell you is that they'll be left in good hands. I've seen to that."

A typical Hank Wiescamp answer. Straightforward, yet ambiguous; like the man himself.

For now, life does go on for Hank Wiescamp the horse breeder much the same as it has for 70 years. His hand is still felt on every aspect of his horse breeding program. He still makes all breeding decisions, he still evaluates the young horses, he still decides which horses stay and which horses go.

Hank still holds court to an almost daily stream of people in the office on the south side of his house. He advises, he entertains, and he conducts business from the same room where he has done those things for the last 50 years.

And everyday, he writes another page in the colorful and unique book that is *The Hank Wiescamp Story.*

PROFILE

FRANK HOLMES has been writing historical articles involving the western horse since the mid-1960s.

His interests have always been centered on the historical aspects of the western horse breeds, including Appaloosas, Quarter Horses, Paints, and Palominos. This broad-based background served him especially well as he tackled the biography of Hank Wiescamp.

A native of Kenmare, N.D., Frank worked for the federal government for 18 years before turning to a career as a full-time writer in 1991. In addition to *The Hank Wiescamp Story,* he recently co-authored *Legends 2.*

Frank was a staff writer for *Western Horseman* magazine for 17 months. Now living in north Texas, Frank serves as associate editor of *Paint Horse Journal.* He has two sons, Eric and Craig.

Photo by Darol Dickinson

Wiescamp Honor Roll

Wiescamp-Bred AQHA Champions

1. Nye's Barney Google
2. Spanish Nick
3. Skipper Jr.
4. Skipity Scoot
5. Skipity Skip
6. Silver Skip
7. General Skip
8. Sir Teddy
9. Sailalong
10. Skip Cash
11. Skipper's Image
12. Skipper's Smoke
13. Skip On
14. Spanish Prince
15. Shawnee Skip
16. Skip's Princess
17. Skipette
18. Skipper Bar
19. Copperelm Queen
20. Silver Son
21. Skip A Barb
22. Skip Bart
23. Skip 3 Bar
24. Skip's Pride
25. Skip O Bar
26. Skip's Admiral
27. Skip's Ink
28. Skippit Bar
29. St Three Bar
31. Skip Sir Bar
30. Scoot Baron
32. Skip Tres Bar
33. Skip Beau
34. Skip's Dilly
35. Skip's Trama
36. Spanish Ruler
37. Skip Thrush
38. Skip Veto
39. Skip's Waiter
40. String Of Gold
41. Sheik's Jewel
42. Skippa Cord
43. Skip's Depth
44. Skip Relic
45. Sir Colonel
46. Skip N Go
47. Skip Jet
48. Skip Rita
49. Skip School Day
50. Skip's Chita
51. Skip's Style
52. Stage Kid
53. Spanish Fair
54. Scotch Supreme
55. Skip O Pay
56. Skip N Jay
57. Skips Ego
58. Sierra Scheme

Wiescamp-Bred Superior Halter Horses

1. Skipper's Image (188 points)
2. Skipper's Prince (60 points)
3. Skipper's Smoke (100 points)
4. Spanish Prince (98 points)
5. Skip's Princess (71 points)
6. Skip's Glory (65 points)
7. Skipette (113 points)
8. Roanwood Nick (64 points)
9. Silver Son (176 points)
10. Skip 3 Bar (62 points)
11. Skip's Champ (73 points)
12. Elm's Bar Maid (77 points)
13. Skip's Ink (54 points)
14. Whispering Elm (125 points)
15. Skip Sir Bar (54 points)
16. Skip Flash (66 points)
17. Skip's Trama (62 points)
18. Skip Thrush (154 points)
19. Skip Veto (163 points)
20. String Of Gold (601 points)
21. Skip Barba (52 points)
22. Skip's Count (65 points)
23. Sheik's Jewel (56 points)
24. Skip Ima (161 points)
25. Skippa Cord (76 points)
26. Skippanee (53 points)
27. Skip's Depth (72 points)
28. Skip N Go (75 points)
29. Skip Rita (53 points)
30. Skip's Chita (65 points)
31. Skip's Style (56 points)
32. Silent Sheila (92 points)
33. Skips Mist (94 points)
34. Spanish Array (66 points)
35. St Jean (51 points)
36. Skips Targa (64.5 points)

Wiescamp-Bred Superior Performance Horses

1. Speedster (cutting)
2. Skip's Princess (reining)
3. Silver Son (calf roping, reining)
4. Skip's Dilly (western pleasure)
5. Skip Thrush (western pleasure)
6. Skip's Waiter (steer roping)
7. Shastanee (western pleasure)
8. Skip N Go (western pleasure)
9. Skip Jet (western pleasure)
10. Scotch Supreme (western pleasure)
11. Silent Sheila (western pleasure)

Horse Photo Index

T

W

With his golden palomino color and typical Wiescamp-look, Sir Colonel, a 1968 stallion by Sir Teddy and out of Skip's Aid by Skipper W, is one more example of one of the most enduring Quarter Horse lines in the history of the breed.

The *Western Horseman*, established in 1936, is the world's leading horse publication.
For subscription information: 800-877-5278. To order other *Western Horseman* books: 800-874-6774.
Western Horseman, Box 7980, Colorado Springs, CO 80933-7980. Web-site: www.westernhorseman.com.

Books Published by Western Horseman Inc.

BACON & BEANS by Stella Hughes
144 pages and 200-plus recipes for delicious western chow.

BARREL RACING by Sharon Camarillo
144 pages and 200 photographs. Tells how to train and compete successfully.

CALF ROPING by Roy Cooper
144 pages and 280 photographs covering roping and tying.

CUTTING by Leon Harrel
144 pages and 200 photographs. Complete guide on this popular sport.

FIRST HORSE by Fran Devereux Smith
176 pages, 160 black-and-white photos, about 40 illustrations. Step-by-step information for the first-time horse owner and/or novice rider.

HEALTH PROBLEMS by Robert M. Miller, D.V.M.
144 pages on management, illness and injuries, lameness, mares and foals, and more.

HORSEMAN'S SCRAPBOOK by Randy Steffen
144 pages and 250 illustrations. A collection of handy hints.

IMPRINT TRAINING by Robert M. Miller, D.V.M.
144 pages and 250 photographs. Learn to "program" newborn foals.

LEGENDS by Diane C. Simmons
168 pages and 214 photographs. Barbra B, Bert, Chicaro Bill, Cowboy P-12, Depth Charge (TB), Doc Bar, Go Man Go, Hard Twist, Hollywood Gold, Joe Hancock, Joe Reed P-3, Joe Reed II, King P-234, King Fritz, Leo, Peppy, Plaudit, Poco Bueno, Poco Tivio, Queenie, Quick M Silver, Shue Fly, Star Duster, Three Bars (TB), Top Deck (TB), and Wimpy P-1.

LEGENDS 2 by Jim Goodhue, Frank Holmes, Phil Livingston, Diane C. Simmons
192 pages and 224 photographs. Clabber, Driftwood, Easy Jet, Grey Badger II, Jessie James, Jet Deck, Joe Bailey P-4 (Gonzales), Joe Bailey (Weatherford), King's Pistol, Lena's Bar, Lightning Bar, Lucky Blanton, Midnight, Midnight Jr, Moon Deck, My Texas Dandy, Oklahoma Star, Oklahoma Star Jr., Peter McCue, Rocket Bar (TB), Skipper W, Sugar Bars, and Traveler.

LEGENDS 3 by Jim Goodhue, Frank Holmes, Diane Ciarloni, Kim Guenther, Larry Thornton, Betsy Lynch
208 pages and 196 photographs. Flying Bob, Hollywood Jac 86, Jackstraw (TB), Maddon's Bright Eyes, Mr Gun Smoke, Old Sorrel, Piggin String (TB), Poco Lena, Poco Pine, Poco Dell, Question Mark, Quo Vadis, Royal King, Showdown, Steel Dust, and Two Eyed Jack.

PROBLEM-SOLVING by Marty Marten
248 pages and over 250 photos and illustrations. How to develop a willing partnership between horse and human to handle trailer-loading, hard-to-catch, barn-sour, spooking, water-crossing, herd-bound, and pull-back problems.

NATURAL HORSE-MAN-SHIP by Pat Parelli
232 pages and 275 photographs. Parelli's six keys to a natural horse-human relationship.

REINING, Completely Revised by Al Dunning
216 pages and over 300 photographs showing how to train horses for this exciting event.

ROOFS AND RAILS by Gavin Ehringer
144 pages, 128 black-and-white photographs plus drawings, charts, and floor plans. How to plan and build your ideal horse facility.

STARTING COLTS by Mike Kevil
168 pages and 400 photographs. Step-by-step process in starting colts.

THE HANK WIESCAMP STORY by Frank Holmes
208 pages and over 260 photographs. The biography of the legendary breeder of Quarter Horses, Appaloosas, and Paints.

TEAM PENNING by Phil Livingston
144 pages and 200 photographs. How to compete in this popular family sport.

TEAM ROPING WITH JAKE AND CLAY
by Fran Devereux Smith
224 pages and over 200 photographs and illustrations. Learn about fast times from champions Jake Barnes and Clay O'Brien Cooper. Solid information about handling a rope, roping dummies, and heading and heeling for practice and in competition. Also sound advice about rope horses, roping steers, gear, and horsemanship.

WELL-SHOD by Don Baskins
160 pages, 300 black-and-white photos and illustrations. A horseshoeing guide for owners and farriers. The easy-to-read text, illustrations, and photos show step-by-step how to trim and shoe a horse for a variety of uses. Special attention is paid to corrective shoeing techniques for horses with various foot and leg problems.

WESTERN HORSEMANSHIP by Richard Shrake
144 pages and 150 photographs. Complete guide to riding western horses.

WESTERN TRAINING by Jack Brainard
With Peter Phinny. 136 pages. Stresses the foundation for western training.